M'sieu André's

COUNTRY

P9-ASL-059

L. Pontchartrain

L. Borgne

Mississippi

NEW ORLEANS

River

CHALMETTE

Pakenham Oaks

Salvadore

BARATARIA

LAFITTE

POINTE A LA HACHE

Breton Sound

Bayou Lafourche

ISLE JEAN CHARLES

BURAS

OSTRICA

GOLDEN MEADOW

LEEVILLE

GRAND ISLE

Mexico

Cajuns on
the Bayous

Cajuns on the Bayous

BY

CAROLYN RAMSEY

ILLUSTRATED WITH DRAWINGS BY

ALEX IMPHANG

AND

PHOTOGRAPHS BY THE AUTHOR

HASTINGS HOUSE, PUBLISHERS, NEW YORK

TO MOTHER AND DAD

*Whose love and faith have enriched all my
life's adventures.*

Acknowledgments

The indebtedness incurred in putting together this book has not been of the usual literary nature, so I have no long-suffering friends to thank for doing research, nor typing, nor giving criticism, nor reading proof. For better or for worse, I have managed to do all this for myself.

I am indebted to the *Saturday Evening Post, Liberty* Magazine and the *Reader's Digest* for portions of this book which were first published by them. I am grateful to *Holiday* Magazine for permission to use passages from my article, "Cajun Cruise," published by them in October, 1955. Particular thanks are due to Irène Thérèse Whitfield for permission to quote verses from her invaluable book, *Acadian Folk Songs* (Louisiana State University Press, 1955).

Of thanks for non-literary assistance there is plenty.

And so it gives me pleasure here to express deepest gratitude to Alex Imphang, my illustrator, who knows the bayou country as well as I and puts his love of it into tender, nostalgic drawings which are as gay and bright as his own heart; to Roy Trahan, a masterful photographer with a fine old Cajun name, who took stained and musty negatives from my very oldest files and printed them in his own lab—greater loyalty than this hath no photographer for another; to Toni Strassman,

author's representative, who "sat up all night reading" the first
half of this manuscript, then sold it and pinned me to a deadline to finish the job; to Kay and James Register, my neighbors in the Vieux Carré, who kept up my strength with steak
suppers for the last three hectic weeks before deadline; to
Eleanor Gillespie (Mrs. Eugene), my erstwhile assistant fore-
man at Old Bonita Ranch in Marshall, Texas, who fed the
horse, tended the new calves, harvested walnuts, got winter
pastures planted, while I was holed up in my New Orleans
French-quarter apartment fighting the finish line; and to my
Dad, who mailed the home-town gossip sheet along with cheery
notes of his own good health and happiness, thus giving peace
of mind without which Toni Strassman's commitment could
not have been fulfilled.

Finally, I wish to thank all the lovely characters who have
made possible my adventures in the bayou country. The characters of this book are mostly real and carry their own names.
In some instances, as in the case of the Boudreaux family, they
are composites of many different real-life personalities. In the
opinion of the author these are no less "for-true"; their activities are reported accurately from experiences lived through,
or—as in the case of *Tante* Cloe's funeral—told so vividly to
the author that she can report as though it had actually happened to her. For obvious reasons, and for the protection of
their many real-life cousins, it was necessary to create the
Boudreaux family. Their trapping camp on the marsh is described faithfully by the author, who once lived in a campboat
on Little Bayou Black and operated a *chalon,* or traveling
grocery boat, on the marshlands during one trapping season.

Thanks to all these good and true!

CAROLYN RAMSEY

Contents

Preface

Along the winding bayous of South Louisiana, deep in the heavily moss-draped country, live a people who are half myth, half reality. In mansions and in hovels, among the rich green cane fields and far back among the murky swamps, their lives move on in a strangely foreign pattern.

By custom and tradition, by speech and action, the people are French. Somewhere among them are the pure-blooded descendants of the first French refugees in America, those Acadians whom the British drove out of Nova Scotia two centuries ago, the first North American DP's. Their hazardous wanderings over half a continent rivaled the miseries of European displaced persons of our own century. Most of these first exiles found no easy welcome to the American Colonial states and many of them were destined to roam for thirty years over this foreign soil before they found peace again in a new home.

The story of the original exiles is well known to readers of Longfellow's *Evangeline*. The poem's heroine is a symbol of thousands of tragic Acadian women who suffered through the Great Deportation. Less familiar and equally tragic is the true story.

The Acadian colony in Nova Scotia, established in 1604, was the first French colony in the New World, the second

permanent European settlement in America. Frenchmen from
the northern provinces of Brittany, Normandy and Picardy
lived in old *Acadie* for a hundred years before Louisiana was
colonized. In 1713, following the War of the Spanish Succes-
sion, France lost the colony to the British. By the terms of the
Treaty of Utrecht the Acadians were granted permission to
leave the lost colony, with all their goods, any time during the
following year. But the British, desiring settlers for their newly
acquired territory, prevented them from leaving during that
year and for forty years to follow. The Acadians were held to
the lands by force, until the British were equal to the task of
civilizing the wilderness and making the colony commercially
successful.

Acadians were docile, peasant, law-abiding folk and sub-
mitted to their oppressors. In 1744, when France fought another
war with the British and attempted to get the Acadian colony
to revolt, the colony refused to break the original treaty.
Through their honor Nova Scotia was saved for the British.
Forty years after the treaty there were still less than a dozen
English families in the whole province, and the land was really
Acadian as it had been for a century and a half.

Then, in 1748, the British brought over twenty-five hundred
settlers from England, established the city of Halifax, and
matured the plan they had formulated many years before—to
evacuate the Acadian colony. The Acadians, having completed
their usefulness in pioneering the land, were to be deported.

In the year 1755 in all the villages of Nova Scotia—in Grand
Pré, Minas, Minard, Port Royal, Beaubassin, St. Gabriel and
others—men and women were called into the church houses
on a certain Sunday morning to hear the proclamation which
spoke their doom. The words were slowly absorbed, the people
stunned almost past believing. Acadians were to be driven
away from their lands and goods, scattered along the Atlantic
coast. And it was to be done immediately!

A few days later began *le Grand Dérangement,* as it is still
called by Acadians of Louisiana. Hundreds of helpless exiles
were crowded onto small ships which bore them away from

their native land. Families were separated, never to be joined again. With their villages burning behind them and their beaches crowded with despairing comrades and friends, the Acadians of the first deportation presented a picture as tragic as any in history.

For eleven years the British actively continued their pursuit and deportation of the Acadians, exiling more than eight thousand. Ships that carried them were infested with smallpox and other diseases. Four thousand of them died at sea. Those that survived were scattered along the coast in the American Colonies of Pennsylvania, Massachusetts, Georgia, the Carolinas, Connecticut, New York and Maryland. For thirty years in all they were doomed to wander over a continent far more inhospitable to them than it was to the European DP's who followed them by almost two hundred years.

From all these Atlantic coast Colonies except Maryland the Acadians were driven away with bitterness and resentment. Maryland received the exiles with kindness. From there Acadians drifted gradually down into the more southerly states. Most of them pushed toward Louisiana, seeking to join other French people in that state.

Louisiana welcomed them. The first party arrived in 1756 and aroused such sympathy among the French people that Baron de Kerlerec, Governor of Louisiana, gave them lands, seed and provisions for establishing in the interior. They were permitted to choose their lands. An engineer was appointed to locate the sites for their settlements, along navigable streams. Land was distributed according to the number in the family. Other Acadians poured into Louisiana from all parts of the United States, with due bills for services, issued by the government of France and by Canada. Thirty years after the *Grand Dérangement* a group of fifteen hundred Acadians who had been living for a quarter century in France came to join their relatives in Louisiana.

At last the wandering exiles had found a home. In the midst of a great unexplored state, among the primitive Indian settlements, they carved out a land which they claimed for their

own. They made good citizens, justifying the faith placed in
them by one official who declared: "They are reborn in
Louisiana, and they will perform marvels if they are given a
little assistance. Thus, at a time when least expected, this
country will flourish." Filled with the natural energy of their
race and with a love of honest toil, they soon transformed the
wilderness into a garden land.

The Acadians, being originally from the northern provinces of
Normandy, Brittany and Picardy, were possessed of a rugged
physical constitution and a Celtic, almost Nordic civilization
completely at variance with the Latin attributes dominating
early Louisiana settlers from France. It was the physical
hardihood of these people which enabled them to colonize and
survive the rigors of the Canadian winters. And it was this
physical strength combined with a robust quality of self-
reliance which set them apart in Louisiana from the Latin
colonists coming from the temperate climes of central and
southern France. Acadians were peasant fisherfolk whose ancestors had fished for cod off Nova Scotia banks long before
Columbus discovered America. The other French settlers of
Louisiana were younger sons of nobility, urban shopkeepers,
entrepreneurs and petty officials, long accustomed to finer
social amenities and the acceptance of a monarchial government almost unknown to the onetime Bretons and Normans.

Once in the new land, Acadians did not remain aloof as a
separate group. They mixed their blood with other French
people, the "originals" from the mother country, and with the
Spanish and the Creoles. With the Indians even, and with the
few *américains* they found there. Some of them settled along
winding bayous, some sought farm lands away from water,
some wandered along coastal marshes and became trappers;
others settled along the Gulf where they found good fishing.

They scattered their seed afar in this warm friendly land.
They became farmers in the rice fields, alligator hunters on
the bayous, trappers hip-deep in the cold, wet marsh, fishermen for crab and crayfish, shrimp and oysters, cane planters
"along the front" of the big bayous and moss gatherers "in the

back" . . . and always they were a warm-blooded, laughter-loving people, rich in a heritage of courage and strength.
For two centuries it has been thus in Louisiana.
And where are the children of those original Acadian exiles today? Where does one go to find the true Louisiana Acadian? Where *are* Evangeline's people and what have they become?

These questions entangled my imagination. And so, a few years ago, I determined to go into the new Acadia of South Louisiana, into the land and among the people descended from the early exiles—to settle for myself the truth and the mystery of these peoples, to find the real children of Evangeline's land.
I thought I knew what Acadians would be like when I found them. They would be physically attractive people—lithe, agile and strong, with a dark French beauty. They would be full of peasant sturdiness, but softened with the grace of life in a warm, lush climate. They would be courageous people, happy people, satisfied with simple things, honestly proud of their tradition and the customs they carried from far old *Acadie*. They would live close to the land without losing sight of water, and live close to the water while always loving the land—for water and land were as closely blended in their new country as in their old.
These were the Acadians I sought.
Early I ran across a difficulty. If I sought the Acadians, who were the "Cajuns" . . . and who were the Creoles? That, I found, was the puzzling mystery of this land.
For no matter where one goes in the Cajun country, one seems to be searching for something which does not exist. The "Cajun" is always the other fellow. Sentiment everywhere seems to be: "Me, I'm Creole . . . that other fellow, he's Cajun."
I found that today the term "Cajun," a contraction of Acadian, has lost its racial meaning and taken on social connotations. It is used by some as a term of disregard, applied to the most ignorant of the lower classes. The city dweller refers to his country cousin as "a simple Cajun." The country

farmer refers to a neighbor as a "down-the-bayou Cajun"
and even the swamper speaks of "dem damn Cajuns in de
back"—by which he means the water dwellers in deep interior
swamp country. Occasionally a flippant sophisticate refers to
himself as a Cajun, but when a stranger speaks of him in the
same way the stranger must smile, and smile broadly.

The Creole, on the other hand, stands for all that is fine,
rich and noble. Creoles are descendants of the first French and
Spanish settlers of Louisiana, the "originals." Those earliest
settlers were noblemen, dashing romantics, the elite and cul-
tured of Continental Europe. They established a culture dis-
tinctly their own in the New World. Their glamorous traditions
contrasted strongly with the peasant background of the early
Acadians. Creoles were gallants, extravagant cavaliers. Acadians were sturdy, plodding peasants. This resulted in a distinction of terms which is not borne out actually in the blood
mixture of the two peoples. Today in Louisiana there are few
Creole families who do not have Acadian forebears, few
Acadian families whose blood is not mixed with the Creoles.
Yet the terms are used as referring to two distinct racial groups
and cultures.

It is now two hundred years since Acadians began the
wanderings which led them finally to Louisiana's friendly
bayou country. Today Acadians possess South Louisiana completely. The Acadian blood is thick, and strong in a great
tradition of suffering and triumph. For two centuries the fire
of the French heritage has burned in the hearts of these people.
The fire will not soon grow dim.

The future of the Acadians is as shrouded in mystery as is
their past and present. Changes are coming fast to Louisiana,
the old rural ways yielding to a booming industrialization.
Everywhere Acadians are losing their distinctive foreign ways.
Roads are being built into the deepest interior villages. Schools
are reaching the furthest marshy islands. Children of French
settlements are speaking English, are teaching their parents a
new language, and taking pride in the ways of a changing outside world.

Yet for centuries to come the spirit of this people's great courage will be an inspiration wherever tales of brave men are told. And certainly the Acadians as much as any group of people in history exemplify the words of the poet Ronsard:

> *Le français ressemble au saule verdissant:*
> *Plus on le coupe et plus il est naissant.*
>
> (The French resemble a growing willow:
> The more you cut it the more it grows.)

This is the story of my search for the true Cajun of Evangeline's land. It began more than a decade ago and with an erratic insistency which Cajuns appreciate and condone, it still goes on today. I hope it never ends.

The search has brought many, many adventures. Things I've seen . . . people I've met! . . . But that is my story.

Some of those who guided me have gone now. Some of the trails themselves have changed. Time moves on, more swiftly now, even in the bayou country, and the new industrialization is bringing change here as elsewhere.

Yet the basic elements of drama have not changed in this fabulous land-and-water country. Wherever Gallic traditions of the good life remain—and that is everywhere in the bayou land—there is romance aplenty to share.

It is only necessary that you remember one thing—that in the Cajun country, as in all life, your experiences are expanded by what your heart brings to them. For many of us the horizon of travel does not stretch to golden lands of Tamerlane, nor to hidden heights of Tibet, nor to jungles of Cambodia. Yet adventure is ours on closer shores of home, along a thousand water trails of winding bayous, in a dozen Cajun villages within close range of New Orleans. For wherever there are our fellows, living out the intricate patterns of their own charmed lives, there is experience waiting for us to explore.

So you will find your own adventures in Evangeline's enchanted land. But first, read some of mine.

Bon voyage, mon ami!

Cajuns on

the Bayous

M'sieu André's Prophecy

i

On a sultry night in June my search began.

I stood talking with a Creole gentleman on the verandah of the Frederick Hotel in New Iberia. It was the time of early evening known as "first dark." Lights were beginning to come on in store windows along the street which curved gently toward that lovely old plantation home, Shadows on the Teche. From three blocks away I could hear the starlings chattering in the high bamboo hedge which hid that home from the street. Down on Bayou Teche bullfrogs and katydids were beginning their evening symphony. From one silver-voiced mourning dove, harbored in a giant live oak along the bayou bank, come a poignant call of loneliness and wonder.

As the Creole gentleman murmured *"bonsoir"* to passing friends, I tried to be casually destructive to the monstrous mosquitoes attacking us from all sides.

Feeling a little apologetic for speaking in English—and, insult to injury, without even a trace of French accent!—I told him exactly why I was there.

"Mon dieu, Mam'selle! It is something, this thing you want

1

to do. You desire to see the Acadian country—*all* of it? And you want to know Evangeline's people?"

He looked at me a little queerly, I thought, then waited a long time to answer.

"*Mam'selle,* you search for a myth," the Creole gentleman said. "You will find many, many peoples, but who is to say if you will find the true Acadian? In all South Louisiana I know only one man who can define for you the true Acadian. You will find him in St. Martinville. Go there and ask for Monsieur André Olivier."

He paused and stood quietly, his head tilted slightly to one side as if listening to the night sounds from the bayou and considering some other sounds which I might not have heard.

"*Mais oui, Mam'selle,* you search for a myth of land and of people. But I envy you the searching!"

Next morning saw the start of the fabulous journey which was to begin so sanely in the "heart of the Evangeline country" and was to lead into so many strange paths before it was done.

From New Iberia it was a short seven miles, along an oak-lined road, to St. Martinville. Through this little town Bayou Teche flowed indolently, glistening blue-white in the morning sun save for the deep green shadows of the willows and the brooding darkness of the live oaks along its banks.

I crossed the main bridge to find a small notion shop, its windows crowded with a mad miscellanea of goods and bearing over its door a huge sign: "Evangeline Enshrined Here."

Inside I knew I would find Monsieur André Olivier, recognized historian of the Acadian country, the man who had preserved the relics of his people in a hodgepodge country store-museum which is one of the strangest in the world.

As the wiry little gentleman came out of the recesses of his store's back quarters, approaching with a delicate step and bowing in a courtly manner, I knew that here was living legend.

Straight out of a Molière comedy was *M'sieu* André, or perhaps a tragedy of Racine; but quite, quite French of the seventeenth century. His brilliant black eyes were set in a thin, dark face, and he had a look about him of one always seeking something. "Highly-tuned as a Stradivarius," I was later to hear him called, and this is what I felt on our first meeting. You could see M'sieu André flicking snuff from a lace handkerchief and leading the minuet with the daintiest of them. Or, in more serious mood, you could see him adjusting his lorgnette, hem-hawing a bit, and reading a paper before the French Academy.

With a gesture of graciousness worthy of an invitation to Versailles or Fontainebleau, M'sieu bowed me into the crowded aisles of his shop. Counters on either side were stacked high with an assortment of truly staggering diversity. Newly-knitted fish nets, shiny cane poles, old-fashioned gas street lamps, antique hardware, wood stoves, coils of rope, assorted groceries, and a thousand other minutia crowded the counters and the musty shelves.

In a back corner of this strange country store-museum was M'sieu André's shrine to Evangeline. While my eyes were still straining into the dimness, he flicked on a small spotlight and flooded the shelves with brilliant light. This, I realized, was his big moment. With thin blue-veined fingers M'sieu André picked up a pince-nez which hung by a black ribbon around his neck. Solemnly he placed the pince-nez on his finely-shaped nose, cleared his throat and began a lecture. His voice was dry, strained, monotonous—the voice of the museum curator the world over. But when I interrupted with a question, seeking to get things off the other-world plane, it became soft, smooth, strongly-accented and beautiful. Much as I enjoyed the information he gave me, I realized that he enjoyed it more, this seance with his beloved Evangeliana—his prized spinning wheels, hand-wrought chests, baskets, hand-woven hats, couche-couche bowls, the old St. Martinville Gazette published on wallpaper during Reconstruction days, and other hoary documents.

Then it was over and M'sieu André sighed as he switched off the spotlight. We blinked at each other a moment in the sudden darkness, then *M'sieu* André invited me into his quaint Acadian garden which lay between the store and his adjoining cottage. There he served thick, black, drip coffee which I drank with alacrity, remembering my Creole friend's advice: "Only two things you must remember. Always drink their coffee, and never to their faces call them 'Cajun.' "

He told me how he, André Olivier—sired by Hughes Charles Honoré Olivier de Vezin, a French nobleman, and by the earliest of the Acadian exiles—was from childhood enthralled by the Evangeline legend, how years of work and research had gained him the title of Historian of the Teche.

And he told me many tales of his people: How the Acadian French was actually the old French as it was spoken by the elite of France in the seventeenth century; how the *code Napoléon* was still the law of his people; how the purest-blooded Acadians mixed their blood with two other French groups who first settled Louisiana, the "originals" from France and the Creoles who refugeed from the Haiti Revolution.

He told me about the fifty Acadian citizens of St. Martinville who made a pilgrimage to their ancestral homes in Nova Scotia in 1930—how cousins met cousins after one hundred and seventy-five years. And how one hundred and fifty Acadians from Nova Scotia returned the visit the next year to *l'Acadie louisianaise*. How five years later, in 1936, the Louisiana cousins made yet another visit to the fabled land of their forefathers. And how the visits continued to go on, the old ties growing stronger among a people who loved and revered their ancestral traditions.

For *M'sieu* André these episodes were equalled in drama only by the terrifying flood of 1927 in which all his people fled from Bayou Teche and there were left in St. Martinville only the priests, the valiant newspaper editor, Lazaire Bienvenue, and himself.

"When the waters flood Evangeline's Oak we will leave," the townspeople had said.

And when the waters sucked around the huge oak's limbs, only the priests, the editor and *M'sieu* André had stayed on.

He had gathered his museum about him in the attic *garçon-nière* of his Acadian cottage and watched the water creep up and up. When the flood receded at last, it left the Teche a devastated and wasted valley which has never completely regained its beauty.

M'sieu André's story of the "real Evangeline," the gentle one his grandparents remembered and told him about, differs from that of Longfellow's poem. Separated from her fiancé at the time of *le Grand Dérangement,* she endured the same terrible hardships suffered by all the wandering Acadian exiles. Many mothers, wives and sweethearts spent lifetimes in fruitless searches for their loved ones. Battling the terrors of an unknown land, they walked barefoot or combed the streams in pirogues, going backward and forward upon rumors that in this or that place was a settlement where son, daughter or wife, husband or lover had been found.

Such a girl was Emmaline Labiche who was torn from the arms of her love, Louis Arcinaux, on that dread morning in 1755. Louis found his way to the bayou country of South Louisiana. Despairing of ever finding his lost fiancée, he married another Acadian exile and settled in St. Martinville.

Then one morning several years later, a crowd gathered under the huge oak trees near the wharf on the bayou banks and cheered lustily as another group of exiles stepped off a barge and was welcomed into the hospitable new land. Among those who walked down the gangplank was frail, beautiful Emmaline Labiche, her eyes searching feverishly among the crowds lining the bank. With a hoarse cry Louis rushed forward, forgetting his new wife, and took her in his arms. Then came the shocking news, so unbelievably cruel to the delicate Emmaline that she fell unconscious. She was never well again, spent her few remaining months in gentle madness, dancing and picking flowers up and down the bayou banks, and died finally in the mournfully beautiful new land where she had found her lover at last, then lost him forever.

This is the true story as it was told to Longfellow by a

young St. Martinville student attending Harvard law school.
The young man told Emmaline's story first to Hawthorne,
who was unimpressed, then to Longfellow who recognized its
dramatic possibilities and reworked the story into one of
America's immortal love poems.

Having successfully drained my first tiny demitasse of black
Acadian coffee, and feeling somehow like one who had joined
a great fraternity, I began to wonder if I could persuade
M'sieu André to give me a personalized tour of his city. Perhaps, after all, my search would not be as complicated as I had
been led to believe. It might, in fact, be a *fait accompli* in very
short order if I could only have *M'sieu* André as my guide!
For surely Evangeline's land and its people held no mysteries
for him.

Seeming to anticipate my question, the Acadian gentleman
rose and said, "Would *Mam'selle* want to see our *Petit Paris?*"

He took me first to Evangeline's grave and monument, in
the old Attakapas Cemetery where Indians had once buried
their dead. Here was a quiet tomb marked by a bronze monument of exquisite simplicity and beauty. The young girl sat
peacefully there, resting from all her weary wanderings, her
hands folded in her lap, her cape falling from her shoulders,
and a look of serenity on her face. For her, one knows, the
search is over.

M'sieu André cleared his throat as he read the inscription
beneath the statue.

"*Mais oui,* is it not beautiful, *Mam'selle?*"

He told me how this statue was given by the cast of the
motion picture "Evangeline" after they filmed the story at
nearby Catahoula Lake in 1929. It was dedicated by Dolores
del Rio whom all the people of St. Martinville grew to love
during the weeks when she worked there.

It was then I felt a strange sensation which seemed to suffuse
the air around this spot, to engulf me with a startling vivid-
ness. Perhaps it was compounded of the vitality in the statue,
of *M'sieu* André's reference to 1929 and Dolores del Rio as if
they were yesterday, of the brightness and sunlit freshness of

the air around the old St. Martin Church and the high-pitched children's laughter that rang across the lawn from the nearby convent school. It was for a moment an overwhelming sensation of the meeting and merging at this spot of the lives of gentle folk of two centuries past.

Perhaps it was nothing but the usual air in *le Petit Paris*, I decided, when *M'sieu* André turned from the shaded tomb and led me into the cool, shadowy aisles of old St. Martin Church.

Within these walls, completed in 1832, was the original chapel built in 1765 when Father Jean François of the Capuchin Order became the first resident priest of the pioneer outpost.

Among the pews, though it was mid-afternoon, I saw a dozen or more people kneeling at their prayers. For the people of St. Martinville are as deeply religious today as in those bitter days two hundred years ago. Sermons here are still delivered in French to a people whose faith is strong in the tradition of their forefathers.

M'sieu André pointed out three outstanding features of the church before he told me the story of the bells. Above the main altar was a painting showing the patron saint of the town, St. Martin of Tours and the beggar with whom he divided his cloak. The painting was done by Jean François Mouchet, son of the great eighteenth-century artist, François Marie Mouchet. Painted sometime between 1830 and 1840, it pictured a figure on horseback, Martinius, a Roman soldier who later became a priest, a bishop, and finally was canonized as St. Martin of Tours.

M'sieu André pointed out next the elaborate baptismal fount of sculptured marble, with its beautifully carved wooden lid. This fount, in which thousands of Acadian and Creole babes have been christened, was a gift of King Louis XVI, the unfortunate monarch who was beheaded before his royal gift ever reached its destination at the mission church of his faraway subjects.

I liked best *M'sieu* André's story of the bells and their christening day. It was many years ago that, from miles

around, the Acadians swarmed into St. Martinville for the
christening of the bells. Before the altar, on a long table
clothed in white, the three bronze bells stood bedecked in
ribbons and flowers. The largest of the bells, weighing 2100
pounds, was christened Marie Angeli. It was presented by its
godparents, Monsieur and Madame John Ferran. The middle-
sized bell, weighing 1050 pounds, was christened Stéphanie.
Its godparents were Monsieur and Madame Albert Levert.
The smallest bell, was named Father Auguste Thébault, after
a beloved priest of the parish. Its godparents were Monsieur
and Madame Auguste Maraist.

After the solemn christening, the bells had been lifted to
their places high in the spire of St. Martin Church. And ever
since that day they have been a part of all the lives in *Petit
Paris*. They have rung proudly for christenings of beloved
infants, have called joyously for weddings and mournfully
tolled for funerals. Down through the decades they have rung
out the Angelus in the morning, at noon and in the evening.
All who live within the sound of the bells know well their
familiar voices—the delicate call of Auguste as she rings a
full hour before High Mass on Sunday mornings; the deeper
tone of Stéphanie ringing half an hour later; and finally the
full, vibrant tones of Marie Angeli joining the other two to
make a trio of glorious, golden calls, hastening all to worship.

As we walked out of the church onto its oak- and palm-
shaded lawn, I realized again that we were in the very heart
of the little town, with post office, courthouse, parochial
school and business buildings all grouped within a few blocks,
as if they clustered attentively around the church which was
so important a part of their lives.

We had only to stroll a block to the post office which *M'sieu*
André showed me with pride. Once a stately plantation home,
this is the only post office in the nation to be used and preserved as a Federal building. Originally it was the home of
Eugène Duchamp de Chastagnier, émigré from the Haitian
rebellion in the West Indies. Out of native cypress and bricks
made from the claybanks of Bayou Teche, he built a replica

Under this oak tree the original Evangeline is said to have ended her long search for her lover when her ship docked here. There is an inscribed plaque on the tree, dedicated by citizens of St. Martinville, and there is a statue of Evangeline in the churchyard nearby.

of his sugar plantation home in Martinique. Many years later, rather than see it neglected or destroyed, the people of St. Martinville purchased it by popular donation and made it their post office.

Inside, over the mantelpiece in the postmaster's office, was a mural of the Evangeline story. Here *M'sieu* André stood and mused, as though trying to determine if it suited his exquisite sense of fittingness for all things related to the unfortunate heroine whose memory he treasured.

The pretentious building, with its lofty grandeur, its lace iron grillwork, was completely unlike the simple Acadian architecture that I had seen elsewhere in the town.

"What does it mean?" I asked *M'sieu* André, "and what is meant when you say *le Petit Paris?*"

The question seemed to please him and he launched into a capsule history of his native city. It gave the answer to the differing cultural patterns which were so plainly evident throughout the little town.

According to *M'sieu* André, Frenchmen from three far, different lands settled the early outpost which in its later, more sophisticated days was to become known as *Petit Paris*. First were *les originals* who came direct from France in the early 1700's. They built a military post, called Poste des Attakapas, in wild lands inhabited only by hostile Attakapas Indians. These first settlers carved out huge indigo plantations along the rich Techelands. Living in this small oasis in the wilderness, surrounded by fierce Indians, they enjoyed a life of comparative luxury.

By 1765 the poor exiled Acadians began to reach the Poste des Attakapas. They trapped furs, fished, raised cattle, farmed the bayou banks. With courage, hard work and independent spirit they rebuilt their lives in this beautiful new homeland.

A third group of settlers arrived at the close of the eighteenth century, also French refugees. These émigrés, so different from the simple Acadian folk, were the aristocracy who had fled the bitter French Revolution. Intending to make only temporary residence here until their monarch and court were restored in France, they nevertheless began to like their new home, and they remained as colonists.

It was their influence which caused the pioneer outpost to assume the flavor and the name of *le Petit Paris*. In their adopted city the nobility resumed the same extravagant social formalities they had enjoyed in their brilliant European capital. Barons, marquis and counts gave great balls where their ladies displayed court gowns and rare, precious jewels. At their *fêtes champêtres* the exiled nobility dazzled the eyes of simple Acadians. Spending fortunes on a single ball, they followed extravagant social patterns modeled on Marie Antoinette's court.

But the wilderness was never far away and eventually the sophisticated splendors began to fade under the rugged pioneer necessities. Noble-born ladies sold their jewels to support husbands and sons who were unable to meet the hard physical tests of the pioneer land. A few hardier families adapted to a life of trading or farming, but most sank to poverty-stricken gentility. Pride and memories of the old glorious days sustained them. Their descendants married with humble Acadians and today there is a fusion of the two cultures which gives St. Martinville its unique cultural flavor.

Through the bewildering changes of government which made the Poste des Attakapas first a French settlement, then a Spanish post, then French again, and finally, in 1803, a United States purchase, the little town prospered and made outstanding contributions to the state. When Louisiana was admitted to the Union as a state, the town's name was changed to St. Martinville.

It was a steamboat town in the 1800's, its life built on the busy traffic along twisting Bayou Teche. As long as the proud white steamboats brought their cargoes, their sophisticated passengers, their showboats and their exciting, glamorous days, St. Martinville retained its importance as the leading river port of the beautiful Teche. When the river traffic died and railroads chose to bestow their lusty blessings on New Iberia, nine miles away, *le Petit Paris* began to fade. Its gracious people mourned the passing of the steamboats, but did not regret loss of the railways. Today, *M'sieu* André told me, they are extremely happy with their town as it is. Here a Frenchman, be he descendant of Parisian nobility, Haitian planter or Acadian peasant—or, as is likely, a blending of the three— can feel at home, close to the good rich land which welcomed the ancient exiles and gave them a new good life.

From the post office *M'sieu* André walked me past the nearby courthouse, a white-columned classic structure, slave-built before the War between the States.

His eyes glistened as he spoke.

"Her vaults, *Mam'selle*, hold more exciting records than my own museum. They hold papers of the Poste des Attakapas going back to 1760. Many of the later papers, particularly wills and testaments, were written on backs of wallpaper during the War between the States."

We walked inside to see, emblemmed in the lobby of the old courthouse, the coats of arms of some of the post commandants and other families of French nobility who were ancestors of the present day citizens of *le Petit Paris*.

Then *M'sieu* André bowed me into his automobile and continued our tour to the outskirts of town, to the Longfellow Evangeline State Park. The flavor changed quickly from the grandeur of early nobility to the humble Acadian accouterments of a peasant people exiled to rough wilderness life.

The park gave a picture of what life was like in the days of early Louisiana Acadia.

"In the park, *Mam'selle*, you see the homes of poor Acadians and rich Acadians also," said *M'sieu* André as we stood before a tiny fenced-in cottage.

This charming cottage was a reproduction of those built by the Acadian peasants two hundred years ago, and in its simple lines I saw the same pattern I was to see many times later throughout the Evangeline country.

Originally the houses were of hand-hewn lumber, mortised with wooden pegs, and built with a combination dining room and kitchen separated from the main house. A staircase on the

front porch led to the attic, which was called the *garçonnière*,
or boys' room. In wealthier homes the *garçonnière* was a separate building, but in modest homes like this the attic served
nicely for the boys' dormitory. Every Acadian boy, rich or
poor, was entitled to these private quarters.

Today this little house serves as a *boutique* where one can
see demonstrations of spinning, weaving and other early
Acadian crafts. Also one can buy finely-woven materials, huge
straw hats made from palmetto leaves, bonnets and aprons of
the type used by Acadians. These are made by local craftsmen
who have not lost the skill nor the knowledge of their forebears.

I saw the charming curator of this little *boutique* lean out
the screenless window, so typical of every Acadian home, and
wave her hand in the direction of some nearby oak trees. This
signal called forth a rather startling apparition. Suddenly a
horse and a big-wheeled buggy appeared at the gate of the
split-cypress fence surrounding the cottage.

M'sieu André was as pleased as I when a youth hopped out
of the buggy and said,

"Would *M'sieu* and *Mam'selle* like a ride through the park
in our Acadian flivver?"

The invitation was such a combination of old and modern
Acadia that I had to laugh as we boarded the "flivver." The
horsedrawn buggy was similar to those still in common use
throughout Evangeline's land of today.

In a delightful clop-clop ride through the park I felt what
it must have been like in the older days. We rode over graveled
roads winding among Gargantuan moss-draped oak trees,
along a shining little coulee or *petit* bayou, which glistened
in the sunlight. Finally we arrived at the Acadia House
Museum, surrounded by great oak trees, a handsome home of
the type built by wealthier Acadians.

This home and the surrounding park through which we had
ridden, was once the estate of an *original* named d'Hauterive,
who arrived from France in 1763. The big house and the small
kitchen lying to its rear was beautifully restored after the state

This Cajun cottage is the boutique of the Acadian State Park in St. Martinville, where visitors may purchase handiwork done today by descendants of the original Acadians. Note the outside stairway and the mud chimney, both typical of Acadian homes in the Louisiana bayou country.

purchased the property in 1931. Inside we saw many tools, household furnishings and other evidences of life among early Acadian settlers.

Back in *M'sieu* André's car, we left the park and drove still further down the highway leading away from St. Martinville.

"*Mam'selle*, I will show you now a different story, one you will find hard to believe," he said.

Looking at my guide as he sat stiffly behind the wheel of his modern automobile, I wanted to say, "But, *M'sieu* André, I find them *all* hard to believe . . . and hardest of all is *you.*"

For it was true that the sight of *M'sieu* André—his slender, blue-veined fingers gripping the wheel, his straw hat resting gingerly on his high, white forehead, his black-rimmed pince-nez gripped on his nose—seemed thoroughly incongruous to this day and this occasion. He looked, somehow, ill at ease in his modern dress and sitting behind the wheel of an automobile. It seemed to me he would be more at home behind a coach-and-four, gesturing imperiously for a coachman to turn a span of blooded mares into this lane of giant oaks which we were approaching.

Suddenly we slowed and turned into the lane of oaks and moss-bearded pine trees which stretched ahead for a mile. Branches of the magnificent old trees met overhead. Moss hung down almost to our car top.

I got a startling impression that the oaks and pines were as human as we, and that they were lonely as *M'sieu* André looked lonely—for older, better days, for the white-columned plantation mansion which once had stood at their head, and for one glorious night when they were festooned with gold . . .

"Wait," exclaimed *M'sieu* André, "don't put the cart before the story."

Then he told me of days and nights which these old giants must remember and sigh for always.

Once, at the head of this mile-long tunnel of trees, stood the magnificent mansion of Monsieur Charles Durande. This fabulously wealthy *bon vivant*, who arrived in *le Petit Paris* in 1820, was forever startling the gay colony with mad and beautiful extravagances which endeared and enchanted the pleasure-loving French.

Not content with the usual planter's dream, a handsome lane of live oaks before the façade of his home, he planted *two* lanes of oaks and pines. These crossed each other at right angles, making the form of a cross. One alley, three miles long, led from his doorstep to the family wharf on Bayou Teche.

The pride of this flamboyant gentleman's heart were his two daughters, whose beauty, naturally, surpassed that of all other girls of the colony. When his daughters were still little girls he made them a promise.

"I will give you the most beautiful wedding that ever was in all Louisiana!" he said. Then *"Non, mon dieu,* the most beautiful in the whole world!"

The girls grew up, fell in love, and it was time—*voilà!*—to plan a double wedding.

Papa Durande's imagination proved equal to the fulfillment of his promise.

"Bring me a million spiders!" he commanded, and his daughters shook their heads in wonderment.

Some say he sent his slaves into the murky swamps of nearby Catahoula Lake to find them. Others say he sent to China for a whole boatload of spiders and had them shipped up Bayou Teche from New Orleans.

Anyway, thousands of spiders were delivered to the plantation and released among the moss-draped limbs of giant trees along the alleys of oaks and pines. Soon the trees were webbed with millions of yards of filmy lace. From California special couriers brought hundreds of pounds of silver and gold dust. Negro slaves sprayed the glittering metal over the spider webs, making a glistening mile-long fairy canopy!

Two thousand guests sauntered down the silver-and-gold alley to the altar which stood at its head, in front of the white-columned mansion. There never was a day like this, nor a night like the one when guests danced till dawn under the glittering canopy!

Grandchildren of the Durandes, and those of the guests who

were part of the glorious spectacle, will tell the tale forever.

The mansion gone now, only the Gargantuan oaks and pines are left to live on another hundred years or so in memory of that glorious night.

Slight wonder I felt enchantment in that haunted lane. The ghosts that wander there are touched with a golden wand. And the happiest ghost of all is doubtless *Papa* Durande who wanders contentedly along the tree lanes and smiles as he remembers how he kept his promise to his beautiful daughters.

There was one more stop on *M'sieu* André's tour.

Back in St. Martinville, he drove to the old Castillo Hotel, hard by the banks of Bayou Teche. This building, which now houses the Convent of Mercy School, is the oldest in town, said to date back to 1795 when it was an Indian trading post. For generations it served as an inn, until a certain Monsieur Castillo renovated it and gave it his family name. Close by the busy wharves of Bayou Teche, where cargo lay stacked high and passengers picked their way daintily to the hotel's hospitable portals, the old Castillo was a vital part of *le Petit Paris*. Troupers of the French opera lived here on their annual visits to the sophisticated city in the wilderness. French Royalists gave great balls here, trying with music, wine, and laughter to silence the noises of the wilderness and recapture the glory of the European capital they had lost.

Since 1896 the building has housed a school run by Catholic Sisters of Mercy. Today children's voices mix their echoes with those of days long gone.

M'sieu André had saved the Evangeline Oak for the last.

Our afternoon was gone. Dusk crept slowly through the willows and oaks, along the bayou banks. We felt it in the darkening limbs of Evangeline's oak, under which we stood. The ancient tree stood proudly within its little iron-chain fence, set apart from the rest, as was fitting.

M'sieu André spoke quietly:

"It is said that here under this oak tree, Louis Arcenaux

spoke to Emmaline Labiche the words that broke her heart."

Leaving the oak, we walked along the bank of the bayou called "Teche," or snake, because it winds and twists in reptilian strides through the whole Acadian country and down to the sprawling Atchafalaya.

My mind was crowded with the afternoon's experiences, the contrasting, conflicting tales of *le Petit Paris* and the strangely mixed pattern of its cultures. I was as confused, maybe more so, as when we started our tour. The changing patterns whirled about in a kind of kaleidoscope, and the only thing that seemed to be sure, certain and definite was this Bayou Teche on whose bank we stood.

Perhaps *M'sieu* André had read my thoughts.

"Mam'selle," he said, "you have now met some of our Acadians. There are many others. My people crowd the banks of the Teche for miles below. They live in mansions and in hovels along this bayou which first led them into their new land, the bayou they have traveled by steamboat and johnboat, by shanty boat and . . ."

A daring thought flashed into my mind and I interrupted him in my excitement.

"M'sieu André! I want to follow down the Teche!"

And as the idea leaped stronger into my imagination, "I want to go on an old steamboat . . . to sit on the long white decks and watch the paddle wheel churn the winding bayou. I want . . ."

His expression stopped me from getting more lyrical. He stood there, sad-eyed and glum, and shook his head.

"Ah, *Mam'selle,"* he murmured. "It is too late. All the great white steamboats are gone. Only one is left, a plodding packet turned freighter, which the law prevents from carrying passengers. No, *Mam'selle,* to go by steamboat . . ." He paused, his face lighting up for a moment. ". . . But it is quite, quite impossible."

His hands fell expressively in a gesture of resignation.

"Come back now to my garden," he said, "and I will give you something else which may help in your searching."

We sat again in the small Acadian garden adjoining the country store-museum. *M'sieu* André lit the first of several coach lanterns which stood on antique lamp posts within the tranquil enclosure. It cut a circle of brightness in the blackening dusk.

M'sieu André disappeared into his cottage, returned in a moment with a small tray and liqueur glasses. We were tired and drank the fine liqueur in silence.

Then he drew from his pocket a frazzled old map that carried many penciled and ink-stained markings. He spread it out on the coffee table before us.

"*Mam'selle*, when you ask me to define you the Acadian, you have asked me a difficult question." He spoke with some ceremony and I realized that he was relishing this chance to say a final word on his favorite subject. He drew his finger along an imaginary triangle over the weather-beaten map.

"There will be many to tell you different, but this is the land of Evangeline's people: west from where the Black River bends from the Mississippi, south to where the Sabine flows into the Gulf, and east again to far below New Orleans.

"Go here and here and here," he said, flicking his finger from one end of the map to another, "and you will know Evangeline's people. You will find Acadian and Creole, Spanish and German, Portugese, Italian, Manilamen, Indian-men, and God-knows-what-men . . . But they'll be Frenchmen all. And much of their blood will be from Evangeline's Acadia. You'll find them on the land and you'll find them far down the winding bayous that brought them to this land. You'll find them on farms and in shanty boats. You'll find them in hovels along the bayous. You'll find them everywhere . . . and yet, when you have finished, you will have found them nowhere. For that which you seek, *Mam'selle*, is everywhere, and . . ."

He stopped, his glass poised, and looked at me quizzically.

"Yes?" I asked.

He did not go on, but filled the tiny glasses again with the fine sweet liqueur.

"You must go and search for yourself," he said. "Go and search for my people and when you have finished come back to me . . ."

Then *M'sieu* André lifted his glass and said goodbye with a toast:

"There will be others like me to show you the way. There will be someone in each place to guide you. May the map I give you lead to many places of happiness, and may you find, at last, the true Acadian!"

"Steamin' at de Moon"

ii

Down through Evangeline's country Bayou Teche winds like a silvery thread. The other bayous that cross, join and merge with it are a hundred other silver threads which twist and twine like a great fish net over the interior and down into the Gulf parishes of Louisiana. Through rich farmlands and peaceful meadows, through throbbing oil fields and through the ancient watery mysteries of the far, dim swamps these bayous flow quietly to the sea.

To travel these waterways is to know the secrets of scores of Evangeline's people who ended their exile and made their homes by the banks of these beautiful streams.

And what better way to travel than by a chugging old stern-wheeler?

From the moment that *M'sieu* André had said, *"Non, Mam'selle,* to go by steamboat is quite, quite impossible," I had known what I must do. It had proved only a *little* difficult —getting a trip that was forbidden by government and insurance regulations.

At New Iberia, nine miles from *M'sieu* André's tranquil garden, the *Str. V. J. Kursweg* made its last landing on the Teche, unloaded its cargo at the Teche Wholesale Grocery Company, picked up a load of "groceries and bulk goods" and turned about to set its stubby nose toward faraway New Orleans. The stern-wheeler was the last of its kind anywhere on the bayous of South Louisiana and one of the few left in the whole United States.

A doughty old lady beloved by her captain and crew, she led the life of another century. Except that her staterooms were empty now and her long white cabins, once resplendent with many lights and music, were stacked high with freight, she was as much a replica of the steamboat era as was to be found in America. Dusky-skinned roustabouts still carried her freight at the landings, singing their rhythmic chants as they toted the loads. Her paddle wheel still stirred the slumbrous Teche—and the Atchafalaya, the Black, Boeuf, Chene, Pigeon, and the mighty Mississippi itself—by the doors of splendid mansions, by lean grey shacks of bayou Cajuns and by thatched huts of the half-breeds.

It was dusk and the *Kursweg* stood ready to lift her stage from the wharf at New Iberia. A storm-clouded sun cast strange lights on Captain Brown Blakeman's face. He stood in the pilothouse, shouting through his megaphone at the black-skinned roustabouts below.

"Cast 'er off, Willie! Lift 'er steady! Now . . . pull 'er in!"

The roustabouts moved swiftly, pulling the hausers to haul aboard the big stage, which is the riverman's gangplank. Our stiff-beamed old boat groaned as she cleared the landing. Now she reversed, with dignity and a certain semblance of her ancient grace. She stood a moment against the other bank of the bayou, as if to bid farewell to her home port and to gather strength for the long voyage ahead.

"Stand to go ahead," shouted red-faced Cap'n Brown. He swung the pilot wheel with a rolling motion that almost lifted him off his feet.

The steamboat creaked, shuddered in her rusty joints, then

leaped forward with a swiftness and ease that left me gasping.

"We're off!" I shouted, then looked quickly at Captain Brown to see if I had disturbed his concentration.

But he smiled broadly at me, nodding with pride and satisfaction. From below decks the crew echoed my shout with their own.

Suddenly I felt a deep pang of regret—for all those thousands of poor mortals who had not stood in a pilothouse and felt that surge of eager motion as some ancient riverboat slid through deep bayou waters and headed downstream.

I rested a hand lightly on the great pilot wheel and silently sent my prayer of thanks to the river gods, wherever they lived in watery splendor, for looking kindly on me and welcoming me to the *Str. Kursweg*.

Would they smile too on my search along the winding bayous for the true Acadian? Surely these waters had meant much to Evangeline's people—had meant highways into the land, roads to and from the markets, had meant life itself to thousands of Cajuns who settled along the twisting streams and lived off the water's harvest of fish and game. The Acadians of the land whom I had seen around St. Martinville were healthy peasant stock of Nova Scotia or fastidious French gentility remembering luxurious Creole days. But they lacked the love of water which most of Evangeline's people had developed in their years of wanderings through the myriad bayous, streams and coulees of their adopted land.

Now I was to know the Acadians who made their homes on the waters—people whose gardens were the blue hyacinths on still bayous, whose front porches were boat decks, and whose streets were water trails. Were these, perhaps, the true Acadians, the real descendants of Evangeline's harassed exiles?

From the pilothouse I walked onto the hurricane deck and watched as the sun dropped behind the bearded oaks, casting long shadows across the limpid bayou. From a high embankment to starboard I saw resplendent columns of the same great old plantation home I had visited earlier in New Iberia. At Shadows on the Teche, the ancestral home of artist Weeks

Hall, lived a Creole-Acadian gentleman whose inherited knowledge of this land would surpass whatever I could learn.

Dusk dropped swiftly now on the splendid columns, as I stood on the hurricane deck and bid goodbye to Cajuns of the land.

The first night aboard was always a quiet one. Even the *Kursweg's* ancient engines seemed to whisper in the darkness. From below came no sounds of the crew, not even enough to make me wonder about them and what manner of men they were. In the pilothouse Captain Brown Blakeman, known affectionately to all along the bayous as "Cap'n Brown," brooded over his thoughts. Occasionally he cocked his head to one side as though to listen and wonder at the old riverboat's silence. I was tired, glad to go early to my small neat cabin with its white-painted wooden walls and its comfortable bunk. The only sound as I fell asleep was that of bayou waters churning through the blades of the huge paddle wheel on our stern.

I wakened abruptly to noise and turmoil, to sounds of the captain's hoarse shouting, to bells ringing in the engine room, to rushing feet of roustabouts on the deck below, and to slapping of waves against the low-slung bow.

Sun streamed into the cabin, reflecting against the ceiling the bright, curving bands of river waves.

"Morgan City, we's comin'," I heard a deckman shout, and realized we had left the languid Teche in the night.

Then a shudder ran through the steamboat's hull and there was a rasping sound as the stage made contact with the wharf and the *Kursweg* warped into its landing.

Outside my window I saw crewmen rush down the stage, and from overhead heard Captain Brown's warning shout.

"Watch the clock, you danged webfeets. Me, I'm gonna pull this here boat outa this here danged shrimp town in half an hour flat."

It was a short stop, just long enough for the Negro warehouse workers of the Teche Wholesale Grocery Company to load a couple of dozen crates of soap and for our crew to

"Shadows on the Teche" is the home of a well-known Creole
gentleman, Weeks Hall of New Iberia. Its gardens run down to
the bayou in back where the old stern-wheeler, the V. J.
Kursweg, *used to ply the water of Bayou Teche.*

scamper happily aboard with two cases of beer.

From where the *Str. Kursweg* lay tied to the wharf, I saw
the Morgan City bridge towering over us, spanning the Atchafalaya River like a steel-limbed Colossus. Under its monstrous
legs river traffic flowed ceaselessly, the shrimp boats surging
past with black nets swinging against their masts, big luggers
and little luggers plodding by with their half-cabins and full-
cabins gleaming white in the morning's sun, johnboats putt-
putting across the wake of the luggers, and far against the
other bank a line of crab boats loaded high with their wooden
crates looking like water-borne chicken coops.

Truly, Morgan City was a riverman's town. I longed to
linger here, to know the life of the shrimp fishermen and crab
fishermen, the oilmen and the swampers who made it their
home.

"You got time, Miss," Captain Brown assured me. "This
here ole town been aroun' these parts for a stretch o' years now
and she ain't afixin' to do nuttin' but keep on growin' bigger.
Them danged Portagees on big shrimp boats call this the
Shrimp Capital o' the Worl' and act like no Cajuns was
catchin' shrimp here before *they* ever moved over from
Floridy. But the Cajuns is learnin' about jumbo shrimp they-
selves, Miss, and ain't no Dago gonna out-shrimp a Cajun
once dat Frenchmens decides to go jumbo-in' out into the
Gulf."

I had heard something earlier about the contest of shrimp
fishermen—the "Floridy-mens" with their heavy-hulled, sixty-
foot luggers blazing deep-water trails into the Gulf and breeding discontent among the "Frenchmens" whose shallow-draft
luggers worked only the inside waters.

But this, as Captain Brown reminded me, must wait for
another day.

As the *Kursweg* left its Morgan City wharf, I stood on the
aftdeck watching her paddle wheel push us away from the
bridge. Hearing a peculiar clump-clump sound, I turned to
see approaching a maimed giant of a man. He towered to a

good six-foot-six but one shoulder slumped down in a sharp slant and he wore at his knee a heavily-padded wooden leg. This was Mr. Joré, the watchman and the first member I was to meet of the enchanted crew which tended and adored the creaky old *Kursweg*.

Although Mr. Joré was well past sixty, his voice was still changing. He addressed me first in a blasting foghorn that shook the timbers beneath us.

"Bonjour, Mam'selle," he said, and I felt the deck quiver with his reverberating tones. He took off his battered riverman's cap and bowed, bracing his wooden leg firmly in a deck seam. His manner reminded me of the courtliness of *M'sieu* André, and I was delighted to find that the gallantry sprang, like *M'sieu* André's, from rich Gallic blood.

"Eh bien, and how you like our tough ole lady, *hein?"*

In the midst of his question, Mr. Joré's voice broke, and he ended in a high mousy squeak. I tried not to look startled at the squeak nor at the question either.

"She been around a long time, her." He paused, seemed to consider the thought and to wonder if his voice would go foghorn or mouse-squeak as he continued. "But not so long as my *grandpère's* schooner, *mais non."*

This conversation, I thought, is beginning to sound like *Alice in Wonderland.* I looked closely to see if Mr. Joré's cap would change into a high hat as quickly as his voice changed on a puzzling remark.

It didn't, and soon I realized that Mr. Joré's comments always made sense, if one only knew a key or two.

"Mon dieu, Mam'selle, she musta been a beauty, her," meaning, naturally, his grandfather's three-masted schooner.

"She done sail straight outa de ole country, that is Brittany, *Mam'selle,* and she come straight into this very river port, her . . . an' tied to bank down there below that blasted big bridge . . . It were a hunnerd years ago, yes, and many times my *p'père* tole me how Morgan City was nuttin' but a little bit of 'er town then. He were a real Frenchmens, him. He married him a pretty lil Cajun lady what came floatin' down the Atchafalaya on a raft with her dad and a coupla sisters. They wus plenty happy and raise fifteen lil childerns and fifty-five gran'childerns. But my *grandpère* have one beeg sorrow. He losted that schooner on a reef at the mouth of the river. My lil *grandmère* say she was glad, her, because now he would have to stay home and learn to crabfish and farm that levee behind their campboat home. But it broke his heart, *Mam'selle.* My *p'père* was a real sailor, him, and he die before he farm a levee bank behind no campboat, him."

It was a sad story, I said, and Mr. Joré said it was not finished yet.

"Once when I was leetle boy, *Mam'selle,* not much taller'n a whooping crane, my *p'père* took me downriver in his pirogue, down to where his schooner got wrecked on that reef. We could see her timbers stickin' out of the marsh. They was ragged and grey from the Gulf winds whipping water against 'em for a year or so. They looked like the ribs of a whale. My *p'père* rested his paddle on the pirogue's side and tried to tell me something. But he couldn't talk 'cause the tears ran out of his eyes. Finally, he got his courage back, and he say, '*Cher,* some mens loves a boat like they loves a woman . . . and if you be that kind of man you can die from a sight like this 'un.

"Then my *p'père* turn round and row like crazy fifteen miles back upriver to his campboat home, and never stopped to res' til we tied up to our front deck. That night *grandmère* heard him cry in his sleep and when the sun came up in the campboat next morning he was dead."

When Mr. Joré stopped, it seemed very still on the stern deck, and I couldn't think of anything to say. We stood there awhile, watched the paddle wheel whirl crests of foam into the air and saw the foamy wake lengthen as the *Kursweg* steamed upriver. The Morgan City bridge became a tiny pigmy against the distant horizon and dwindled away at last.

In the high, white pilothouse above the old hurricane deck Captain Brown was king. A cozy kind of autocrat, with a Cajun accent thick as bayou coffee, he could roar out a belly laugh at one of his own jokes, then change instantly to lacerate a fumbling deckman with a series of biting sarcasms, then could laugh the culprit into good humor again before he had time to sulk. Most of the time Captain Brown looked and acted like a five-year-old's vision of Santa Claus, and he was greatly beloved by the collection of pixilated old coots who were his crewmen.

Standing his watches with him, listening to his tales of the old days on the Atchafalaya and the bayous of the Great Basin, I learned things that stretched credulity far.

"This danged Atchafalaya Basin ain't water and it ain't land. And still it's both. It's the river . . . I guess that's the main thing . . . the deepest river in the whole worl' . . . ninety feet at the bridge in Morgan City, Miss, and so fer down that the fishes busts they lungs when they comes outa there on a line!"

"Yes, and it's a whole mess of bayous too," he continued, "and sloughs and cuts and such. It's one danged monstrous big lake . . . we're comin' into her right now . . . Grand Lake, we calls her . . . and it's God knows how many islands . . ."

Later, confirming the fantastic tales that Captain Brown was to tell me of the Great Basin, I learned that even the river scientists had difficulty putting the mysterious, broad and sprawling waters of Louisiana's Atchafalaya Basin into their proper place.

It was still a primeval wilderness, still unexplored in many of its more remote and inaccessible regions. Bayou Mongoulouis, the Bayou of the Little Bears, Whiskey Bay, Dead Man's Slough, and the Eleven-Mouths-of-the-Atchafalaya into Grand Lake were still spoken of with awe by rivermen from Pittsburgh to New Orleans. The Great Basin, created by devious windings of the short, deep Atchafalaya, was a region of haunting beauty, of tropical, tantalizing silences.

It was a hot green and amber world of great trees and mysterious waters sparsely peopled by strange, wary, suspicious men. You might see a blond, bearded giant of Scandinavian mien smoking his pipe on the deck of a houseboat snugly harbored up some quiet bayou, or a beady-eyed Chitimacha Indian paddling a pirogue loaded with Spanish moss across the open reaches of Grand Lake.

Lying west of Baton Rouge and east of New Iberia, the Great Basin of the Atchafalaya stretches seventy miles long and forty miles wide, a sprawling question mark of shifting waters and islands. No roads penetrated its labyrinths of jungle and stream. A railroad which once traversed the area was abandoned long ago, and from my comfortable chair in the *Kursweg*'s pilothouse I saw swirling waters of the great river wash at ruined piers which once supported a bridge.

The Atchafalaya probably has given more nightmares to more U.S. Engineers than any other stream in America. Even to the river scientists it is still a River of Doubt. For who is to say exactly what will happen when the great Morganza Floodway gates are opened, three hundred miles above New Orleans, and the mighty Mississippi pours its millions of tons of water through the Atchafalaya Basin? Some geologists think the Atchafalaya was the old way of the Mississippi to the sea.

"They's plenty of rivermens like me," said Captain Brown, "who thinks the Old Man will change his course some day and bus' down this short alley to hit the Gulf. And when he do decide . . ." the Captain sobered and his chubby face looked troubled.

"God help us all pore Cajuns, in campboats and in the cities too. They's not enuff boats in the worl' to float us out!"

It was a staggering thought and I was glad to turn from it and walk to the hurricane deck for a better look at the broad, flat waters of Grand Lake, which we entered after passing through a channel from Six Mile Lake.

The character of Grand Lake was constantly changing, the captain said. New land, big and little islands, were built up by silt that poured in with the floods each spring. These same floods gouged new channels through older islands or mud flats. Tall cottonwood trees stood where there was only open water five years before. A large island covered the spot where gunboats battled to the death in the War between the States. The new land was easily discernible by the greener foliage of the trees it supported. Snow white sand bars, river-sculptured forms of streamlined beauty, lay along some of the water courses.

To me there was something thrilling about looking at this new land, as if we were closer than we ever expected to be to the creating of God's earth.

Captain Brown expressed no such poetical view, but complained that river traffic, which once assumed such proportions that Government navigation lights were needed on Grand Lake, was being ruined. He pointed out one long island, extending down the center of the lake, which impeded traffic from east to west. Big boat traffic from the east side of the lake had to be directed through miles of tortuously winding bayous before it could reach the western shore.

"Use to be some good mens . . . Yankees mostly they was from the north country, but good mens too and mixin' in fine wit da Cajuns . . . what came in here to tend the navigation lights. Now they ain't no navigation lights and the families o' dem mens is poor fishermens like the res' of da Cajuns."

Captain Brown continued, considering this.

"All except 'Our Saviour' . . . he's still a general mixtry, mostly quarter-Irish, quarter-Cajun and quarter-sonofa . . . *pardon*, Miss, I forgets myself wit a lady aboard . . ."

" 'Our Saviour'? You mean he's aboard the *Kursweg* right now?" I asked.

"You ain't met 'Our Saviour,' Miss? Why, you ain't begun to live rightly on the *Kursweg!*"

He asked me to hold the wheel while he stepped outside the pilothouse and bawled to a roustabout below.

"Hey, Willie, you . . . tell 'Our Saviour' to leave them Gawd-danged engines alone fer a minute and come up to meet a lady."

From the deck below there appeared a tiny little red-haired man with blue eyes popping from under bushy white brows, his face streaked with grease and his tobacco-stained mouth stretched in an ear-to-ear grin.

"Enchanté, Mam'selle," he said and bent his knees in a jerky bow.

Well! A general mixtry, indeed, I thought and listened with fascination as the little man talked with an accent half-French, half-Irish.

This was the *Kursweg's* engineer, the man who tended her engines ceaselessly with blind love and that special kind of fanatical devotion which only such a man could bring to the creaky old boilers. He could not be long from her side, so I must hurry and get the story of his nickname.

" 'Our Saviour,' *Mam'selle?* Captain Brown was fooling you wit fun, him . . . the boys all call me 'Kelly.' "

Captain Brown leaned over from the pilot wheel and shook his finger in the face of the engineer.

"Listen, you danged-blasted Irishman . . . you tell thet young lady how you got to be 'Our Saviour.' "

Kelly's greasy face split into that ear-stretching grin again.

"It really warn't nuttin', *Mam'selle* . . . but them Cajuns got funny ideas, them, and they likes to remember the day way back in 1915 when they gives me thet name.

"I guess it was the biggest tidal wave them Gulf-island Cajuns ever seen, them, and to tell the truth she look mighty big to me too. I had me a swimp lugger then . . . jus' a thirty-footer, but as sound as steel all through . . . and fer two days I rode 'er through that storm . . . A fearful wind it was, *Mam'selle,* an' waves as tall as schooner masts pounding along thet marsh.

"Them fishermens' families had run clean outa hopefulness, when me and my lugger hove to. Someways or other I got the whole bunch on thet lugger, *Mam'selle* . . . We was jammed like canned swimps, tied to the rigging . . . and da lugger rockin' in them waves like a wobbling beer can . . . but I got them folkses to Morgan City, me, and ever after thet they call me 'Our Saviour.' They don't mean it should be funny, *Mam'selle,* nor either irre . . ." he stumbled over the word . . . "nor either disrespectful, *mon dieu,* no, but that is what they calls me."

The engineer finished, and Captain Brown gave his big belly-shaking laugh.

"That what *we* calls him too now, Miss, 'cause it takes a danged-blasted saint of a man to wrestle wit these engines we got on our old gal here."

The engineer brought his fingertips together under his chin and rolled his eyes heavenward in a gesture half-gay, half-serious.

"It takes prayer, *Mam'selle*, it does, for sure."

Then 'Our Saviour' bent his knees in that funny little bow again and scurried below decks, into the cavernous chambers of the *Kursweg*'s engine room.

Along the shell-lined shore of Grand Lake's east bank I had noticed at intervals several cone-shaped mounds, each with a large oak growing from its crest.

Captain Brown said these were ancient kitchen middens of the Chitimacha Indians who once lived here and had great feasts on these spots, throwing the bones and refuse onto the mound. Bones and seafood shells built the mounds higher through the years and left them as monuments to the aborigines' civilization long after the red men had been dissipated through wars and disasters.

Somewhere among the older islands of the lake grew the sacred cypress tree of the Chitimachas, he told me. The legend was that whenever a careless boatman's wake splashed water on the sacred tree, thunderous clouds appeared in the sky and storms beat for many days upon the waters. He had never found that tree but if he ever did, he'd be mighty careful, him, to turn the *Kursweg* away. Don't need no storm out here abeatin' waves over our ole gal's nose!

From out of the choppy water of Grand Lake the *Kursweg* turned now into the first of many quiet, sparsely inhabited bayous of the Great Basin. Only occasionally we passed a few fish camps and some campboat communities. At the sound of the *Kursweg*'s whistle the dark, lithe fishermen stood up on their johnboats and grasped hold of the willow branches above them, to steady themselves. Their womenfolk rushed to the decks of the campboats to watch and their children jumped up and down gleefully and waved to the big white steamboat as she floated high above them.

Captain Brown gave a gay tootle of response with the steamboat whistle and smiled nostalgically as he said, "They allus 'minds me of my days on the fishboat *Florence,* Miss, the sweetest little fishboat what ever sailed these here bayous, I guarantee you."

Then he launched into his favorite subject and for hours I listened to fabulous tales of the fishboat *Florence* which had been Captain Brown's very own in the days when the Great Basin was alive with many swampers and many lumbermen, when he traveled the lost and tenuous bayous trading groceries and trinkets for fish and furs and logs.

He never tired of these tales, especially those involving his Cajun mate, Bobo.

"Dat Bobo!" Captain Brown would say, and the name itself was enough to conjure up another story.

"Did I ever tell you the time dat Bobo got himself married, him? I give him one trip off and he jump the broomstick wit a pretty lil bougalis gal. He built him a one-room campboat, no bigger'n a card table, much. Then the next trip he lef' his little gal and came back wit me on the *Florence.* He warn't no real good to me, though, apinin' away fer dat gal like he was. Finally, when we got to Morgan City I told him to grab a johnboat and go back to 'er quick and I'd pick 'im up the next trip. Bobo was a very jealous man, him, and he worried plenty 'bout leavin' dat gal alone. Anyways, when he finally tied that johnboat to his front *galerie* it was ten o'clock at night. The campboat is all dark and he try the door and it's lock. Then he start pounding the door, loud, loud. His wife call out, 'Is dat you, Bobo?' And he says, 'by damn, it better be me!' "

Captain Brown's laughter shook the pilothouse and the wheel popped out of his shaking hands and I had to grab and steady it.

"Another time Bobo decided to leave the *Florence* and make

some of that big swimp money. He move his little campboat down to the Borrow Pit near Morgan City and he done so well with them danged swimps that he bought an old flivver automobile. Bobo was livin' high on the hog. One trip he stayed out trawling two weeks and made $700. His wife wasn't home when he got in and it was Saturday night so he took his flivver down to the Cut Grass Inn to celebrate *un petit* with the boys. He come back after midnight and when he try to get on his campboat he fall off the deck into the Borrow Pit. This make a big splash and wake up Bobo's wife and she look out the window. It's clear moonlight and she see the front of his car up there on the levee, all smash in. She yell, 'Bobo, what happen to the car?' Old Bobo, he think fast, him, and he yell back, 'A drunk cow is fall out of a tree and bus' my radiator!' "

Captain Brown always ended a *Florence* session with, "Miss, they's jus' one man in the worl' what I envy, me, and that is Dew Robert Vuillemont, him what runs the fishboat *Elaine* into this here danged swamp."

I thought I knew what he meant. By the time our creaky stern-wheeler had reached Bayou Plaquemine, I had seen many swamp dwellers in their floating campboats, had caught glimpses of them "tarring up" their huge, black hoop nets and watched the lonely paths of their johnboats cut an arrow-head wake before our approaching bow. These swamp Cajuns were a different breed of Evangeline's people, their blood mixed generously with outlaws from the Outside, and I felt that I must know them better. I wanted to learn the secrets of their crab fishing, their cat fishing and alligator hunting, wanted to gather moss with them from the cypress giants and stack it along the sagging fences for drying, wanted to sit on the "front *galeries*" of their campboats in the long twilights and watch the swamp night come swiftly through the slumbrous bayou waters.

Early on our last day in the swamps we passed the fishboat *Elaine* and Cap'n Brown nearly blew the whistle off the *Kursweg* signalling joyfully to Dew Robert Vuillemont as he stood before his big scales on the foredeck and weighed in a swamper's load of fish. The fishboat captain waved back as though he had no envy for a steamboat captain riding high on the top deck in his pilothouse. The thought came to me that someday I might hitchhike a trip on the fishboat *Elaine* and get a closer look at the Cajuns of the Atchafalaya's Great Basin.

Now our stern-wheeler drew closer to Old Man River. Sitting alone on the aft deck, I watched as her paddle wheel splashed its curving wake through the bayou waters. We had passed through an old, old land, from Bayou Teche into the surging Atchafalaya, the Great Basin lakes, Bayou Chene and Bayou Bouttee, Little Pigeon, and finally Bayou Plaquemine.

Ancient live oaks bent wearily over and dripped their mossy tresses in the still waters. Or they twined protectively around desolate ruins of old plantation homes and abandoned sugar mills. Deep in the swamps were rotting acres of cypress stumps —mute remains of the lumbering days of another century. Then the lumbermen felled forest giants by the millions and fortunes were made and lost on log rafts pulled busily down the bayous.

Yet this was a young land too. Beside the decaying hulk of some ancient steamboat wreck, close by the walls of a crumbling mansion, rose the steel derricks and the silvery towers of an oil company's loading station. The bayous and swamps were ringing again with the pulsing song of industry. Sugar and rice might be hauled by truck, but oil was traveling by water, in deep-swung, heavily-loaded barges.

Down through this pageantry of old and new, past the decadent farms and abandoned mills, past the shining new derricks rising out of blue water hyacinths, and past the fishing villages of the mysterious Great Basin, our old stern-wheeler rolled on. High up in the pilothouse or down on the foredeck close to the water, I watched strange things and strange people go by as in a kaleidoscopic dream. I saw whole towns of campboats, saw communities built on stilts and scaffolds, saw the clumsy boats of the moss gatherers.

Now we approached the Cajun town of Plaquemine where

the *Kursweg* would lock through, leave the bayous behind and bear down on Ole Man River.

I went below to the first deck, which lay flat on the water, not ten inches above the surface, and asked Preacher to lead the rousters in a last jam session for me. He tried, but they were not in the mood.

"Miss, dere nerves done sot down on 'em," he apologized.

I got the point of that, remembering that the two cases of beer from Morgan City could not have lasted long among such a thirsty crew. As soon as the boat tied up to wait her turn at the Plaquemine lock, I sent one of the boys off for a couple of gallons of wine.

First Captain Brown, Mr. Joré and I tried it out in the pilothouse and decided it was just what all of us needed. After a little while there was a clatter of bells and blowing of whistles and a great commotion ahead of us.

"Danged if I didn't fergit all about that danged lock," said Cap'n Brown.

"A little more o' that stuff and you'll fergit about the river," said Mr. Joré.

We passed through the lock with no trouble at all. It was heavy dark on Old Man River, but even in the black night I could feel the difference in the water. There was a feeling of broad spaces around us, as though we moved on a great highway. And suddenly it seemed to me that the *Kursweg* was growing smaller, shrinking fast to Lilliputian dimensions. The loose-jointed old hulk suddenly became a small craft floating on broad, strange waters. Our little family of crew and rousters seemed to pull together for company. I listened to their hushed murmurs from below and wished their nerves had not sot down on 'em.

Cap'n Brown said, "Well, how you like the Ole Man, Miss? Ain't he a monster, him?"

Then, our passage through the lock safely over, he sent the second bottle of wine down to the rousters.

In no time at all their nerves bucked up and they were

rocking, swaying, shouting and singing. Preacher led them in his high, thin tenor. The rhythm of the old river chants gripped us in a sort of enchantment:

"Oh, rollin' down the riber, steamin' at de moon,
Chase de possum up de bank and cook de grizzlum coon!"

Then the rousters stretched out on a longer one:

"Got the riverfront blues, baby, and I'm blue as I can be,
Got the riverfront blues, baby, and I'm blue as I can be,
That ole Mississippi sure is makin' a fool out of me.
My baby is there when the man gives me my check,
Oh, my baby is there when the man gives me my check,
When I looks at the river I feel like cuttin' my neck.
That river, that river, ole man riverfront blues.

Oh, the riverfront blues, talk about havin' them riverfront
blues . . ."

Between songs I could hear Alvin and Frank arguing. By his own admittance Alvin, the tar-black cabin boy, was "a little teched in de haid." He was forever bragging about the days when he had served on bigger, better boats on broader, swifter streams.

Frank was Cap'n Brown's pet deck hand, a seventy-year-old darky who lived in a tiny private cabin under the pilot-house. On murky nights he sang his own haunting, mournful chant that the captain said meant "it's agointa rain fo' sho."

Preacher, the shouting song leader, shot craps with the roustabouts all day and preached hell-fire and damnation all night. I knew that as soon as the song session was over he would launch into his fire-crackling sermon. He led the rousters now in one of their favorites:

"A hook on a cistern is boun' to rust,
Lots of N'Awlins wimmen is hard to trust.
If we two was like we three
We'd all git together and then agree.

A nickel is a nickel,
An' a dime is a dime,
The best work is on the riverfront,
All the time."

They wound up finally with a work song:

"Let's truck this here cotton, unload this ship,
Boys, let's truck this cotton, unload this ship,
'Cause when we finish I'm gonna look for my wench."

All quiet now on the deck below. Even Preacher seemed awed by the immensity of black night on the river, and decided to withhold his sermon.

I was asleep in my stateroom (which is never called "cabin" on a steamboat) when something awakened me. I listened, heard no sound, and was suddenly aware of the boat's lack of motion. The *Kursweg*'s engines were still, her paddle wheel inert. In a flash I rushed to the hurricane deck, but from there I had to creep. Fog, damp, heavy and impenetrable, lay like a white shroud on the river. Our gallant stern-wheeler was silent as death. Helplessly the arc light threw its beam in a circle to right and left, searching for a shore that was not to be found.

How long we lay helpless on the white river I cannot say, for the fog cast an eerie, other-worldly air over the whole scene. It was a shout from Mr. Joré on the foredeck below that waked me to reality.

"Wind's comin' up!"

In an incredibly short time the wind had blown the fog upriver behind us, and our rousters were shouting at their ropes and chains as the big anchor came in and we got underway again.

But the Ole Man was full of tricks that night, and his show was not yet over.

There was a tenseness and excitement in the air that I could not understand. Preacher had come up from below to stand motionless on the hurricane deck; and on the lower deck a black boy stood with rope coiled in his hand.

In a moment I knew. The deep, thrilling tones of the sounder's voice came from below, to be echoed by Preacher so that Captain Brown, silent now and solemn in the old pilothouse, could hear.

"NO-O-O BOTTOM!" came the encouraging message.

"No-o-o bottom!" echoed Preacher.

Rhythmically the roustabout below threw his weighted rope and pulled it in to feel the leather tags and know the depth of the river.

"QUARTER LESS THREE!"

"Quarter less three!"

I heard a grunt from Cap'n Brown.

"HALF TWAIN!"

"Half Twain!"

"QUARTER TWAIN!"

"Quarter Twain!"

A pause, and I waited breathlessly for the enchanting words . . .

"MA-A-RK TWAIN!"

"Ma-a-rk Twain!"

Captain Brown groaned. But a thrill ran over me. How many times, on who knows how many fog-bound old riverboats, had the phrase been called from lower deck to pilothouse! How many times had it echoed, rich-voiced and rhythmical as this, in the heart of a youth from Hannibal, Missouri, who had made it great!

"DEEP FOUR!" came the call from below, and the engines began to throb a little stronger, until the comforting "No-o-o bottom!" rang out.

The shoal was passed, the leading over, and we were once again on our way. The *Kursweg* was wrapped in silence again, except for the muted pulse of her engines. Dimly and silently the river flowed below us. The moon rose lazily over willows on the eastern bank and pushed the last of the haze away.

Magic lay on the river that night, and reached up to the high white pilothouse, holding me enthralled. For when Cap'n

Brown said, "They's the Acadian Coast on our starboard, Miss, for a hunnerd miles on down," I didn't even question him.

"Let it wait another day," I thought.

A shadow stood on the hurricane deck between the moon and me. It was a great giant of a man, with legs braced far apart, staring moodily down to the river below. Mr. Joré, looking like Captain Ahab alone and desolate on the deck of his whaler.

Silence on the river engulfed us all as we plowed on down toward New Orleans.

Next morning I wakened to find us tied to the Toulouse Street wharf. River traffic was busy and noisy on our port side, and just a few blocks away to starboard the city's skyscrapers towered.

I packed and left the boat mournfully, to return to a different world. All my fine old, hoary characters were slicking themselves out in city clothes, preparing to wander up to Canal Street.

Only the roustabouts were left, beginning their forty-eight-hour stretch of loading freight.

Their songs echoed down the wharves as I crossed Decatur Street and wandered over to Jackson Square. Weary, rhythmic chants of their own making, they helped to lighten their burdens and to pace their toil:

> "I don't know, but I'se been tole
> *Kursweg*'s comin' down wid a heaby load . . ."

Faintly now the sound, led by Preacher's thin tenor:

> "Cap'n Brown, Cap'n Brown . . .
> I'd like to see dis white man's town . . ."

"General Mixtry" on an

Isle of Paradise

...
iii

By the time our creaky old *Kursweg* had stuck her stages into the Toulouse Street wharf, I had seen many kinds of Evangeline's people. There were, Captain Brown said, many kinds more. None seemed to fascinate him more than what he called "the general mixtry on the Isle of Paradise."

"They won't be your true Acadian, Miss, but you'll find plenty Cajuns there in the general mixtry, and you'll have more danged funny sights to see than you ever laid eyes on yet."

He added, "Go to Houma and find a little lady named Madame Marie Louise Duval. Tell her I said to help you."

At Houma I watched the Intracoastal Canal cross Bayou Terrebonne and saw small thirty- and forty-foot shrimp luggers turn into the canals of the town as if they were sailing down the streets of Venice.

Half a generation ago, I was told, nothing but French was spoken along lazy Bayou Terrebonne which was the real Main street of this town. But as I wandered along the bayou bank, close by the shrimp canneries, the ice plants and the trappers' equipment stores, I now found citizens who could direct me to Madame Marie Louise Duval in English.

She sat at her desk in the Public Welfare Office, listening by the hour to the troubles and tribulations of those who found living hard along the twisting bayous surrounding this town. Her black, curly head nodded sympathetically as she heard their woes. Her dark eyes flashed and burned as they reported their injustices.

When I told her I wanted to see the Isle of Paradise, she smiled and looked at me searchingly, as if to see if I deserved such a trip.

"If l'Isle au Jean Charles has such a name," she said, "it is to those who have never been there."

I did not understand what she meant at the time, but later I came to agree.

Five bayous stretched out from Houma like five wet fingers of a giant hand. At the foot of one of these lay l'Isle au Jean Charles, a weird knoll rising out of the coastal marshes.

Here lived a group that the French people of Houma called "Sabines," that other Louisianians called Indians and that Captain Brown Blakeman called "general mixtry." I was told there were many such groups among the coastal regions—mixtures of Indian and Spanish and French and Acadian and Italian and Portuguese and Chinese and Manilaman and Negro. Their group was a tragic one in most communities, since they were accepted as belonging neither to the white race nor to the red or the black. Schools they seldom had, as they could not go with the white people and would not go with the black.

But on l'Isle au Jean Charles the Sabine had found a home. He seldom left the island. The only persons who came from the outside were the priest who visited every three weeks and Madame Marie Louise who came with her assistant to make a call on her clients every two months.

At a beautiful spot called Pointe au Chêne, lying at the end

of oak-lined, moss-draped Bayou Pointe au Chêne, we came to the end of the road.

From here the marsh stretched for miles and miles, lying green and hot under the summer sun, its tall grasses hiding the trappers' *traînasses* and their campboat homes in a world where the only highways were water trails.

Two Sabines from the Isle of Paradise met our car at the road's end on Pointe au Chêne. They took us aboard a tiny top-heavy lugger that reeled and swayed down the winding bayous in a most disconcerting way. For six miles we rode through the flat, green world of floating marshes, through an area that was neither land nor water.

A strange, inexplicable sense of drama pervaded this marsh country. It was as if we rode a mystic boat in a land suspended between two worlds. The air was too still and too quiet. The marsh enclosed us in green as vivid as a mad painter's dream. The sky was far above and of an eerie blue. Except for our group in the shuddering little boat, the only living things, as far as eye could see, were the black crows that looked like exclamation points on the landscape and the white gulls occasionally flying in from the sea. There was a weird feeling of unreality about it all.

I was not sorry when we sighted the island in the distance. The oaks that rose like sentinels to stand silhouetted against the hot, marsh sky meant that there was solid earth underneath.

In another mile, with the marsh creeping closer in upon us like a menacing green monster, we had gone as far as the small lugger would go. From here our travel must be by pirogue, those tiny dugouts fashioned by the natives out of cypress logs and used like Model-T's in the swamps.

Half a dozen pirogues appeared with lightning swiftness out of the tree-bordered island, as if conjured up by the same magic hand which had painted this strange and dramatic day. Sharp and narrow as a trapper's knife, the hand-hewn craft sprang forward, each one propelled by the flashing poles of a grinning native who stood up in the stern, balancing precariously. They were lined decoratively with palmetto leaves which draped over the gunnels and made rippling waves along the narrow waterway. This, I learned, was to protect their insides from the bitterly burning sun.

The Sabines poling the pirogues smiled broadly in welcome to their beloved Madame Marie Louise, she whom they loved so much that they burned candles daily for her safe return.

We left the lugger and rode each in a pirogue, with a native behind us poling the craft through the narrow canal.

It was a pirogue processional of some grandeur. Not exactly as impressive an escort as that for the *Queen Mary*'s christening, but for l'Isle au Jean Charles a rather spectacular show.

All too quickly we had arrived at the Isle of Paradise, had crossed beautiful 'Ti Canal which cuts through the middle of the island, and had banked our pirogues before the neat home of Chief Victor Naquin, patriarch of this strange place. The Chief, who was "da bos" of the island through heritage, came down to greet our processional.

"C'est magnifique!" he shouted in welcome and, with a sweeping gesture, he gave us the island.

Chief Naquin was tall, broad-shouldered, copper-skinned, a man of great calmness and solemnity. In spite of the primitive crudeness of his surroundings, he wore an almost regal air. Certain it was that he was born to be ruler of this little island, a man who stood for his humble people against the onslaughts of an unappreciative world.

He ushered us to the gallery of his *Maison Blanche,* the only painted board house on the island, and sent his bronze-skinned wife to bring us coffee.

On the shaded porch, drinking the strong black brew, I listened while Chief Naquin told the stories of his island.

It was not true, he said, what was told by the city folk at Houma—that his father's grandfather had been a Lafitte-man escaping the fury of the corsair's wrath when he discovered the marshy island which was to bear his name.

"My great *grandpère* was Monsieur Jean Charles Naquin who came from France with his brother, Monsieur Jean Marie Naquin, in 1783. They walked the prairie to come here."

There were no written records on the island. History had been handed down by word of mouth. As he spoke, I thought I could imagine the coming of these two brothers to the island. A tiny channel, known now as Bayou Jean Charles, rose out of the marshlands south and east of Houma, and found its way after much wandering into the channel of Pass Felicity and thence to the Gulf of Mexico. Whatever their origin and whatever their motive for seeking fortunes in this unknown part of the world, the Naquin brothers must have landed at Lafitte's headquarters on Grand Isle or perhaps on the Timbalier Islands. Seeking a home and headquarters, they might have come by pirogue, inland through the marshes and up the meandering little bayou now known as Bayou Jean Charles. Across the shifting grasses they might have sighted this island as we had done an hour before, by silhouettes of the great oak trees rising from out the flat green prairies.

On the little ridge they found beauty in the stately trees, the rich soil, the abundance of fish and game, and in the tiny bayou which ran down the center of the island to provide transportation along its whole length. For them it was the Isle of Paradise they had been seeking, and here they made their home.

Chief Naquin, proud of the French grandfathers of his tribe, seemed reluctant to discuss the womenfolk who joined them in their Island of Paradise. Without doubt, though, these were handsome, copper-skinned Indian girls whom they found scattered along the marshy bayous. Perhaps some came from the Houma tribe only a few miles away, or from the Chitimachas of Bayou Teche and Grand Lake, or even from the strong and fierce Attakapas who had a great nation near St. Martinville. These, mixing their blood with early French explorers, with other self-exiled Europeans, and with the wandering Acadian exiles, produced the Sabines who today inhabit the secluded island.

Chief Victor's son, Willie, an intelligent youth who forsook the island for a life in New Orleans, has been heard to speak more directly than his proud father. Once when he was guiding a friend of mine on a hunting trip, he said:

"I have listened to the old people since I am as big as a raccoon. All the time, it was of the great Lafitte that they spoke. They say it was some of Lafitte's big men that came here. The great Jean would sail his ships into hiding around the island and slip away from those that were on his tail. One time our people search from one end of the island to the other for gold. All they find was prairie water that seeped into the holes."

But all the youths of l'Isle au Jean Charles were not so sophisticated as stern Chief Naquin's son. Many were content with the old ways of their fathers—eager to dig their *traînasses* through the trembling prairies, to learn the muskrat's trails and how to catch the little beast in sharp, silvery traps, glad to paddle their pirogues for fifteen or twenty miles a day and sell fish and crabs at Pointe au Chêne—if they could return at night to the comforting Island of Paradise where their forefathers had found peace and contentment.

Such a youth was Tony Dardar, whom Chief Naquin assigned to guide me over the island. The name of Dardar, like that of Vardin, Billiot and Chaisson, went back to early days on the island, and Tony's own great-grandfather might have been the famous chief of the Houmas known as "Dardin."

Tony Dardar was tall and lithe, his Indian features strong and handsome. Standing in the end of his palmetto-lined pirogue and leaning against the pushing pole with long, slow strokes, he had the grace of an early-American brave in his own pioneer wilderness.

He spoke, in a beautiful cadenced rhythm, a French-Indian patois that was different from any I had heard in South Louisiana.

"About the treasure, *Mam'selle*," he said, continuing the conversation Chief Naquin had been reluctant to pursue, "We looka for her, yes . . . but da bad spirits no like that. They drive us away . . ."

Then he told me about the spirits of the island. How the bad spirits set the earth to trembling when natives searched for treasure, how they sent red streaks of lightning when they were displeased. He told how fathers would not let their sons attend a group gathering when the moon was full, how he must be careful always to make an exit from a house over the same threshold that he had entered. How every person had a good spirit to watch over him as long as he lived straight. How the good spirits guarded the muskrat traps . . .

By this time I was staring open-mouthed at Tony Dardar. He was Chief Naquin's favorite youth, said to be the smartest man on l'Isle au Jean Charles. Had he not, the Chief said proudly, gone to school for three months on the mainland, and did he not speak the English?

Yet here was Tony Dardar, in broad open daylight on a bright sunny day, telling me as dark superstitions as ever came out of a primitive land.

I knew then that I must meet the other natives of this

island. So we banked our pirogue and started visiting back-
and forth at the humble, worn-out houses that lined both sides
of 'Ti Canal.

Walking was difficult. Tropic growths sprang up from the
ground to catch my feet, leaned down from trees to snare my
hair. Sand flies bit at me fiercely, and mosquitoes swarmed
blackly around my ankles.

The air was damp-hot and sticky. Yet it was heavy, too,
with the scent of wild cape jasmine blossoms. And by the side
of all the poor little thatched-roofed homes there were vivid
oleander trees, red as fire and bright as courage.

There was a welcome in every house.

"Entrez, Mam'selle . . . entrez . . . entrez . . ."

The homes were a good bit alike inside. Bare walls and
floors polished smooth and turned a golden tan from much
scrubbing. A crude open fireplace and a few fat, black pots
for cooking. Statues of the Virgin Mary and of the saints clinging to rickety shelves. Overhead some sacks of flour and
staples. Occasionally a picture of Franklin Roosevelt sharing
the shelves with the saints. In a few of these humble homes the
armoires were large and impressive, beds were well-carved
four-posters. Most of them possessed hide-bottom chairs and
other furnishings made by Antoine Naquin, the island crafts-
man who had inherited his gift from his father and built most
of the furniture in the island homes. His work was of simple,
good design and fine workmanship, graceful and French.

Underfoot in all these houses was a scrambled collection
of chickens, cats, puppies, and babies, all seeming to be equally
at home on the bare scrubbed floors.

From Tony I took a cue and learned the magic word.

"Portrait . . . portrait . . . donnez vous portrait . . ."

It brought out the whole family, giggling and shy. After
that it was easy making friends, with my camera serving as
the great leveler.

"Donnez . . . portrait . . . bébé . . ."

And when the babies were proudly caught up from the litter

of pups, kittens and chickens . . . *"très joli, très joli . . . c'est bon . . . bien merci . . ."*

With babies and cameras it is the same in any language.

Faces of these islanders were of a startling mixture. Brown of Indian, white of French, tawny Portuguese, mulatto-slate, Asiatic yellow . . . all the nondescript inheritance of long-ago Lafitte men . . . they were here, in various combinations, pure in some and faded in others. And all these in the children of a single family. I realized in that swift instant how true was Captain Brown's naming of these islanders—the general mixtry.

In some cases a pure strain would assert itself and there would be a little pickaninny scampering about with his brown and yellow brothers, or a pure white child looking pale and odd among the multi-skinned brood.

Such a child was Michel, a pale, blue-eyed youngster whose swarthy mother was so proud of his ability to read that he had to dig out the primer from under the box with the setting hen and give me a demonstration. Michel had gone to school for the whole six-months term last year, but this year the teacher had not come back to the island and the schoolhouse had gone empty.

Michel's mother was a widow, with seven children to feed. From the looks of their thin faces she found the job none too easy.

"They cries, sometimes, the leetle ones, when they get tired o' fried-potato sandwiches," she told the welfare worker. Yet she was saving money to buy First Communion for the second oldest lad.

There was an even larger family next door. A widow with eight children had just married a widower with nine. When Tony asked about one of the daughters, she said, *"Mon dieu,* she take up with her a man, yes . . . like dey all do."

Later I asked my guide about weddings on the island. The people here "no like" the words the priest has to say over a couple; they prefer to *sauter l' balai,* the "jump-the-broomstick" method which was the way of their fathers.

Tony grinned broadly as he explained courtships on l'Isle au Jean Charles.

"First dey make de moon-eyes," he said. "Den dey make da promenade together. If dey make da promenade twice, it is engagement. Next, dey tell all de folks on da island that on Thursday Jacques will take Marianne for wife. On Thursday night Marianne go to Jacques' home to live and den dey are married."

From the few outsiders who know these people, I learned later that their marriages stick. They don't jump the broomstick but once and family life is a very stable affair on the Isle of Paradise.

The promenade is the only form of entertainment on the island, though natives once held weekly dances which lasted all night and on into the second day. On Sunday afternoon every one of the one hundred and sixty persons on l'Isle au Jean Charles dresses in his best bib and tucker and "promenades" up and down the small levee, or *banquette,* on either side of 'Ti Canal. Then half the crowd serves coffee in their homes to the other half—and such visiting, such side-splitting laughter, such tall-tale telling, and flirting and fun making!

Next best thing to a promenade, I learned, was to have a picture-making machine on the island.

By the time Tony and I boarded the pirogue again, news had spread that "a white lady with a picture box" was on the way. Now the *banquette* was lined with children, faces scrubbed and hair slicked down, grinning invitingly at *"le portrait* box."

At the last house on three-mile long 'Ti Canal we caught up with Madame Marie Louise. In the doorway of a tired old house a lively little lady of eighty was leaning on her cane, swinging a rosary from her arm and signing a document which would bring her a few more dollars of pension money. I was intrigued with her method of giving a signature. Because she could not write, Madame Chaisson simply touched the pencil of the welfare worker, thus giving her consent for the signature.

The old lady was very proud and had the welfare worker explain carefully to me in English that the reason she could not sign her name was because she had been too sick to attend school the last term. It seems that school had been held for children in the morning, women in the afternoon, and men at night. That way nearly every person on l'Isle au Jean Charles had learned to write his name and many to speak the English (though none talked so well as Tony Dardar, and understanding him was no easy task).

With Madame Marie Louise following in her own pole-propelled pirogue, we turned about and headed back up 'Ti Canal toward the head of the island.

It would be impossible to leave, said Madame Marie Louise, until we had paid our final visit to Chief Naquin. We found him sitting on the front gallery of his *Maison Blanche,* ready to serve us a feast. There was a red-plaid table cloth spread over one of Antoine Naquin's good square tables. A gallon of claret wine stood at one corner and as we took our places Madame Naquin—I wondered if they called her "chieftess"?— brought from the kitchen a platter piled high with boiled crabs, their steamy fumes sending up that delicious aroma that rivals all other fine foods of South Louisiana. Madame Naquin whipped the plaid cloth from the table—it had fulfilled its purpose in making a good first impression—and laid the platter on the bare board table.

What a feast it was! Never till then had I eaten such crabs and never again since leaving l'Isle au Jean Charles. Madame Marie Louise said these islanders inherit the cooking arts from both their French and Indian ancestry. I only know that the pungency of spices in the delicate white meat of these blue-claw crabs gave us a meal surpassing anything I have eaten in the finest restaurants of the Creoles.

It was late afternoon when we finished the fabulous meal. Yet Chief Naquin would not let us go. He, his broadly-smiling wife and the dozen-or-so favored islanders who gathered on the *banquette* as we ate, were loathe to see their beloved Madame Marie Louise depart.

"It ees so long before she come again," said our hostess.

Chief Naquin, seeking to hold us longer, began to tell more old tales of the island.

"Things change since forty years ago," he reminisced. "Then my people were all happy, things were better on the prairies, more game and more fish for eating. Our boys stayed with us then, did not know nor care about the cities far away. We had no riches but what we wanted and what we needed. Some of our people made gardens. Others fished or hunted, or trapped the furs that we used for clothing.

"When heavy work was to be done, we did it together. We all help each other in everything. We trade work for work and food from our gardens for meat and fish. We have no need for money.

"My father told me that when the first people, his father and uncle, came to the island, there were buffaloes, deer, bears and panthers here, but they all gone now, since many years ago. We have cattle here on the island as long as anyone can remember, but no horses."

The communal society he described, which existed until three or four decades ago on l'Isle au Jean Charles, was that of the early Indian wherever you found him in America. Until so recently, these islanders had followed the traditions and primitive customs of their forefathers. There were evidences here, too, of the ways and manners of the early French explorers, and Frenchmen of a later day, who mixed their blood with these primitives.

Some of the pure-blooded Acadian stock must have filtered through this flat marsh country during the days following the Great Migration. But the Acadian strain is very thin among the islanders today.

The sun was sinking behind the dark silhouettes of the oak trees before Chief Naquin would let us say goodbye. The hospitable, lonely people of the Isle of Paradise stood along the *banquette* of 'Ti Canal and waved till our pirogues disappeared behind the sentinel oaks.

As we left, we met half a dozen pirogues filled with island

men coming in from the potato and bean fields of the mainland. Their pirogues were loaded with rolls of bedding and cooking utensils. They were coming home from the few weeks' farm employment which supplemented trapping and crab fishing as a source of income for them.

Soon we cleared the shallowest prairies surrounding the island and saw our saucy little lugger waiting to bear us toward Pointe au Chêne. We climbed aboard wearily and sat on deck as an islander steered the lugger up the winding bayou.

Tony Dardar tied his pirogue on behind us and climbed up on the roof of the lugger's half-cabin. The motor sputtered, coughed, then pushed forward doggedly, leaving a shimmering wake in the black-green water of the darkening water prairies. This was the magical *feu follet*, the trail of gleaming phosphorous that comes to life when the still marsh waters are disturbed by the island men's boats at twilight.

Then, above and around us, floated a haunting melody. Tony sang in a thin, high tenor such a song as I had never heard. Half-Indian and half-French it was, a pagan sort of song that seemed to blend into all we had seen and all we would remember of l'Isle au Jean Charles, the Island of Paradise.

Moss Pickers of the

Lafourche Interior

iv

Next morning I sat with Madame Marie Louise Duval, drinking a final demitasse at the Seabreeze Restaurant by the bank of Bayou Terrebonne.

I showed her the battered map that *M'sieu* André had given me and asked where she thought I should take up my search. We agreed it was a very old map, and one of considerable value, for there were large blank stretches here and there, as if the map maker himself had not unpuzzled many parts of the land he sought to chart.

Madame Marie Louise pointed out a section lying to the north of Houma, and to the west of those well-marked Bayou Lafourche cities of Thibodaux and Napoleonville.

"See, like on all old maps this is marked 'the Lafourche Interior.' Until a few years ago no roads led into these bayou villages from the outside. Folks along the front of Bayou Lafourche believed that 'them damn Cajuns in the back' were wild and fierce, little better than savages. Occasionally a few hunters and fishermen found a way to the deep interior bayous.

They told of seeing villages there of unbelievable beauty."

Madame Marie Louise paused, considering.

"Why don't you go into the Lafourche Interior? Yes, that will be it!" Her black eyes flashed with enthusiasm.

"You must go to Pierre Part, and ask there for Father Toups."

Pierre Part! Father Toups! The words themselves had a fascinating ring.

I got there by moss truck, one belonging to the merchant, Honoré St. Germaine, who is known as "the moss king of Pierre Part." A kindly friend in Napoleonville arranged for me to ride in the seat of an empty truck that was returning to its village after delivering a load of moss "on the front."

As we bounced along the rutted, oyster-shell road, the driver told me something of the moss industry. I was to learn that this was not only the chief support of his village, but the

favorite conversational topic of his fellow-villagers of Pierre Part.

Near the end of the road the landscape took on an unreal, story-book picturesqueness. It was like something off a picture postcard, or an illustration out of a children's book. Everything seemed to be in miniature. We crossed on a curving bridge over the tiniest bayou I had ever seen—next, of course, to 'Ti Canal of l'Isle au Jean Charles, which was not a real bayou at all. The houses which lined these banks were quaintly-shaped, small as model houses, and had little yellow curtains flying out the windows and doors. The pirogues seemed infinitesimal. The campboats were strange one-room affairs with open, sunken, barge-like decks. These were the boats of the moss pickers who towed them behind sputtering johnboats into the deeper cypress swamps to pull the grey shrouds from the trees.

Only the oaks seemed of normal size, and they were enormous, stretching their tortured feet along the bayou bank, dipping into the musky earth for support, and swinging their huge limbs out boldly to join with limbs of other oak trees across the narrow bayou.

With a tremendous shudder the moss truck came to a stop beside the long, white wooden bridge which stretched across Pierre Part Bay. It seemed to me I had never seen such a beautiful village as Pierre Part, which lay on either side of the wide stream.

"*Eh bien, Mam'selle,*" said the weary, dark-skinned lad who drove the truck. "Me, I mus' leave da truck 'ere by the sto' *galerie* for tonight. You find Father Toups over dere, by the church, him."

Across the river, dominating the village landscape, stood the Catholic Church, its stark white beauty reflected in the bayou waters. Here, I was told, the natives rowed in to Mass from miles around, from settlements that never had seen a gravel road or an automobile.

I walked across the bridge toward the church, watching youngsters and oldsters alike standing up to propel the big

A moss picker rows his heavily loaded péniche *past the Catholic Church at Pierre Part. Tied before the church is the floating chapel,* Mary Star of the Sea, *and its towboat launch,* St. Francis Xavier.

skiffs which the truck driver had called *péniches*. They rowed with peculiarly graceful strokes, bending forward on the long oars, straightening up to pull strongly and send the *péniche* foward with a steady rhythm.

Tied to a landing in front of the church was one of the strangest chapels I have ever seen. It was built on a houseboat with a roomy porch deck running all way round, a wooden cross nailed to its roof peak. It was painted shining white with green-trimmed windows. *Mary Star of the Sea* was her name, painted in neat red letters on her roomy sides.

At tiny communities all along the deep interior bayous, at

every place *Mary Star of the Sea* could safely make a landing, the Cajuns flocked out of the swamps and came joyfully to Mass in this trim chapel. Inside she had a small but fully appointed altar and benches for fifty worshippers. Others stood along the bayou banks and listened as the priest said the solemn words. Here too, Father Toups performed weddings, held funerals, christenings and confirmations, and here he give them counsel on all matters spiritual and temporal.

Beside the floating chapel I found Father Toups, buried elbow-deep in the motor of a long bateau tied near by. This bateau bore the name *St. Francis Xavier* and was the boat that Father Toups used to tow his chapel to faraway, down-the-bayou missions accessible only by water.

The broad-shouldered priest laid down his monkey wrench, ran a big hand over his sweaty, grease-stained brow, straightened his crumpled cassock, and smiled at me. Though he was a strong, brusque man with deep-set, intense eyes, his smile glowed like a child's. In an instant I thought I knew why he was the best-loved man in the bayou country.

"This is my penance, *Mam'selle*," he said. "*St. Francis Xavier* leads me a bad life, him."

Father Toups found a hospitable family who agreed to let me stay in their home, for of course there was no regular place for an outsider from "the front" to stay in Pierre Part.

For three days I slept in the master bedroom, with a mosquito net shrouding the sides of the four-poster. The family served me coffee in bed at dawn, and chocolate at breakfast out of a big steaming bowl in the center of the table from which each member of the family dipped his own. They told me their oldest yarns, their latest gossips. Let me sit on their sto' *galerie* which was the center of life in Pierre Part. Took me with them crab fishing and alligator hunting.

I met Elijah Miller, historian of the swamps, the only man who was "set on book-larnin'." I soon was haunted by a charming little sprite, Anita Foret, an intelligent and ambitious child of twelve. She volunteered her services as guide for the chance to practice on me "da Engleesh" which she had learned in six months' schooling in Napoleonville. Anita lived with her mother, the village dressmaker, and her little brother of whom she was intensely proud. Their home was a one-room house set up a foot off the ground on six round logs.

Through these friends I made many others—oldsters full of superstitions and youngsters eager over the new school bus which was taking them "to the front" to school. All of them spoke constantly of the moss—picking, drying, ginning—which was their chief source of income. Like the French I met all over the bayou country, these moss pickers seemed to derive as much pleasure from their work as from their play.

"*Mam'selle,* I have many *noncs* (uncles)," Anita told me one day. "All da bes' moss pickers in Pierre Part is my *noncs, oui.* My *nonc* Étienne, he aks me yesterday if you like to go wid the moss fleet nex' Monday. He say he take you and me and *maman,* and we leave lil Antoine with *Tante* Suzette. You like that, *Mam'selle?*"

While it was still dark on Monday morning we gathered on Étienne's barge. They had given him the place of honor, the lead barge, because he had guests aboard. *Nonc* Étienne turned out to be a mere youth of nineteen, young like most of the moss pickers, for this was arduous work. He had a slim grace, powerful shoulders, and a way of tossing his dark head back in laughter that was beautiful.

We sat on the deck of the broad, flat craft, slapped at monstrous mosquitoes and waited for the sun to rise.

On six days of every week dawn crept slowly out of the swamp mists and lighted Pierre Part quietly, delicately. But on Monday mornings it crashed along the bayous, full of violent noises and swift, flashing colors. Gasboats spluttered, motors kicked and spewed, skiffs banged their sides together, towlines cracked along the boats' flanks. In all the bayous of South Louisiana there was hardly a village so busy as Pierre Part on a Monday morning.

"Hey, Jacques, hurry wit' de gasoline," shouted Étienne

to his partner. "Time, she get wasted and pretty soon dat sun pop up like crazy."

"Jean, bring da lanterns," came a shout from the barge behind us, "an' don' forget your spikes, like las' time."

"*Allons*, Étienne, and we will follow you. . ."

"Jean-Jacques, we meet at the big split cypress on Flat Lake, *hein?*"

"*Oui*, Cyprien, watch yo' derrick boat. She fix to get caught on dat line."

"Mother of God, my motor she's stuck again. Why must I suffer wit dese t'ing, *hein?*"

The moss fleet, leaving for its week's work in the swamps, was a sight worth seeing. We were off at last, moving slowly down the winding, hyacinth-lined Bayou Pierre Part. From off the wider stretches of Pierre Part Bay came more gasboats, moss barges, derricks and skiffs, all to join our parade. We made a strange procession. In the muggy dawn the barges loomed up like monsters, with squat ugly cabins and lean empty flanks. Following these were swaying skiffs which held the spindly legs of derrick platforms from which the moss pickers would work. Ahead of all, the stub-nosed gasboats spluttered greasily and pulled at the towlines. Fifteen to twenty barges fell into the weird parade, towed by as many gasboats and followed by as many derrick boats and *péniches*.

I stood up in the barge to watch the fantastic procession wind sinuously along the bayou. The sun rose at last and put a glistening touch to the wakes of our strange craft.

We were heading into the smaller waters of the Atchafalaya Basin, to a region of tortuous bayous, dark, hidden sloughs and wild, shallow lakes which lay to the east of the path I had traveled on the beloved old *Str. Kursweg*.

As we moved slowly toward the inner swamps, the landscape grew more grotesque, its cypress and oaks more heavily laden with long, thick moss. No one knew why the Spanish moss of the Pierre Part swamps was different, richer and stronger, than that from any other region. Some special combination of atmosphere and general terrain perhaps Yet no

one denied that these deep swamps, far from salty Gulf
breezes, produced the finest there was. Long of staple, it averaged five feet when cured, whereas in other regions the average
was as low as five inches. There were a few spots where the
strands grew as long, but of a weaker fibre.

I had lots of time to hear about the moss, for we had to
travel the whole of Monday before we reached the spot where
we were to work. Like great waddling turtles the barges
lurched down the narrow waterways, followed by their brood
of smaller boats. A whole day of such travel and we covered
only thirty miles!

My friends talked incessantly while the sputtering gasboat
pulled us deeper into the swamps through a green and grey
world of trees, moss and water.

We traveled mostly on narrow "float roads" cut many years
ago by lumber companies who had robbed this swamp of its
richest timber. Cypress stumps were not pulled up to make
this watery path. They were simply sawed off at the surface
during low water periods. Covered now by rising spring tides,
the jagged stumps lay treacherous and evil beneath us, ready
to gore the hulls of barges and gasboats if the men should
misjudge the water's depth. Swamps of the Great Basin are
interlaced with such float roads. I wondered what this weird
place must look like to the big white cranes that flew lazily
above and around us—perhaps like a green city, crisscrossed
with murky brown avenues and smaller watery alleys.

Étienne and Jacques were arguing hotly over which trees
produced the best moss.

"*Mais oui*, the cypress she grow da longest, strongest strand
of any," insisted Étienne. "Me, I seen da strands fifteen,
sometimes twenty feet long after they was cured."

"*Mon dieu*, man," said Jacques, "but t'ink of da bulk in
them oak tree. She lose weight in curing, yes, but what you
care when you got the bulk."

Probably, I concluded, it was to the picker's advantage to
gather oak moss for bulk, but to the buyer's and ginner's
advantage to get the more durable cypress moss. Also, I

learned, the loss in poundage varied with the section in which it was picked. Moss grown in Lake Verette and in Des Allemands, both only a few miles from Pierre Part, lost seven-to-one in weight during the curing, while at Pierre Part the loss was only three-to-one.

Although these boys, and their companions on the barges that followed behind us, were following the traditions of their fathers, trained in the trade they loved best, they could tell me little of the beginnings of this industry nor how it developed. The men of today remembered that their fathers were moss pickers before them. They remembered well when the moss was floated out to market on giant barges that would dwarf the little one upon whose deck we sat. Not until 1932 was there any road leading out from Pierre Part to the market towns "along the front" of Bayou Lafourche. In those days, before the gravel road put the village in touch with the outside world, the moss industry was run on the plantation system—one man furnishing supplies and taking a percentage in exactly the same fashion as on a cotton plantation. But the new road brought in more buyers who saw golden opportunities in the moss business. They broke the one-man monopoly. Now there is no gin at all in Pierre Part. The cured moss is carried out by truck to two gins in towns on the front.

There were only about half a dozen moss gins in all South Louisiana. Ginning was a fairly simple process, consisting chiefly of cleaning twigs and extraneous materials from the moss, then baling it for shipment to Eastern markets where it was used for upholstery material in automobiles and furniture.

Étienne said that a good moss picker averaged about seventy-five dollars per month for his work.

Anita's *maman,* a shriveled little woman of forty-five who looked sixty, explained that moss picking was always a family affair. *Papa* found that he could get the most from his children's work in this way, since young boys were agile in the big swamp trees and to them moss picking was a game. A boy could cure the moss as well as a man.

Étienne interrupted, flashing his smile and flexing his muscles proudly.

"Since fo' year now Jacques and me been partners—since my brother Ophille got drowned in the alligator hole—and since we fi'teen year old we can pick more moss in a day than any grown man, for sure. All da boys like dat, can pick more dan mens."

I learned that a barge like the one we rode cost the family about two hundred dollars and that they paid another hundred and fifty for the gasboat and motor, and twenty-five a piece for several derrick boats.

"Dat's our whole rig, *mais oui,* and when da price she drop to da bottom, it seem one helluva lotta rig, *Mam'selle.*"

Dusk crept swiftly upon us now as we drew near to the rich woods which were our destination. Gigantic cypresses stood like ghouls along the float roads, silently dragging their shrouds of heavy moss in the water.

Étienne climbed to the cabin roof and signalled that the fleet should tie up here. The bulky barges stopped, made their towlines fast to trees on the edge of the float road. Night closed down suddenly on our caravan, and each barge became its little world within a sea of blackness. We moved swiftly to tighten our door and window against the dronings of merciless mosquitoes. I looked through the cracked pane of our single window. Lamps glowed dimly in the small opening of our sister barges.

"*C'est bon,*" said Étienne as he looked around to see that all was shipshape. We felt very cozy inside the little cabin with its narrow bunks double-decked against the walls and bedrolls on the floor for the boys.

Jacques ducked outside and brought in the catfish he had caught that afternoon on a troll line and which we had towed for three hours along the barge's shank.

"*C'est magnifique!*" shouted Étienne, catching the catfish away from Jacques and dancing a little jig with it as he presented it to *Maman* Foret.

The stoop-shouldered little lady bent coaxingly over the one-burner oil stove. Anita worked on the tiny table nearby, cutting onions, green peppers, opening cans of tomato paste and tomato purée. Her mother put the rice in the big black iron pot. The catfish went into a stew with the delicacies cut up by Anita.

Étienne and Jacques did everything they could to hurry the cooks, and soon the feast was ready—two big pots placed in the center of the table and each fellow serving his own plate.

The food was wonderful.

"*Maman's coobyawn*, it's da best in all Pierre Part," bragged Anita.

Étienne slapped his stomach and groaned with delight.

"Da bes' in da worl' is what you mean, *chère*, and I'm here to guarantee ya."

I hastened to agree. By now I felt myself something of a connoisseur of French bayou cookery. Catfish court bouillon was without doubt the ultimate delicacy in a land where every woman, and most of "the mens," excelled in cookery magic. And of all the catfish court bouillons I had eaten none seemed to compare with *Maman* Foret's, cooked on that one-burner oil stove in the moss picker's cabin.

After the meal we sat quietly for awhile, then turned to the bunks and crawled in with our clothes on. Étienne and Jacques sighed wearily and soon their heavy breathing told they slept. From the other barges came the faint echoes of keen, high laughter ringing across the waters. Then faintly came the sounds of music from an accordion and a young voice singing a plaintive French love song:

> "*Ma demoiselle faites votre idée faites votre paquet*
> *Allons à la maison.*
> *Quand on est chez nous autres on fait comme on veut,*
> *Quand on est chez les autres on fait comme on peut.*
> *Oh! Toi, la belle, ne dis donc pas ça tu*
> *Sais toi-même mon coeur est malade.*"

Now a guitar joined the accordion and several youthful voices sang together a favorite song of the bayou country:

"Jolie blonde, gardez donc quoi c'est t'as fait.
Tu m'as quitté pour t'en aller,
Pour t'en aller avec un autre que moi.
Quel espoir et quel avenir je peux m'en avoir.

"Jolie blonde, tu m'as quitté, moi, tout seul pour t'en aller avec ta
*   famille.*
Si t'aurais pas écouté les conseils des autres,
Tu serais ici avec moi aujourd'hui.

"Jolie blonde, tu croyais qu'il y avait juste toi que j'aimais dans ce
*   pays.*
Il y a pas juste toi dans le pays que, moi, j'aimais
J'ai trouvé une autre, jolie blonde,
Bon Dieu sait moi j'aime d'autres."

The boys sang another, telling of their dreams of sweethearts back home:

"Mon amour est barré dans l'armoire,
Et la clef est cachée dans mon coeur.
Hier au soir j'avais toi dans mes bras
Mais j'ai trouvé que c'était un rêve."

Now the songs grew softer, sadder and more mournful:

" 'Tite fille quand je vas mour-rir, enterre moi pas dans le cimitière.
Enterre moi dans le coin de la cour, dans le coin de la cour chez ton
*   papa.*
Laisse-moi donc les 'tits yeux sortir
C'est pour voir tes chers 'tits yeux
Je vas rester si canaille
Tout le temps de ta vie tu ris.

Allons à la Queue de Tortue,
C'est pour vivre sur le pain perdu

Maudite 'tite criminelle, maudite 'tite bouteille
C'est la cause de si la belle veut pas de moi."

Finally the songs grew fainter still and after a little while they stopped.

From out in the swamps came the growls of the big bull 'gators and the piercing wails of screech owls. Gradually the swamp came alive with night sounds, as lights blinked out in the cabins and sleep settled on the moss fleet.

The moss pickers were up in the early dawn. Some of them detached gasboats from the barges and, with derrick boats and skiffs in tow, set out along the many small alleys which cut off from the main float road. Some moved barges and whole rigs further into the woods and went their separate ways to seek the rich moss harvest.

Étienne and Jacques moved our barge a little way down the float road and, with two other rigs nearby, prepared to detach the derrick boats and climb onto their spindly ladders. Anita, *Maman* and I watched from the barge deck.

Soon the great, silent trees were alive with little men. They stood aloft in the tall derrick boats and gathered moss in armloads. They stood in swaying skiffs and fished the moss from the trees with long, hooked poles. They dug their spiked boots into trunks and clambered up to the highest limbs, tearing off the clinging moss and throwing it to the tiny boats below.

The trees were tall and sometimes the little men climbed a hundred feet into the air. I shuddered as I watched. *Maman* smiled sadly at me, seeing that, and spoke very quietly. "My husban', *Mam'selle*, he fall out a tree taller than dat one dere. Ninety feet down, he fell. He broke 'is back, him, and die before they can get him into the barge. Anita was only *une petite* girl, maybe four-five, when it happen."

Anita patted her *maman's* shoulder.

"Many mens fall from da trees, *Mam'selle*, and sometimes they get drowned. But mens they love da trees. Father Toups he say it's not jus' to make da money they climb 'em. He say the mens sometimes t'ink the bigges' trees is . . . how you say, dat, *Mam'selle* . . . a challeenge?"

Then Anita told about the time Father Toups himself was gathering moss with his parishioners. He fell from the top of a fifty foot tree. He sprang out of the water, shook his fist at the giant cypress, dug his spiked boots into the trunk and cried:

"*Tonnerre!* So you t'row me out, *hein?* Well, *un* moment, my fine, sweet cypress. I show you who clim' who!"

By now the derrick boats and skiffs were stacked high with the silvery parasite. Moss pickers towed smaller boats back to the barges, piled their load into big empty decks and cooked their lunches on cabin stoves. In the afternoon they set out again, and returned at dusk with their second boatload for the day.

A man could pick one thousand pounds of green moss in a day, but in the evening his back ached fearfully and he lay down wearily on his hard cabin floor, thankful for the protective folds of his mosquito nets.

For two days our pickers combed the cypress brakes. Sometimes the group stayed out three or four days, but because Anita, *Maman* Foret and I were along they made this a shorter trip.

Now, with barges of the whole fleet stacked high—for the boys had worked hard and this had been a good trip—they made tow lines fast to the gasboats and turned our caravan back toward the village.

Thursday nights and Friday mornings the fleet usually returned, in pairs, trios and larger groups, creeping carefully along the bayous. The most exciting part of the work was over. Now came the drudgery of unloading and the long slow process of curing.

I had noticed that each time Étienne or Jacques brought in a skiff-load of moss, they stacked their own moss in a separate place on the barge deck. So with every man in the fleet. Although to me the barge loads looked like one big unit when they were complete, each of the boys knew exactly where his "rank" began and ended.

We made the long trip in from the moss-picking grounds even more slowly than we had gone out. With the barges loaded ten to fifteen feet in the air with solid blocks of grey moss, and pulled by gasboats followed by the swaying derrick boats, we must have been a weird and beautiful sight to behold. Sitting on the roof of our cabin I had a fair view. But I kept wishing I had the wings of the big white cranes which flew down the quiet bayou waters ahead of us. What a view *they* must have had!

Home from the swamps, boy moss pickers unload their barges in front of their bayou homes and stack it on the bank where Grandpère *and the littler brothers will take over the curing operation.*

The moss pickers use stilted platform boats to gather the moss in the swamps above Pierre Part.

By Thursday noon we were back in the village. Along Bayou Pierre Part the clumsy barges dropped one by one out of the procession, as each was tied to the landing in front of its own home.

Each man unloaded his own part of the crop, dumping it first into the bayou waters. Here it must soak for a week. After Étienne and Jacques had each unloaded his week's harvest into the bayou, they took the afternoon off to spend it over a few beers in Honoré St. Germaine's café by the bank of Pierre Part Bay.

Next morning they were back at work. Many of the boys in the moss fleet did not have the laborious job of curing their own moss, for this was usually handled by fathers, grandfathers and little brothers. But Étienne and Jacques had both been orphaned, by the same fierce hurricane that had swept over the village five years before, and although Étienne had a bright-faced little wife and a laughing baby son of five months in his tiny houseboat home on the bay, he had no older man to share his labors.

Now the two young fellows must drag their last week's load from out of the bayou. This moss, streaked a sickly yellow from its week-long soaking, must be stacked in beds for curing along the bayou bank. In front of all the houses along the bayou were many of these beds. They looked like giant toadstools or like big black igloos, adding to the strangeness of the village landscape. Each bed represented a week's picking in the swamps. A man's prosperity was measured by the number of moss beds lying before his cabin, and Étienne was proud of those which lay on the bank beside his campboat home. He figured he must have two to four hundred dollars there—and this, *Mam'selle,* was no little fortune for a family man of nineteen!

To moss pickers the curing process was still filled with mystery and wonder. Though for generations they have seen the velvety bark shed from the strong, wiry, black inner strands, a moss bed was still something of a miracle to them.

There was an art in this curing, as in turning any rough

material into a finished product. Old men must know and must teach the boys just *when* the bed should be "turned." Sun and rain and wind must be judged. A man must know the seasons and must be able to judge the effects of slow heat engendered by nature. In winter the process took longer. Sometimes the bed was left for two months before it was turned. After this turning it might stay another month in beds before it was completely cured. In summer the same process might be completed with two turnings in a mere six weeks. When sun and inner heat have dried the moss completely, it must be wet with bucket-loads of water from the bayou, so that the sun can steam again into the bed.

The heat inside one of these moss beds is blistering. Étienne showed me how he could hardly hold his hand in the heart of a moss bed without being scorched.

When curing was completed, the moss was hung out to dry. Now the village took on its fantastic look, like a fairy town in a child's picture book. Lacy black draperies festooned every fence. Finally the product was ready for sale.

Étienne and Jacques had a favorite among the four moss buyers who operated out of Pierre Part. This man always bragged on their moss, how clean it was, how free of sticks and twigs that would add to the poundage once it reached the gin in Napoleonville. This buyer made half a cent per pound for carrying their product to the moss gins, and he had to be careful of his buying if he was to keep a profit. Each time the moss was handled, loading into the trucks, unloading at the gins, it lost weight.

It was time to say goodbye to Étienne and Jacques, to little Anita and *Maman* Foret. All of us felt sad. Anita turned her face away so I wouldn't see her tears.

I walked by the church for the last time, and found Father Toups again fussing with the motor of *St. Francis Xavier.*

Covered with grease to his elbows, the husky priest pulled his hands from the engine, lifted them palm-up to the heavens and sighed.

"It is my penance, *Mam'selle. St. Francis*, he do me bad again!" Then his face lighted up in that wonderful child's smile of his, and he said:

"And how you find it wit da moss pickers, *Mam'selle?* You find yo' true Cajun out there in the moss grounds, *hein?*"

I knew he was teasing me, and was chagrined that I could give him no real answer. The kind priest must have seen my disappointment, for he suddenly became thoughtful, and said:

"*Mam'selle,* you should know *les petits habitants* of Bayou Lafourche. You go back to Napoleonville and you see *Grand-père* Théophile Verret. He's quite a scholar, him, and he got a son, Jules, what is a *marchand-charrette.* Together they know all you want to know about Bayou Lafourche and the Frenchmen there."

I said goodbye to Father Toups and was glad to have another lead to follow. For the natives of Pierre Part had left me confused indeed. These people were all gracious, glowing, charming. Dusky-skinned and limpid-eyed, they were French to the heart, full of gayety and wit, full of peasant love of work. And they were brave as the hardiest Acadians. Using the resources of the wild swamplands they had built a simple but sustaining industry.

But few of them—not Jacques nor Étienne nor even *Maman* Foret whom I had asked on that first night in the little barge —had ever heard of Evangeline. And "Cajun" was a word I had not heard spoken at all! No one but old Elijah Miller and Father Toups knew what I was seeking. For them, and for the rest of these contented ones of Pierre Part, it was enough that the good grey moss still grew long in the swamps, and that their bayous flowed quietly by the curing beds.

I left in the same truck which had brought me in a week ago, knowing a lot more about the bayou dwellers than when I came in, and knowing too, that my search was far from ending. Father Toups had given me a note to *Grandpère* Verret. If I could find him somewhere along Bayou Lafourche he might be able to help.

Les Petits Habitants

v

I had by now heard much of the Bayou Lafourche Acadians
and of the "longest village street in the world" which was
their home. It was time I searched among them and saw for
myself *la vie lafourchaise*. This most distinctive of South
Louisiana bayous stretches for one hundred and twenty miles,
from Donaldsonville to the Gulf of Mexico, through the most
thickly populated rural district in America. *Les petits habitants*
(as the Lafourchais were called by a visitor in the early
1800's) line the curving bayou banks with their farms and
live a life so different from their neighbors that to say a man
is Lafourchais is to tell a thousand patterns of his thoughts,
deeds, dreams, and actions.

There are several ways to describe *la vie lafourchaise* and
I heard them all.

"You can throw a baseball from one house to the next for
more than a hundred miles on Bayou Lafourche," I was told.
And a favorite story was of the day in 1918 when the news
of the First World War Armistice reached Bayou Lafourche.

Couzan (cousin) Octave, at the northern end of the bayou, received a telegram out of Donaldsonville. He must rush the news to Alcide, who lived at the southernmost part near Leeville and had a son in the Argonne. As Octave jumped in his car he shouted the good news to his nextdoor neighbor, Arsène, *"La guerre est finie!"* Arsène ran to his fence and shouted the news to Gustave, his neighbor on the other side. From house to house the joyful tidings sped along. By the time Octave pulled his steaming flivver into Alcide's yard one hundred miles below, at the lower end of the bayou, his cousin rushed out to shout, "Octave, you have heard the big news? *La guerre est finie!*"

Viewed from the air, Bayou Lafourche is patterned like a long, silver necklace stretched out in gentle curves waiting to be picked up and clasped around the neck of some legendary French giant.

The silver body of the necklace, the bayou, is thin and narrow as bayous go in Louisiana. It is little more than a canal, crisscrossed with many bridges of wood and steel. In places it is clogged completely with the stifling lavender beauty of the water hyacinth plant.

Paralleling the necklace are the tiny dots of multicolored jewels. These are the farmhouses which follow the curving bayou banks—painted red, green, blue, grey, white, brown, pink, and oftentimes two or three of the colors at once.

Each farm, with its house adding to the chain "on the front" of the bayou, has its land lying to the back in a long, narrow strip of arpents, or French acres. For generations *les petits habitants* have divided and redivided their original farms among sons and grandsons, until the farms have grown smaller, narrower—some of them becoming mere slits in the long necklace chain of Lafourche.

There is great similarity in the farmhouses, as in all things, on Bayou Lafourche. They are built for big families and for good living. Oftentimes the front of the house is painted a different color from the sides. This might originally have been an economic measure before it became an artistic tradition on Bayou Lafourche. A house is usually painted in three colors.

The most important room of the house is the open *galerie*, deep, wide, running the whole width across the front. This is the social center of the home, big enough to accommodate the large numbers of visiting cousins, *tantes* (aunts), *noncs* (uncles), *parrains* (godfathers) and *nainaines* (godmothers) who gather here constantly.

Visiting is the real life of the Lafourchais, and it goes on ceaselessly. Afternoons and particularly evenings are given over to the visiting of one clan with another. There are *'ti*-calls

Clothes, groceries and kerosene from "underneath" can all be had when the marchand-charrette *rolls by on Bayou Lafourche.*

and *grande*-calls. There are *passer la journée* visits in the morning, and *passer l'après-midi* visits in the afternoon, and the big calls at night known as *causeries*. At least once a week the whole household must call on the "old family." Twice a month, a *causerie* for brother and sister; once a month for *tante* and *nonc, parrain* and *nainaine*.

There is further need of the large *galerie*, the *garçonnière* or bachelors' quarters in the attic, and for other added rooms. Families are large among *les petits habitants*. Seven or eight children is average, ten is a sign of God's pleasure, and there is real joy when *le bon dieu* sends twelve or fifteen little ones. The Lafourchais are proud of their fecundity.

"Stand anywhere on the bayou, throw a brick and you'll

Petits fermiers *work their gardens on the levees on upper Bayou Lafourche, while a fisherman floats by in his pirogue.*

hit a child," they tell you proudly.

With such riches bestowed by *le bon dieu*, there is little wonder that *les petits habitants* must exercise their imagination in the matter of family names. One family will try to outdo the other in this fine art, and the results are often astonishing. There is, for example, the racy habit of selecting names beginning with a certain letter or syllable. One family named its children Valmir, Valmore, Valsin, Valcour, Valérien. One Bayou Lafourche family selected Carm, Carmel, Carmélite, Carmadelle. This intriguing sport seemed to have spread to other bayous as well, for I heard one Lafourchais speak wistfully of the colorful Mayards of Abbéville who chose the "O" line for Odile, Odélia, Odalia, Olive, Olivier, Olivia,

Ophélia, Odélin, Octave, Octavia, Ovide, Onesia, Olite, Otta, Oméa, and Opta. Not to be outdone, a Lafourche family featured a line of "R"s: Rita, Réus, Réna, Rayo, Rayance, Ray John, Régile, Raybe, Rhea, Raymal, and Ramide.

There are probably more direct descendants of the original Acadian exiles along Bayou Lafourche than on any other bayou of Louisiana. I felt that my search was coming near to its ending, that the scent grew warmer and the trail grew clearer. Yet there were things I needed to know about *les petits habitants*, before I could claim success. *La vie lafourchaise* could be digested by a stranger, but not in one gulp. I determined to take it slowly, to absorb what I could of it gradually and fully. Some of my search would find completion here, but how much? I must find *Grandpère Verret* and see if he could tell me.

Everybody knew *Grandpère* Verret.

"Jus' ten mile below Napoleonville, you find him, *Mam'selle*. You see da old red house with the new-paint cistern and maybe Jules' truck by da fence. Jules is *un marchand-charrette*, him, and mostly this time o'day he stop to visit his *papa* and *maman*. If you not see Jules, jus' aks anybody where at is Le Settlement à Verret.

It was easy to find the "Settlement à Verret" for the family was well-known.

I had already traveled the bayou road enough to sense the thickening of houses, the kind of unconscious clustering which marked a "settlement" of a certain clan. The Settlement à Verret was easily distinguishable because one of the more energetic members of the clan had recently over-bought on green paint and had done the several families honor by re-painting all the big wooden cisterns in the settlement a livid green.

Besides, the grocery truck of Jules, *marchand-charrette*, was parked beside the picket fence of the largest house in the center of the cluster of homes.

It was late afternoon, the sun already beginning to dip

behind the towering cypress trees of the swamp "in the back" of the bayou farms, when I opened the wooden gate and heard its pleasant clunk-clunk announce my call to *Grandpère* Verret and Jules. The two men sat at one end of the wide *galerie*, bent earnestly over a *'ti* game of *bourée*, that dangerous card game which was the consuming passion of all Cajun men.

I hesitated to spoil their game. But they pushed the table back with no reluctance—there were days and months and years ahead for many, many games of *bourée*. Jules came down the steps to greet me. I handed my note to *Grandpère* Verret, who read it painstakingly.

Suddenly the old gentleman jerked his glasses off his nose and stared me over from head to toe, then plopped his glasses back onto his nose, re-read the note, slapped his hand on his thin thigh and roared with such laughter that I thought he would fall out of his chair. He held the note up for Jules to see. I peeked curiously over Jules' shoulder, not knowing whether to laugh with them or be righteously embarrassed. Father Toups had written:

"*La petite Mam'selle cherche un* true *Acadien*. Does he live on Bayou Lafourche?"

Grandpère Verret clamped Jules on the shoulder and said, "Take it inside to *Maman*. She know that Father Toups too! What a rascal, him. *Mais* sho, *un* true *Acadien* live on Bayou Lafourche. Thirty thousand true *Acadiens*, all live on Bayou Lafourche!"

Well! This was something more than I had bargained for. I felt a sudden elation, then a rushing sense of letdown. It just couldn't be this easy, I thought. And yet . . . maybe . . .

Grandmère Verret appeared in the door and dropped a jerky curtsy. Her eyes wrinkled in laughter as she stared at me.

"*Bonjour, Mam'selle*," she said formally, then her whole face broke into a broad grin.

"*S'il vous plaît, Mam'selle . . . café noir* or *café au lait?*"

As we filed into the house her shoulders shook a little with laughter and she continued to chuckle as she poured into the ever-waiting coffee cups which seemed to have a permanent place on the red-checked table cloth.

"That Father Toups, he some man, him. He love to joke 'bout *un* true *Acadien*."

It was no time to unravel this puzzle, I decided, so I gratefully sipped the *café noir* and gave a closer look to my three gracious hosts.

Grandpère Verret was short, thin, handsome in a rough-diamond fashion. His features were delicate, dominated by a high-ridged nose and by deep-set blue eyes which twinkled with mirth most of the time but occasionally mellowed and darkened as he lapsed into thought. At such times I felt greatness of soul about this man and a depth of wisdom which seemed to go beyond the realm of his experience on this isolated bayou. This must have been the quality which attracted many Lafourchais to him and caused all the many Verrets, old and young, to depend on him so completely.

For undoubtedly *Grandpère* Verret was the patriarch of Le Settlement à Verret, a fabled kind of great father to the many sons, grandsons and great-grandsons who cultivated ancestral lands on either side of his rambling old house. He sat on his wide *galerie* all day and far into the night, dispensing wisdom and advice in all matters big and small, not only to members of his large family but to neighbors on all sides and particularly those "in the back" of Le Settlement à Verret. His clan included twelve sons, three daughters, ninety grandchildren, and six great-grandchildren—all living in wide-galleried homes duplicating his and within two five-mile stretches of bayou on either side of him.

Grandmère Verret, or *Maman* as her spouse called her, sitting there at the table beside us, looked like a Daumier drawing, one that the artist might have just finished and sat upright in the chair while he went to pour himself a glass of wine, the better to study and consider his handiwork. Her broad, flushed face was that of the good-natured peasant—her low brow creased with wrinkles, her fat pug nose tipped by a large brown wart out of which a grey hair grew to a facinating, eye-catching length. I couldn't help wondering what she had looked like in her youth, sixty years ago, when she and *Grandpère* Verret flirted, danced together at the *fais-dodos*, wooed and wed at the little church in Napoleonville and settled down to start their family. Had she been a plump, black-haired French belle with flashing dark eyes and a saucy nose bearing its brown mole like a beauty spot?

At any rate she had held his family together for a lifetime, had borne his children proudly and loved them well, as they loved her—and all lived happily together, ever after.

For this is the way of *la vie lafourchaise*.

As if to prove the fact, there came the sounds of many voices approaching the house, footsteps mounting the *galerie* stairs, and shouts of *"Allo, Grandpère! Comment ça va?* Where you at, you?"

The voices and footsteps rushed inside and soon the room was crowded with Verrets of all ages and sizes. Two of the sons had brought their large families for a *'ti* call on the "old family."

I was introduced all around. Jacques . . . Jean-Pierre . . . Marie-Thérèse . . . 'Toinette . . . Alcidore . . . Noo-Noo . . . Too-Too . . . Minette . . . Térence . . .

There was a great deal of laughter and joshing, many chairs pulled to the great round table or leaned against the walls, many more demitasse cups half-filled with black liquid magic which caused these Gallic tongues to spin. Youngsters and toddling *bébés* raced outside to enjoy the swings which hung from the pecan trees. Four or five teenaged cousins sought the dark cool corner of the *galerie* for their whispered, giggling conferences. The back room bulged with adult Verrets. enjoying their favorite sport—visiting con familia. During the hour another son and daughter arrived, to add their assorted families to the various groups. At each new entrance I was introduced, and a great deal of fun was had over *"Mam'selle's* billet-doux from Father Toups." The Verrets took my search and my mission on Bayou Lafourche as a great joke, as they seemed to take everything else within their ken.

After an hour of visiting the whole crowd departed at once. "Les' go make *causerie* on the Jeanfreaux, up the bayou, *hein?*" someone said. "Is been mos' a month since we called on *parrain* and *nainaine*. They gointa wonder where is we."

The Verrets set forth, four families of them, plus Jules and *Grandmère*. I wondered if the Jeanfreaux would really welcome such a confederation, but got the impression that these visits were the common thing among the folk of Bayou Lafourche.

I sat with *Grandpère* Verret on the wide cool *galerie* and asked him many questions about Bayou Lafourche and *les petits habitants*.

First, the bayou itself. What was the origin of its name and what of its early history? Who were the first inhabitants and when did the Acadian exiles claim it for their own?

Lafourche, *Grandpère* Verret told me, was once the bed of the Mississippi itself, before that mighty river jumped to the eastward some twenty-five miles.

First, French explorers along the Mississippi came upon the spot where this bayou split off to the west, found a tribe of Chitimacha Indians living there, and named it Lafourche or The Fork. The Chitimachas were a warlike tribe. They murdered an early-day priest who sought to work among them and they made trouble for fifty years or so, until the French were able to rally other tribes against them and thus defeat them.

A few plantations were scattered near the meeting place of the great Mississippi and The Fork, but few settlers ventured down Lafourche among the unfriendly Indians.

To those who came the stream looked like an artificial canal, its own natural levees built within the wide-reaching ancient levees of the prehistoric Mississippi.

For two or three miles on each side of the bayou the embankments stretched out, making some of the richest land in all Louisiana before they dwindled thinly into the vast swamps that lay westward and eastward. It was on those two or three

rich miles, along both sides of the bayou, that many of the
peasant farmers of old *Acadie* ended their wanderings and
established their homes.

When the first Acadian exiles reached New Orleans, they
were welcomed by generous, kindly French people of that
city. But Acadians were not urban folk. Their hearts yearned
for country sights and sounds and smells. *Voilà!* There was
this vast wilderness to the west, *mes amis,* and what man
could tell the richness of the earth along those quiet flowing
bayou embankments?

Nearest of the Bayous, because of its connection with the
Mississippi, was Lafourche. A few families of various nationalities had preceded the Acadians and there would be other
nationalities to follow, but for the most part Bayou Lafourche
was claimed by the displaced French colonists from *Acadie.*

Even after France was traded to Spain in some *'ti* game
between their European majesties in 1762, the Acadians poured
in. They were given land grants along the bayous in the same
manner as the Mississippi River land grants were made—with
a certain frontage on the river and the remaining land running
in a strip away from the stream.

Along Bayou Lafourche, where Acadians continued to arrive
in a kind of never-ending tidal wave, land grants were smaller,
the bayou frontage often being only a few arpents. Gradually
Bayou Lafourche began to take on the peculiar character it
has held ever since: a chain of small farms, fronting on the
bayou, running back to the less fertile swamplands "in the
back."

Through the years the pattern has been repeated. When an
Acadian farmer dies, he does not want to favor one son over
another, so his will directs that the farm be divided lengthwise.
Each child gets a bit of rich front land and some of the poorer
back land. As generation follows generation, and the fertile
Acadians divide their fertile arpents, farms grow smaller and
smaller and houses grow thicker and thicker along the winding
banks of Bayou Lafourche. So today the bayou is like a long
village street and, *mon dieu,* it *is* possible to toss that baseball

from house to house for a hundred and twenty miles!

And what of other nationalities, I asked *Grandpère* Verret. Were there not others who came in also to mix their blood with the ebullient Acadians?

Yes, there were others. French royalists, exiles of the terrible Revolution, came here in the eighteenth century, turned their snobbish gaze on the peasant-like Acadians and chose lands as far as possible separated from them. Spaniards came too, mostly from the Canary Islands, during the forty years in which *la Louisiane* belonged to the Indian people. But these, like many of *les américains* who came fifty years or so later, were destined to lose their identity, to be absorbed gradually by the jovial, persuasive Acadians—so that by this time it was hard to tell, *mon ami,* where Spanish and American and French began and ended among the gently possessive Cajuns.

Some of the Americans still held aloof, however. *Grandpère* Verret smiled as he told me their story.

"Ah, *Mam'selle,* there are many fine *américains* on Bayou Lafourche and we live as friends, my people and theirs."

"Have you heard, *Mam'selle,*" the old gentleman said with a twinkle in his eye, "why Bayou Lafourche is like the aisles of a church?"

I had heard, twenty times or so thus far, but I let him tell me again for this is a conundrum beloved by all Lafourchais.

"Because there are Pughs on both sides of it!" he said with a guffaw.

Of all the American planters who settled on Bayou Lafourche during the booming 1830's, carving their great sugar plantations out of the rich delta earth, the Pughs were the most fabulous and left the deepest mark.

It was early in the nineteenth century, the era of big sugar and cotton plantations, that a few American families from the older South saw golden harvests to be had in this rich land of the French peasants. Their sophisticated tastes were shocked at the poor, uneducated Acadians who seemed content with their incomprehensible language, their small farms and modest

homes. One early-day planter resented the effect on his Negroes
of the contented Acadians and their blissful lives. He said:
"My slaves, seeing them in comfort without much property
and without steady labor, could not help thinking that it was
unnecessary for men to work as hard as they themselves were
obliged to do, and thought that if they were free, they would
not work."

Other Americans found the Acadians "amiable, kind, law-
abiding, virtuous and honest beyond any population of similar
character to be found anywhere in the country."

Out of North Carolina came the Pughs and the Martins,
both families of wealth already, and with knowledge of how to
increase it in the rich sugar lands of their quiet bayou.

W. W. Pugh, arriving here as a youth, recorded his impres-
sions in a diary. The tiny Acadian cottages, with their mixed
moss-and-mud walls, their wide front galleries, their neat
picket fences, were a curiosity to him. Accustomed to travel
on the great floating palaces of the Mississippi, he was amused
by the toy-like stern-wheelers which plied Bayou Lafourche
and brought glamour and excitement to simple Cajuns who
dashed from their *galeries* and raced to the levee whenever the
old *Eagle* came crashing and splashing down the oak-lined
stream.

It was a time of great excitement and great riches on the
bayou. While *les petits habitants* looked on in amazement,
les américains cleared broad and broader acres, bought more
and more slaves, built large and still larger mansions.

For half a century or so the planters lived out their fabulous lives before tragedy began to haunt them. Tariff laws
broke the sugar market. Planters opened the taps and poured
molasses from sugar mills into ditches and into the bayou.
Then there were the terrible war years, when Yankee troops
ravished the Bayou. The troops burned lumber the Martins'
slaves had cut laboriously and had stacked for building a mansion, and lived two years in Albemarle, the comfortable Martin
cottage which the mansion was planned to replace.

"C'est triste, Mam'selle," said *Grandpère* Verret. "The

grands américains were broken. Most lost their plantations to
the bankers from New Orleans. Today there are only a few
left. And out of all the great plantations of Bayou Lafourche,
only Albemarle still belongs to an original family, the Martins,
who have owned it over a hundred years."

Grandest of all the American mansions were Woodlawn and
Madewood, built by the two Pugh brothers just three miles
apart on the east bank of Bayou Lafourche.

"Would *Mam'selle* wish to see the two great homes?" asked
Grandpère Verret. "It is only *un petit* drive away."

We took the small drive, crossed the bridge at the village of
Paintcourtville, and swung up the gravel road on the east side
of the bayou. Two miles up on the right was Albemarle, home
of the Martin family for five generations. A giant pecan tree,
with its two-hundred-foot spread of limbs hanging heavy with
Spanish moss, almost hid the house from sight although the
moon cast pale shimmers on its lawn.

The plantation gardens lay outlined in the moonlight, darkly
mysterious and fragrant. This was the world of the past. Yet
blending into it was the laughter of the Albemarle darkies in
Petite Street, their little row of cabins back of the plantation
home, and the faint shouts of the men in the fields, working
all through the night to haul the cane to the sugar house.

A few miles further we came to Madewood. Its great Ionic
columns glowed whitely in the moonlight. There was grandeur
and a quiet magnificence about this century-old home which
had been built so lovingly and tended so well through gay and
through tragic years on Bayou Lafourche.

Grandpère Verret told me of its building and its builders.
Early in the 1820's three Pugh brothers—Augustin, Thomas
and Dr. Whitmel H. Pugh—arrived on the bayou, began to
amass a fortune and to establish one of the greatest dynasties
of the rich South Louisiana sugar land. The second brother,
Thomas, married Eliza Foley, daughter of one of the two
English-speaking families which had preceded the Pughs to
Bayou Lafourche—and thus established the tradition that no

Pugh was to intermarry with their French neighbors. In the
1830's the Thomas Pughs began the building of their home.
For four years their slaves labored in the forests, cutting
cypress and òak for the great mansion. Another four years of
building before the splendid house was finished—to stand in
brilliance and magnificence, a marvel to the humble Acadians
who came to admire its glories. They called it Madewood, and
even the slaves were proud that this thing of beauty should
arise from their own crude axes, out of the encroaching dimness of the forests "in the back."

For almost a hundred years Madewood was owned by the
Pughs. Eliza, after Thomas' death by yellow fever, was clever
enough to fend off the pillaging Yankees and keep the house
intact even during the tragic years of the War between the
States. It stood for all to see, the symbol of the Americans'
elegance of living, their superiority to their humbler Latin
neighbors. Finally, in 1916, the home was sold and in 1946
sold again—this time to Bronier Thibaut, a fine and enter-
prising Creole gentleman.

Grandpère Verret smiled wisely as he finished his story.

"You see, *Mam'selle, les français,* they was meant for Bayou
Lafourche, yes?"

So at last the Americans—and their greatest dynasty on
Bayou Lafourche—had yielded to the French. Throughout its
long and useful life Madewood has been loved and tended by
both the Americans and the French. Today it lives on in dignity and beauty, one of the few Louisiana plantation homes
which has kept its integrity against withering time and invading tourists.

As we left the lovely mansion and traveled slowly up the
bayou road, I felt a kind of enchantment descend on us. Except
for the crunch of our tires on the gravel road, there was no
sound. Moonlight filtered through the great moss-hung trees
on our right, casting weirdly-shaped shadows on the road and
on the levee banks. As the road followed the curving bayou
banks, it seemed to be taking us into some mystical land of

mystery. We seemed to travel backward into time, to be possessed by ghosts of other, older years. Mists were beginning to rise off the sleepy bayou waters and these blended with some strangeness in the air to create a sense of unreality, a kind of heavy foreboding through which we traveled silently and curiously alone.

Suddenly *Grandpère* Verret stopped the car. Without the swoosh of our tires on the gravel road, we were engulfed in complete silence. A cloud floated over the moon and we were in darkness. I wondered why we had stopped at this lonely spot, and could not help but feel that we were enveloped by some sinister spell.

As the cloud swept over and moon whiteness came back to the land, I saw a giant oak beside us, its limbs draped in funereal strands of moss, swaying sinuously in the night wind. Then, through the mossy tendrils and beyond, there loomed the haunted ruins of a long-dead magnificence—the tall, desolate columns, the temple-like wings of tragic Woodlawn.

I gasped as I looked for the first time on the magnificent proportions, the cavernous walls, the gaunt somber beauty of the brooding ruins.

Here had been elegance beyond anything Bayou Lafourche had seen. Here the legendary nineteenth-century planters, the faboulous Pughs and other American gentry, had lived out their most grandiloquent dreams. In these high-ceilinged chambers, among Ionic columns of exquisite beauty, their lives had moved in a pattern of gayety and grandeur.

Woodlawn was built in 1839 by William W. Pugh, who had arrived on Bayou Lafourche as a boy of nine and had grown to manhood among the simple charms of this bayouland. Throughout a long life of usefulness as statesman and soldier, this grand old gentleman enjoyed his enviable life on Bayou Lafourche, dying finally at the age of ninety-five, leaving fifteen children and a host of grandchildren—and leaving too, the pride of his heart, beautiful Woodlawn.

Such magnificence as this is more difficult to maintain in modern times than it was to achieve in the nobler years of the

The decayed and ghostly grandeur of "Woodlawn" is a haunting thing to remember.

nineteenth century. In 1910 the Pughs sold their ancestral home, but the new owners were no more able to restore and maintain it than was the original family.

So Woodlawn, like many another Southern mansion, lay a victim of its own grandeur. Its tall, exquisitely proportioned chambers with their carved medallion ceilings were used for storing hay. Cows and stray mules wandered aimlessly among the abandoned garden paths. Transient Negro laborers spread their ragged pallets under the noble pillars of the once-impressive façade.

The very air around Woodlawn seemed to weep. Never had I felt such a poignant melancholy as when I stood in that moonlit night and looked upon this gaunt and dismembered beauty.

Suddenly I felt I must leave, and quickly. Driving up the bayou road toward another of the bridge crossings, I could think of nothing to say to *Grandpère* Verret. Finally we drove out of the black-magic spell of Woodlawn and the air again seemed filled with a sweet liveliness of its own—the crickets and frogs making their dissonant medley along the bayou banks, and far back in the woods the crooning call of the whippoorwills.

On the west side again, where the humble Acadian cottages clustered together like miniature paper-box houses, I could not forget the tragic grandeur I had seen. Now I know I can never forget it. It's decadent beauty and the enchantment of that moonlight night when first I saw it will live forever in my memory.

Next day *Grandpère* Verret sent me ariding the bayou on the rolling grocery store with Jules.

The tradition in which Jules operated was an old and popular one in *la vie lafourchaise*. Doubtless it originated in the *caboteur* tradition of the coastal marshes, where traveling grocery boats served a floating population of trappers and fishermen. On Bayou Lafourche the first *marchand-charrettes* were packet merchants who carried their wares strapped to their backs, visiting bayou wives who preferred to shop from their own front *galeries*. Later, prospering, these ingenious salesmen made their rounds with horse-drawn covered carts. When an excellent hard-surfaced road was built along the length of Bayou Lafourche, many folk predicted that the day of the wandering merchant was over. They failed to remember the strong pull of tradition among *les petits habitants*, and also the Acadian love of economy and convenience. It was so simple, *Mam'selle*—the tradesman just bought a bus and became the *marchand-charrette*.

Jules was the jolliest of merchants and seemed to operate his four-wheeled grocery store as much for the laughs as for the profit. The walls of his big old yellow bus were lined with shelves, each neatly stacked with merchandise. The bayou *mamans* could dress their little ones for school here—suits, shoes, hats, dresses. *Papa* could buy his fish nets, his anchor chain, parts for his putt-putt's motor; medicines, candles, tobacco, candy, *café*, cake, tea, and cookies; brooms and mops, pots and pans—all the necessities and the luxuries of the bayou family were to be found on Jules' crowded shelves.

Lots of these could be bought without any money at all. For what you t'ink, *Mam'selle?* Jules don't carry them empty chicken coops tied to his bumper for nothing, him! He use them for service, yes, for when he gets chicken and geese-fowl in a trade.

More than one bayou wife pays for the family's groceries by bartering with Jules. In town he finds it easy to make a profit on this fresh country produce.

The stops we made at each farmhouse on the bayou road were real social occasions, for the *marchand-charrette* is more than a mere merchant: he is the unofficial social secretary of all his customers up and down the bayou. What better messenger than good ole Jules, him what knows all our secrets anyway, *Mam'selle?* So . . . "Jules, you be sure an' tell *M'sieu* Abadie that the frog gig gonna be tonight, not tomorrow, *hein?*" And . . . "Jules, please let me know if the Dousset twins gonna wear them pink dresses to the *fais-dodo* at Race-

land. Don't want to dress my Too-Too like them saucy flirts!"
And . . . "Jules, ask *Papa* Broussard if he gonna use his lil
throw net tomorrow. Mine is bus' and no time to knit another
before we catch bait for that trot-line in Bayou Pigeon." .

Traveling the bayou road with Jules, I learned many things
about *les petits habitants*. Nothing impressed me more than
the closeness between these simple people and *le bon dieu* to
whom they brought their devotions. There are many cere-
monials on Bayou Lafourche which attest to the Acadians'
devout patterns of thought. Church days are the most important days of the year—Lent, Good Friday, All Saints' Day,
Easter. On Sunday there are several Masses and everyone,
young and old, attends one of these services. On weekdays the
single Mass is heavily attended.

Almost every form of vehicle, for land or sea, is blessed on
Bayou Lafourche, where the protection of St. Christopher is
sought for those who travel by auto, buggy, wagon, or shrimp
boat. The cane crop is blessed too. At the annual ceremonies
for these formal blessings there is a mixture of reverent solemnity and relaxed gayety.

At the end of the day on Jules' rolling store, I realized that
there were many things I must see yet before I had fully
explored the Acadian land of Lafourche. *Grandpère* Verret
must help me still further.

Une 'Tite Journée Down the

Longest Street in the World

vi

Truly to know *la vie lafourchaise*, I said to *Grandpère* Verret,
I should spend a while in the little cities which cling like jewels
to the blue necklace of the bayou.

"Oui, *Mam'selle*," he agreed. "Let us make *une 'tite journée*."

And so we did.

It was a journey that any traveler might make if he wished
to see for himself the charms of that one-hundred-mile stretch
of bayou road known as "the longest street in the world."

It started at the head of the bayou where lay Donaldsonville, a town which dates its history back to 1772. Once this
sleepy little city was the capital of Louisiana.

In the registry of the parish church *Grandpère* Verret showed
me a record inscribed in careful script:

"On the 15th of August, 1772, Father Angelus de Revilla-
godos, a member of the Capuchins, by order of the Very
Reverend Augustin of Toledo, provincial of this province, and
also by order of Charles III of Spain, has taken charge of this
Parish as the first priest."

Then the very reverend father himself records: "This Parish is dedicated to the Ascension of Our Lord. I have this day witnessed its founding."

The good father's parishioners were a few Acadian exiles from Nova Scotia, struggling to build a new home in Spanish territory on lands purchased for them from friendly Houma and unfriendly Chitimacha Indians.

Grandpère Verret showed me how the streets of Donaldsonville were laid out in Anglo-Saxon squares and angles, "Mos' diff'rent from *une ville française, Mam'selle.*"

This was because of the promoter whose name it bore, William Donaldson, who appeared on the scene in the early 1800's with the announced intention of putting this town on the map. He was an American of Scotch-English ancestry who had a decided gift for bestowing presents on the proper people, including the sophisticates and politicos of New Orleans. His industry was rewarded, and within a couple of decades the town bore his name and was the capital of Louisiana. But his glory was brief, the capital was removed after a few years, and Donaldsonville became a sleepy little town again and life there was *très jolie* indeed.

From Donaldsonville to Thibodaux the bayou road wound through the green cane fields—a paved highway on the west bank, a just so-so gravel road along the east levee. I liked the zigzag course we took, first on one side, then across one of Bayou Lafourche's innumerable bridges to the other side, then back again at the slightest excuse. *Grandpère* Verret said there was nothing quite like crossing over a bridge—which he and all Lafourchais called "ferries"—for stirring spice into a man's life. Along Bayou Lafourche it is part of the good life. Crossing a "ferry," like shopping with a *marchand-charrette,* is more than a business matter; it is a chance for a *'ti* call on one's neighbors and friends.

There was a quiet tranquility to the east bank road. It put us back, in feeling, to the leisurely days of the fabulous sugar planters. A few miles down the old road we found Belle Alliance, set in a dense growth of oaks and shrubbery. This was once one of the show places of the bayou. Built in 1846 by Charles Kocke, descendant of a rich Dutch family, the old home combined the massiveness of classic Louisiana plantation homes with the simplicity and functionalism of the raised-cottage type which early bayou settlers built on piers above the marshy land.

Kocke's family lived in splendor here at their country manor —what time they were not in their New Orleans home called Marble House or in their Paris apartment.

Today the big square columns of Belle Alliance soar from the floor of the brick basement to the molded entablature of the roof. Decorative wooden balustrades border the second floor gallery and the flat roofs of the side porches are richly ornamented with grillwork.

We found that the present owners of Belle Alliance were away but *Grandpère* Verret said we were welcome to wander about the remains of the gardens whose camellias had once made it famous and whose paths had been graced by a marble fountain, urns and statuary.

Inside, *Grandpère* Verret said, the long upper hall was paneled in soft pink and there were large ceiling frescoes and plaster medallions over the chandeliers.

Leaving the faded magnificence of the old plantation home, we found our way to the ruins of Belle Alliance sugarhouse. Large piles of crumbling brick and one tall lonely tower, standing like a sentinel over the ruins, were all that was left. This was once one of the most important sugarhouses west of the Mississippi, in the days when each individual plantation had its own mill and Belle Alliance sugar was renowned far and wide. The usefulness of these old sugarhouses is gone, for today the planters truck their cane into half a dozen larger, more efficient mills which serve the whole area.

Grandpère Verret shook his head sadly, regretting those older days.

"C'est triste, Mam'selle."

Like many another passing institution, the change is resented by natives of Bayou Lafourche. They remember nostalgically the gayety of sugarhouse parties which the planters gave each year to celebrate the opening of grinding season—when youthful blades and belles danced all night long on rough floors of the sugarhouses, and took time out only for sipping the sweetness of *la cuite*, dipped from the first cooking of the cane as it boiled and foamed in big kettles alongside their improvised dance floor.

Back on the bayou road, we came in four short miles to Paincourtville, named by an early traveler the "short-of-bread" town. This was one of the original Spanish villages of Assumption Parish. *Grandpère* Verret said many descendants of Spanish settlers still lived here, although they had mixed their blood with the French until no one could tell where

Spanish, French, Creole, or Acadian began or left off.

Dominating the landscape in Paincourtville, as in many a village of Bayou Lafourche, were the sturdy brick towers of the Catholic Church. The red brick of lovely St. Elizabeth's glowed vividly in the warm sunlight, yet even their beauty did not prepare us for the splendors of another church that waited across the bayou.

At Paincourtville we crossed another "ferry" and traveled two miles southward to the early Lafourche village of Plattenville. Here we visited the "Gem of Bayou Lafourche"—the oldest church in the Parish, the Church of the Assumption of the Blessed Virgin Mary, founded here in 1793.

Outside, this church had a true jewel-like quality. Inside, its elaborate appointments gave the same impression of richness. Golden chandeliers and candelabra, bold and brilliantly-painted murals, magnificent carpets, an elaborately carved statue of St. Faustine with relic enshrined nearby—all these gave it an elegance much admired by Acadian and Creole parishioners. Many of these treasures came from France. The inscriptions on stained-glass windows and the Stations of the Cross were in the Gallic language. Yet one could sense something, too, of the Spanish, as if the zealous Capuchins had placed their mark forever on this parish they had clasped from the wilderness.

For the earliest church built upon this spot had been Spanish. In 1793 the first priest, a Capuchin friar named Bernardo de Deva, built a primitive church here and began the keeping of family records in big vellum-bound volumes. In 1819 a more elaborate French church replaced the early structure, but this was destroyed without trace by a violent flood.

In 1856 the present church was built, its elaborate appointments surpassing those of all other bayou towns.

Grandpère Verret spoke with some awe of the annual visit of the Archbishop of New Orleans to the Church of the Assumption. The reverent entourage of churchmen followed a tradition set almost two centuries ago, when youthful Father de Deva received his countryman, Penalver y Cardenas, the first bishop of Louisiana, in his crude uncivilized parish. Since that day every bishop of the diocese and every archbishop of New Orleans has come to officiate once a year at this Gem of Bayou Lafourche. Thus is honored the memory of that early Spanish priest who labored unceasingly among the bayou peoples and who chose to remain among them even when Spain's colonial regime ended and his contemporary brothers returned to the old country.

From Plattenville it was a quick drive through lush green cane fields to Napóleonville. Named by an old soldier of the Great Emperor, Napoleonville was the town on Bayou Lafourche chosen by *les américains* as their favorite.

In Christ Episcopal Church *Grandpère* Verret showed me aisles and small old-fashioned pews where Yankee troops had stabled their horses during the War between the States. Behind the altar were stained-glass windows which the invaders had used for target shooting. So excellently had these been repaired that no damage was now visible. This old church has withstood storms of men and storms of nature. In 1909 a hurricane shattered the windows again and called for another repair job.

Passing down the deeply shaded streets of Napoleonville, we traveled nine more miles through clustering settlements to reach Labadieville, which *Grandpère* Verret said was the earliest of all the Lafourche settlements. Thought to be the site of the chief village of the Washi Indians, this early *ville* saw the intermingling of adventurous souls from France, Spain, Nova Scotia, from American colonies of the North Atlantic states, and from the nearby German Coast along the Mississippi.

A few miles below Labadieville we passed a modest yet beautiful little story-and-half raised cottage which is preserved today because it was the birthplace of Chief Justice Edward Douglas White, who served in the Supreme Court from 1910 to 1921.

Still further down the road we saw ragged remains of a live-oak grove and ruins of another sugarhouse. This marked the site of Leighton Plantation, home of Leonidas Polk, first

Episcopal bishop of Louisiana, the famous "Fighting Bishop" of the War between the States who was killed in an engagement near Marietta, Georgia.

On down the bayou road, watching this intermingling of American and Acadian influences, we came to Thibodaux, largest city on Bayou Lafourche and very definitely the stronghold of the Gauls.

Established early in the 1800's by a Creole statesman, Henry Schuyler Thibodaux, this quiet little city has long been the financial and agricultural center of *les petits habitants*. Its narrow streets, winding to follow the bayou, lined with trees and towering shrubs, are just busy enough, *bien merci*, to suit.

Long ago it had a buzzing water front and its wharves along the bayou echoed shoutings of rivermen as they commanded loadings and unloadings of steamboats. And who would wish it different, said the happy Thibodauxians. So they snubbed the railroaders for wanting to spoil their peaceful streets with the snortings of ugly iron beasts.

"*Avant!* Dispose yourselves elsewhere," they said.

The railroaders did so, putting their line three miles from the little city, and today as then Thibodaux has no railroad. The steamboats are gone too, alas, and only the ghosts of rivermen haunt the crumbling wharves. But the Thibodauxians still stick by their bargain—they are happy, *mes amis*, to have the noisy tracks out of sight and earshot.

It was a different matter, but naturally, when it came to an important thing like the mail delivery. Everybody was happy, yes, when Uncle Sam decided to deliver mail to the wide-flung rural settlements on either side of Thibodaux. On November 1, 1896, from a little post office on St. Phillip Street, this wonderful business was started—the second R.F.D. in the United States. Thus, say the Thibodauxians proudly, we retain our right to be choosy of modern improvements.

This pleasant little town has long been the religious as well as the commercial center of Bayou Lafourche Acadians. More than one well-known ecclesiastic has labored among these parishioners but none so loved as Canon Charles M. Ménard, "the apostle of Lafourche." For over half a century—starting as a young man of twenty-five and laboring until his death at seventy-nine—this good father led his flock in the paths of *le bon dieu*. There are a thousand legends lovingly told about the good man. He was stalwart and rugged in body as in soul, a true man, him. If the need was there, *mais oui*, so was Father Ménard. He traveled in skiffs and in pirogues, on steamboats and in wagons; and often astride his big white horse he sought out the afflicted or the needy.

He was zealous and proud for *les petits habitants*. Once he had a vision and it led him all the way to Rome. There he sought a worthy religious relic for his parishioners, something especially for the young women of Bayou Lafourche, those who would be the mothers of the Lafourchais of the future.

Although the Pope himself discouraged Father Ménard, the priest found a way to acquire a famous relic. A certain cardinal was the owner of a part of the arm of Ste. Valérie, virgin Martyr, one of those sainted ones beheaded in the terrible days of the Flavian Amphitheatre. This was indeed worthy of the innocent maidens of Lafourche!

On his return Father Ménard led a great procession with the relic encased in a richly-dressed statue of the saint, followed by the girls of the parish dressed as "little Martyrs," in gowns of white, with ribbons and head wreaths of red, the colors of martyrdom. The procession wound down the streets along the bayou and out to the old cemetery, followed by thousands of Lafourche men and women. This became an annual ceremonial.

In sentiments and dedication it was equalled only by another ceremony held in the old cemetery on one of the visits of the Archbishop. Here, just after dark one night several years ago, three thousand men stood with lighted candles piercing the gloom of the encircling oaks to renew their baptismal vows in a service long to be remembered for its simplicity and beauty.

Grandpère Verret, standing beside me in the cemetery where we had gone to visit Father Ménard's tomb, said, *"Allons,*

Mam'selle, we must get along with our *'tite journée,* no? One more house you *mus'* visit. A Spanish home, *Mam'selle,* but more beautiful than any you have yet seen."

We crossed the bridge through Thibodaux's heart and found Rienzi just two miles down the bayou. This luxurious eighteenth-century house, perfectly restored and maintained, is truly one of the most gorgeous in the whole South.

Like many another one, it has an intriguing story of mystery and romance. No one knows exactly for whom the house was built, so it holds a secret too. Some historians say it was built by Spanish Queen Maria Louisa at the close of the eighteenth century, as a potential refuge for herself when the Napoleonic Wars might drive her out. Others say the queen had the lovely home built for a favorite lady-in-waiting who considered voluntary exile because of a disappointing love affair. Undoubtedly the house has a look of royalty. Its beauty is exquisite—simple, delicate, feminine.

All that is known, "for *certainement,*" is that the house was occupied for almost half a century by Don Ignacio de Egana, a representative of the Spanish queen.

Another owner, an Italian settler named Giovanni, named the house in honor of his favorite hero, Italian patriot Cola di Rienzi. Today the home is owned by the gracious Creole-Acadian family of Jean Baptiste Levert, sugar planter.

Rienzi, because of its two gracefully curved outside stairways leading to the second floor gallery, is one of the finest examples of the Louisiana raised cottage. Brick piers, rising from the paved lower porch, support the floor of the upper gallery. Small square, wooden colonnettes support the ceiling of the galleries which surround the house on all four sides. These, added to bannisters running around the galleries and on the stairways, give a sense of lightness and airiness which belies the strength of this two-story brick building.

Inside, the large entrance rooms are decorated with elaborate carving and wood paneling. There is a quality of spaciousness about the interior rooms, as if they were built for state and diplomatic functions.

A Bayou Lafourche hand-turned bridge serves for social gatherings as well as for foot, car and boat traffic.

Truly Rienzi is fit for a queen, and if Maria Louisa of Spain never enjoyed its rare beauty, it was her loss and the gain of every one of the *petits habitants* who can drive down the road from Thibodaux and feast his eyes upon it.

On the west-bank road from Thibodaux to Raceland the *pavé* along Bayou Lafourche passes through a land of miniatures—small farms, small houses, small pleasures enjoyed with huge appreciation by *les lafourchais*.

Here one sees the levee bank being put to good use, for with true French economy the Acadians use every arpent of their rich land. Truck gardens flourish on the ancient levees, and many an Acadian wife makes her pin money from produce sold from these short rows of vegetable crops.

Coming into hectic, noisy Raceland—a little village "grown too big for its britch'," according to *Grandpère* Verret—we met traffic from upper and lower Lafourche as well as that from westerly Houma and Morgan City. The bridge stretching over Bayou Lafourche at Raceland is a busy funnel which pours its traffic eastward on Highway 90 toward New Orleans.

We parked and *Grandpère* Verret led me over the footpath to the center of the bridge.

"Look up da bayou, *Mam'selle*," he said, "and then look down. Here you see the diff'rent, *mais* sho. Upper Lafourche belong to the land, lower is for the sea."

From where I stood, I could see no difference. In either direction the bayou was a tranquil slow-moving stream, half-clogged with the menacing beauty of water hyacinths. Half a mile above the bridge was the awkward hulk of a hyacinth-cutting machine, floating on a big barge, its toothy chain chewing into the pesky hyacinths on one side, spitting them out on the other, like some carnivorous, prehistoric monster.

Below the bridge the scene seemed identical, except that the lumbering steel-limbed dinosaur had not broken into the beautiful but deadly carpet of hyacinths.

Grandpère Verret told me a little about the terrible water-hyacinth plant. It is said to have been introduced to Louisiana at the Cotton Exposition in 1884, "a rare and beautiful aquatic plant" from the Orient. Its growth was spectacular beyond anything the bayou folk had ever seen. Too late it was recognized as a menace, a beautiful but evil thing which strangled streams, killing other vegetation, blighting fish, clogging the water paths for boats big and small. Hundreds of thousands of dollars, years of laboratory experimentation—nothing has prevailed against the creeping growth of the terrible plant. Newcomers to the bayou country still find it beautiful, but to natives the purple carpet which spreads over their water paths is horribly repellent.

When we left the bridge at Raceland and continued down

the bayou road, I felt and saw that difference which *Grandpère*
Verret had described.

Down below, the levees grew lower, the bayou seemed to rise
to meet the land, and the narrow canal widened and straightened, became a streamlined kind of chute racing toward the
sea.

At Lockport the small traffic of the bayou, pirogues and
putt-putts, was joined by handsome tugboats pulling barges
loaded with oil and with steel pipe for drilling rigs. Here the
Intra-coastal Canal, bearing its industrial traffic from New
Orleans to Texas, entered Bayou Lafourche—and roaring industrialism invaded pastoral lands of *les petits habitants*.

The peasant feeling remained, though, in wandering herds

*The classic beauty of "Rienzi" remains a symbol of Creole ele-
gance in the sugar lands of Bayou Lafourche.*

A hyacinth-clogged section of Bayou Lafourche. This deadly water plant has ruined navigation on large sections of this and other bayous.

of cows and mules which, because of limited farm land, had to be pastured on the levee banks. And pirogues were still used instead of horses to round up the cattle along the watery pastures! *Grandpère* Verret pointed out narrow, fenced-in lanes called *manches* which were paths of dairy cattle. These led to the *coteaux* (little hills) along the levees where the dairy herds pastured.

Lockport, for all its new industrialism, was still a fishing village, with dozens of gaily-painted shrimp boats unloading at the docks of its "swimp factorie." There was still an old-world flavor about these fishing villages, Lockport, Larose and Cut-Off, which clung to the bayou from here to the Gulf. Shrimp boats—looking like meticulously white, big-bellied water bugs—surged up the bayou, their tar-blackened nets swinging gracefully from short masts. Atop the masts flew brilliantly colored flags, giving the fleet a gayety and charm that was reflected in the dark laughing faces of their Cajun crews. The Lafourchais here were men of the sea, tillers of the blue Gulf waters, cultivators of oyster beds and searchers after the tastiest of "swimps." There was danger and excitement in their trade. They must mark well the howling hurricanes which sweep Gulf waters into mountainous fury. Their wives and sweethearts must know the terror of fisherfolk the world over. Their womenfolk must bend closely over battery radio sets on swaying houseboats, listen for news of the fleet, and pray to *le bon dieu* without ceasing, when autumnal winds began their terrible work.

In summer it was different, *mon ami,* and there was always laughter. After the blessing of the shrimp fleet in August, boats went daily down to the Gulf, many returning each evening to villages where hand-turned drawbridges were lifted time and again for them to pass. Then the bayou shrimp docks buzzed with life, boats leaving and returning. At Golden Meadow a fleet of three-hundred fishing luggers brought in millions of dollars worth of shrimp and oysters, speckled trout, redfish, sheepshead and pompano. Five shrimp-canning factories operated in this one village, shipping their product to every part of the world.

Golden Meadow had the loose-jointed, uncouth look of a gauche boom town. It seemed schizophrenic too, unable to decide whether to be a buzzing fishing village or a booming oil town.

Its wooden stores and frame houses, mixed in among shrimp-drying platforms and packing sheds on land, and the swaying campboat homes on the bayou side, carried the flavor of a fisherman's town. But oil, black gold, and the strange *texiens* who followed in its wake, had left their mark on Golden Meadow. Slush pits and iron-ribbed derricks rose in front yards and on church lawns. Big black barges were tied to the docks for a few days, then floated into nearby lakes and

Golden Meadow is a "lil swimp town" on lower Bayou —
Lafourche.

bayous, sunk and used as bases for drillings into the soft, rich muck.

Since 1931, when oil was discovered at abandoned old Leeville, just a few miles below, Golden Meadow had been a wide-open town. Many of the boldest Cajun youths of the village chose to join the incoming roughnecks, to ride oil rigs out to the flat watery prairies, to climb derricks and wet their hands with black gold which gushed from the holes. Others kept to the ways of their fathers, followed the shrimp, oyster and muskrat seasons, and held to the old Gallic tradition.

Grandpère Verret shook his head sadly. It was plain to see that he did not feel at home in Golden Meadow.

"*Mam'selle,* we go back now," he said. "Below us there is no more of my Bayou Lafourche. Only wasteland, and the ruins of Chênière Caminada, until you reach Grand Isle."

Abruptly he turned the flivver around and headed determinedly up the bayou, sitting silently at the wheel and not relaxing his grip until we came in sight of Raceland.

Here he stopped, in front of a little tavern which hung precariously out over the bayou bank. Inside, heading for a table which gave us a good view upstream, he sighed and seemed more at ease.

"Dispose yourself, *Mam'selle,*" he said, holding a chair for me and ordering our *café noir* with a single well-understood gesture to the proprietor.

As we sipped the coffee, he sighed contentedly and was himself again.

"And how you like down-the-bayou, *Mam'selle?* Is it not terrible, yes? . . . But our *'tite journée,* now that was a good thing, *mais* sho!"

He pushed back his chair, motioned me to stand beside him at the window. Out on the bayou the twilight sun splashed its last brilliant colors into the quiet waters. One lonely putt-putt crossed under the bridge, leaving a funneling wake behind it. A bunch of youngsters dived off the wreck of an old houseboat lying half afloat against the right bank, and their slender arms and legs flashed palely in the waters as they followed the boat's wake. Silhouetted against the sky, far up on the left levee, stood a man leaning against his hoe, looking down the bayou as we were looking up. It was almost as if he waited to hear the angelus—and I knew that, were he close enough to Thibodaux or Napoleonville or the treasured Gem of Lafourche, he *would* hear those comforting chimes ringing in the tranquil dusk, sounding the call through the fields and bringing the *habitants* home for the night.

Driving home in the darkening evening, we were too tired to talk much, but *Grandpère* Verret made one little joke.

"And what you tell Father Toups now, *Mam'selle*, about *le* true *acadien?* You find him on Lafourche, *hein?*"

I was grateful, more than I could say, for the favors of this sweet and gentle old man. I tried to tell him so. But I could not answer his question, for my mind was still confused, uncertain. Driving this day along a hundred miles of Bayou Lafourche, we had seen a pattern of cultures more mixed than any I had seen so far in my search for Evangeline's people.

Acadians there were, for sure, along the upper and lower banks of Lafourche. But were there not also, closely intermingled and fused beyond all separation, the heritage and the blood of the Spanish, the *américain*, the Creole, the German, the Dutch—and even, *mon dieu*, the *texien?*

Grandpère Verret seemed to understand my silence, and forgive it. He even seemed to approve it.

"So you will search further, *Mam'selle? C'est bon!* I give you the name of my cousin, Maxim Terrebonne. You fin' him on Grand Isle. You t'ink you see some mixed peoples on Bayou Lafourche? Wait till you meet the Benoques on Grand Isle, *Mam'selle!* As my little Minette would say . . . you isn't saw nawthin yet, no."

Fais-Dodo with

Grand Isle Baratarians

vii

Luminous brilliance of sea-island sun, wash and surge of billowing surf, a salty tang to southerly winds, and a long, littered stretch of tawny beach—this was Grand Isle, from the Gulf side, as I first saw it.

A single stretch of road—*le pavé*—ran for seven miles down the length of the island. Beach and water lay to the south. To the north majestic palms towered over live oaks dwarfed and tortured by ceaseless winds. Everywhere there were red and white blossomings of giant oleanders.

Some said this island was once the stronghold of Henry Morgan in his buccaneering expeditions along the Spanish Main. Later it was the lair from which Captain Jean Lafitte, king of the corsairs, raided ships in the Gulf and the Caribbean. Stolen cargoes of slaves and shipments of captured merchandise had been hidden here until the captain and his lieutenants could sneak them into New Orleans.

Today the island looked quiet, at peace, as it stretched its sandy limbs to the sun. Its natives, descendants of swashbuckling pirates, had become a pastoral people, tending their small gardens through long, leisurely days or sailing their shrimp boats out of Bay Rigaud into close-by waters of the Gulf of Mexico. Baratarians they called themselves, after winding Bayou Barataria which led a devious trail through the marshes toward New Orleans—the route their wild ancestors had used in going from the island to hidden headquarters in the city. Baratarians was an acceptable, even a flattering name among them, I was told, but do not call them "Benoques" as some outsiders did, thus offering an indefinable insult.

From the beach road tiny lanes led into the center of the island. These were lost in the crossings and crisscrossings of other, still smaller trails which tunneled their way through lush tropical vegetation to weather-beaten houses of the Baratarians. A variation of the Cajun cottages of Lafourche, a few of these little houses retained vivid reds, blues, pinks, yellows, oranges and greens of recent paint jobs. Others were greyed by sea winds. All were propped with long poles against their sides and were thus anchored to the land in prayerful defiance of furious September hurricanes. On galleries and walls of all these island homes hung barometers, thermometers, wind-breakers—such an assortment of weather instruments as I had never seen before. I was to learn that the Grand Islanders had good reason for this fixation on weather-prophesying devices. Tragedy had touched almost every family on the island in more than one catastrophe of wind and wave. Perhaps these instruments would not prevent such a thing, but it helped a man to feel better, *mon ami*, if he had a little warning and gained a little time.

It was Saturday morning, late, time for the shrimp fleet's returning. I was told I would find Maxim at the shrimp docks "to the back." I wandered down half a dozen twisting trails, asking directions of dark-skinned, silent natives who answered my questions with gestures, not words. There, along Bay Rigaud, I found quiet waters, wharves that seemed to be waiting for something to happen.

News of a stranger's coming had preceded me.

A crowd of little boys ran down the shaky dock walks, skipping over the fallen boards and dock-side litter.

"Maxim's coming!" they shouted, and pointed to a trim lugger which was racing up the bay ahead of the rest, flying a big red flag which meant a bulging shrimp hold.

Then the shouts came from every direction.

"Maxim, *ici*" . . . "Maxim, *très bon!*" . . . "Maxim" . . . "Maxim . . ." echoed down the dock and through the shrimp-deheading shed.

I realized then that the boys had not meant their message for me alone, but for all who waited along the shore.

And I felt that I was about to meet a personage. Maxim Terrebonne did not disappoint me.

A great giant of a man, he leapt like a cat from his lugger's net-shrouded deck, and stood before me—a massive fellow, full of grace, vivid and vibrant with a strength born of many days and nights at sea.

His voice was deep and sure.

"*Mais* sho, *Mam'selle*, I show you Grand Isle, I guarantee! And take you trawlin' too!"

He swept his frazzle-brimmed straw hat off a mop of black curls and flung his arm back toward the island.

"Grand Isle, she is yours, *Mam'selle!* I give her to you, me!" He threw his dark head back and roared with laughter at his own generosity. The little boys, standing around Maxim with obvious admiration, tossed their heads too and echoed his laughter.

"But firs' I gotta take care of da swimps, *hein?*"

By this time other boats were tying up to docks all down the line. Shouts of "*Allons*, Maxim . . . Maxim, *ici* . . . quickly, *mon ami* . . . quickly, Maxim . . ."

It seemed that everybody wanted him at once. For in addition to captaining his own boat and crew, Maxim was shrimp buyer for a fleet of fifteen sturdy little luggers. He strode busily about the docks, from one boat to another, supervising the unloading of "swimps" from the holds. Tall wicker baskets were loaded with rich, squirming masses, placed briefly on the dock, then poured into the waiting ice trucks, to be borne to the shrimp factories at Golden Meadow or to the frozen-foods plants at New Orleans. The docks buzzed. Everyone seemed in a fever to get the work done instantly. Finally, a murmured phrase, then an excited shout, told me why.

"Eh, Jean, you playin' yo' ting-a-ling for *fais-dodo* tonight?" . . . then an echoed shouting, running all down the docks . . . "*fais-dodo* tonight" . . . "quickly, man, *fais-dodo* tonight."

The work was finished at last. The final load came out of the holds, the final truck pulled away from the wharves. Fishermen worked deftly to secure their boats for the night, straightening a tangled net, tightening a towline here, a sternline there. Now it was done, and the Baratarians drifted away in twos and threes, turning in to the little lanes which fanned out from the wharves, seeking out their wives and sweethearts —happy to be finished for another week and to rest a little before the *fais-dodo*.

Maxim was almost the last to leave. He stood finally, hands on hips, surveying the fleet with a proprietary air. The sun was setting across Bay Rigaud, a great fiery sphere which hovered just a moment, casting its copper rays along masts and nets of the shrimp fleet, before it slid into the watery horizon. Its mauve and golden afterglow, with deep purple silhouettes of shrimp luggers, made a Japanese print of this placid bay.

We left quietly, walked toward wind-twisted oaks, and when we reached the little lane which led like a green tunnel to Maxim's cottage, we turned for a final look at all this wondrous beauty.

As we stood there we heard the silvery tones of a church bell tolling the angelus. There seemed a special quality in its tones, different from bells I had heard up Bayou Lafourche. Was the quality made by the sea air which bore the music to us?

Maxim took his battered fisherman's hat from his head, crossed himself, and stood for a moment transfixed, a towering silhouette against the vivid sky. Then he turned to me, jammed his hat on his great mop of hair and grinned, breaking the spell of the moment.

"Is it not beautiful, *Mam'selle*, the voice of our bell at the angelus?"

I nodded, not speaking, listening for the last echo of deep-throated tones which seemed richer than any I could remember.

Maxim pushed ahead, motioning me to follow toward his red and white cottage at the end of the lane.

"Come see, *Mam'selle*, and I tell you the story of our bell."

Like other lanes of Grand Isle, Maxim's was tangled with lush tropic growth—ferns and creepers, "angel's trumpers," wild orchids, and everywhere the fragrant oleander bushes which bore the favorite flower of the islanders.

At the end of the lane Maxim's pretty, olive-skinned wife welcomed us to their neatly-painted cottage. She brought me a chair to the wide cool gallery, then rushed back inside to bring us each a tiny demitasse of coffee.

Maxim grunted with pleasure, whiffed the bouquet of the *café noir* before he drank.

"Jus' one leetle cup, *Mam'selle*, before the *fais-dodo*. Then we want somethin' kickier, I guarantee!"

Between sips from the demitasse cups, Maxim told me the story of the bell.

"You must know, *Mam'selle*, she is not *really* our bell at all," he began. "She belong, for true, to oldtime Chênière Caminada. And how we got her . . . *c'est triste, Mam'selle* . . . very, very sad."

It all began in 1893. By then the islanders and the marsh dwellers all along the coast were beginning to forget the agony of hurricane-smashed Isle Dernière. Prosperity had returned to Grand Isle, following bitter Reconstruction days, and speculators with new money were plotting future booms, visualizing vast wealth to be wrung from these Gulf islands.

Close by, on the low sandy island called Chênière Caminada, life was also sweet. The two thousand-odd Italian-French-Portuguese villagers were an easy-going lot, happy with their fishing and hunting, their trapping, gardening, orange groves and vineyards which clung to the flat water prairies. They were a gayer bunch than their neighbors. They laughed and poked a little fun at Grand Islanders, who went about eternally planting oak trees in crisscrossing lanes over the face of *their* island. Is it natural, *mon dieu*, for a man to be forever planting trees to anchor his soil to the earth? Sure, that hurricane on Isle Dernière was a terrible thing, *mon ami*, but *le bon dieu* don't give a thing like that to a man more'n once a lifetime, *hein?*

High-spirited Chênière Caminada natives were solemn about just one thing—their silver-voiced bell which hung high on its platform among the palmettos. Was it not cast from seven hundred pounds of silver, had it not taken ten men to lift it to its place? Now it hung there shining through the happy days, a symbol of the islanders' faith, for all of them had helped to build it. Father Espinosa, before he died, had given his parishioners a great dream: to make a bell whose tone would be the most beautiful of any along the whole coast. He had given his crested family plate, brought from the old country, to make the beginning of the bell. The islanders had brought out their bits of silver and gold. Some of the gifts were long-hidden heirlooms left by their piratical forefathers. Their prized possessions were all melted together and, *voilà*, the beautiful bell! As it pealed across the marshes at morning and eventide, the islanders, good Catholics all, felt pride and devotion in their hearts. Young Father Grimeaux loved their bell as much as they, and he too found days on Chênière Caminada happy and joyful ones.

In September of 1893 even the annual gales seemed more peaceable, less wild and frightening. One or two bitter blows were all, but no terrible hurricane to fight. The vineyards were heavy with grapes, and the luggers' holds were bulging with rich harvests from the sea.

Then, with the hurricane month almost gone, on Friday, September 30, came the storm! Out of a black, ugly dawn the sea rose and made a toy of the island—pushing its weight upon the shallow earth, pulling and tugging and sucking the sands out again, a ceaseless, chilling rhythm. Two days of such terror—with women and children huddled on their knees before crude family altars, lighting holy candles, burning green fronds which had been blessed on Palm Sunday. The skies poured rain upon them, the sea beat endlessly against their southern shore.

At last there came relief. The hush of quieted winds cloaked the island in peace. Villagers offered prayers of thankfulness, and slept for the first time in days.

Then came the real horror. With an angry roar the winds rose, shifted direction, and bore down upon the island with a 125-mile-per-hour blast. Gargantuan tidal waves poured in, one after another and swept over sands, fishdocks, village streets, and over homes and people. In fifteen minutes the island was covered with five feet of water; in half an hour, with eight feet.

Chaos came with the waves. Their homes and boats splintered around them, men, women and children were swept into the sea, grasping for something to cling to, finding nothing. Some clutched at rooftops, found a temporary raft to float on, then felt it smash beneath them and spew them like spray into the sea. Clinging to bits of scattered wreckage, mothers knew the agony of babies snatched from their arms, oldsters saw their grandchildren sink and drown within their reach.

Standing helpless at the windows of his rectory, Father Grimeaux watched as the Caminada church burst before his eyes. He listened in vain to screams of his people as they struggled to reach the lamp he lit in the window. All through the night he prayed and, with a pitying gesture, offered final absolution of the church for those who drowned by scores around him.

And over it all the great silvery tones of the bell tolled achingly.

On other Gulf islands the wild winds raged also, sending thirty-foot waves pouring in upon the marsh dwellers, drowning them by scores as they clung to their frail dwellings.

In all fifteen hundred men, women and children were lost that night. Chênière Caminada, with its laughing people, was dead, never to be revived, destined to become a haunted strip of sand and prairie, a rendezvous of ghosts. Other islanders were forever to shun the spot, cross themselves and murmur a prayer as they hurried past its naked sands.

Grand Islanders, saved from the winds by their oak trees, gave succor to the few survivors. Most of the Chênière Caminadans who remained moved into a village across the river from New Orleans and tried to adjust themselves to town life.

They had only one treasure left—their precious bell. Miraculously they had found it buried in the sands after the hurricane passed. It was all that was left of their happy life on the Chênière. Sadly they stored and guarded its beauty as a symbol of their lost happiness.

Finally, church authorities decreed that the bell should be given to another congregation. Over the ex-islanders' protests the great bell was loaded into a carriage to be taken away.

What happened that night on a lonely road in the swamps will remain forever a mystery. But the bell disappeared. Survivors of Chênière Caminada would say nothing, and for two decades the beautiful bell was lost to usefulness. Would *le bon dieu* wish their bell to ring for other peoples? *Non, certainement, non.*

Finally, twenty-five years after the tragedy of 1893, Grand Islanders made a proposal to the handful of survivors of the Chênière. Would it not be a good thing—to hear the bell ring again over a marshy sea island? A beautiful thing, yes, to see the bell hanging silvery and shiny among the palm trees?

The stubborn ones were persuaded.

They led the way to their cemetery, pointed at a spot on which to dig. Almost, the bell was lost again. The first digging revealed only an empty hole. Then the islanders huddled again, moved to a different area of the graveyard, and pointed to another spot. This time the shovels made a ringing sound against the sides of the bell. One oldster wept as they dug around the big bell and pulled it from the earth.

A celebration was planned on Grand Isle. All along the Gulf, news spread. Father Grimeaux was serving elsewhere—bearing always the scar of the terrible sights he had witnessed at Chênière Caminada. He was invited to return for the ceremony, but was not told about the bell. It was to surprise the good father, yes!

As the boat bore the officiating party toward Grand Isle, silvery tones of the bell rang joyously across the waters. Father Grimeaux knew the tones and fell to his knees on the boat deck, weeping. It was the same bell, the same tone which had haunted his ear for a quarter century! But now it was real again, and ringing for his island people!

That day will never be forgotten on Grand Isle.

The story of the bell will be told over and over again, to each new generation of Baratarians. And so the ghosts of Chênière Caminada may rest in peace.

Even before Maxim ended his story, sounds of music echoed thinly through the island lanes. The *fais-dodo* had begun! Down at the pavilion on the beach the musicians were calling Baratarians to their Saturday night frolic. Maxim told me the dancing would last all night, and all Sunday night too. But we must hurry! Don't miss a minute, *Mam'selle,* for the *fais-dodo* is a wonderful thing, yes.

We were scrubbed, dressed in our finery, and at the pavilion within the hour.

The big wooden dance pavilion was already alive with gayety. Its floor and the benches along its walls were so crowded with people that it seemed to expand and contract as visibly as the French accordion which one white-mustachioed old gentleman played so violently on the orchestra stand On benches around the floor sat gossiping *grandmères, mamans,* and youngsters—all seeming to enjoy the dance as much as the whirling couples. At a long bar running across one end of the pavilion *grandpères* stood cracking jokes with each other, contentedly sipping their apéritifs. A few of them wandered back and forth to the tables in a small adjoining room where 'ti games of *bourée* and dominoes were in progress.

Maxim asked if I would like to see the *parc aux petits*, another small room adjoining the dance hall. Here a chubby, cheerful woman—*Tante* 'Toinette—presided over a roomful of babies, some asleep, some playing on the floor. She held a four-month old infant in her arms, efficiently giving it a bottle while she bent to take a sharp-edged toy away from a toddler.

"Thees Chérie's *bébé*, she one beeg girl now, *hein*, Maxim? Won't be long, no, till she be adancin' like 'er *maman*, the prettiest lil lady on da flo'!"

I had heard of the *parc aux petits* which was a feature of all oldtime Cajun *fais-dodos*. There was always a *Tante* 'Toinette or a *Tante* Zuzu or a *grandmère* or so who was eager to preside at this gathering of the very young. In a land where a girl might be married at thirteen, a mother of two at fifteen, and hardly begun to get her fill of dancing before she was twenty—or, for that matter, for a lifetime—the *parc aux petits* was a great convenience, *n'est-ce pas?*

Maxim told me there was an old Cajun joke about children who grew up not resembling either father or mother. "Must have got mixed up, got the wrong *bébé* at a *fais-dodo*, yes!"

Back inside the pavilion the three-piece band was blasting away at a truly astonishing tempo. It was the oldtime threesome: French accordion, violin, and *'ti fers* or triangles. Bands like this had played the jerky, irregular beats of Cajun tunes as long as any here could remember. The triangle or "ting-a-ling" added a gayety, a kind of childlike abandon to the music. Like many Cajun dance bands, as well as the wandering minstrels known as *célébrités de musique*, this one was composed of three generations of the same family—*grandpère, père,* and *fils*. The gayest of the three was *Grandpère* Babin, whose accordion swelled and shrank and swelled again with intoxicating music for hour upon hour all through the whole night.

Out on the floor the couples, dressed in their brightly colored ginghams, bluejeans and khakis, swirled and dipped and whirled in circles till they made a revolving kaleidoscope of the dance hall. As midnight drew near there was no end to the ceaseless movement, the rhythmic beat of the hopping Cajun two-step and the fast swirling of the waltzes. A kind of frenzy seemed to possess the dancers. These were exotic people, drunk with gayety and romance. Grace was their heritage, and a fierce love of life pulsed through them. Swart, handsome fellows laughed recklessly, sometimes shouted, as they swung their girls round the floor. Some boys wore handkerchiefs round their heads, to show that they were engaged and wanted no one else to dance with their sweethearts. Girls were olive-skinned, dark-eyed, seized by enchantment with the music, moving gracefully through the patterns of the dances.

At midnight the dance was still going on and on, swift-paced and strenuous. Dawn brought the only intermission.

Just at daylight came the tolling of the church bell. The band laid its instruments down, smiling wearily. Couples left the floor, parents and oldsters gathered up the sleeping children and all departed in a muted chorus of weary farewells.

From the all-night dance Baratarians went directly to early Mass and after Mass to their homes for rest. The orchestra went off for a few hours of heavy sleep. At three o'clock on Sunday afternoon the islanders gathered again and the dance went into another breathless swing which lasted until far after midnight. This was every weekend's routine on Grand Isle, Maxim told me.

After early Mass I went to my room at the Hotel Victor, a rambling affair of ancient vintage. Like most of the Grand Islanders, I slept the morning and the early afternoon away.

The sun was lowering behind the tallest palms before I sought out Maxim again. I found him on his *galerie*, sipping coffee and talking with his pleasant-faced wife who was almost too shy to speak with a stranger.

"Allo, *Mam'selle*, the day grows late," he said. "Come sit with us. I keep my promise an' tell you about the old days."

His wife disappeared into the kitchen, returned with the inevitable demitasse, and settled comfortably, like me, to listen to Maxim's stories of their island and some of its people.

Since the days of the French explorers this chain of four

tropical islands—Grand Terre, Grand Isle, Chênière Caminada, and Isle Dernière—had tantalized the imaginations of
adventurers and promoters, luring them into fantastic schemes,
crushing them with gigantic failures. No man had remained
long a conqueror of any of the islands and now only the
smallest, Grand Isle, remained habitable.

Grand Isle had known the dreams and felt the touch of four
strong men. The first, Monsieur François Anfrey, secured the
seven-mile island as a land grant in the 1700's and determined
to operate it as a sugar plantation and a cattle range. Dream-
ers on the other islands were trying the same thing, sending
down large numbers of slaves with overseers, establishing
elaborate quarters. Soon Monsieur Anfrey and other planters
realized that the salty earth would not produce. Grand Isle
and plantations on the other islands were sold and resold.

One of those who came to the island was Jacques Rigaud,
a shrewd Frenchman whose dreams proved more realistic and
faith more tenacious than the rest. His descendants remain
today and are leaders in the island community. The bay to
the north carries his name. His original lands, though divided
many times among his children and grandchildren, remain
sufficient to support his family.

After the big planters left, taking their slaves and their
overseers, the islands began to be settled by little men of many
different nationalities—Frenchmen, Spaniards, Acadians, Germans, Portuguese—who learned how to live happily off the
island's bounty. They fished, trapped, and managed to raise a
few meager vegetables in the salty soil.

They developed another enterprise, a dangerous and exciting
one. From the islands to the south came traders with forbidden
wares, seeking entrance through the devious bayous to New
Orleans and northern markets. No men knew those secret
watery passages so well as the Baratarians, no spot was so
well fitted as their island home for trade in contraband. And,
mon dieu, un pauvre man mus' do what he can to get moneys
for bread so the little ones might eat, yes?

Out in the Caribbean, bands of pirates preyed on defenseless ships which bore the gold and silver prizes of Mexico and Peru. And they cast speculative eyes on the small smugglers of Grand Isle, thinking what a safe retreat this would make if ever England made good her threat to wipe them off the Spanish Main. Early in the 1800's they saw their Caribbean retreats captured, knew they must find a new base of operations.

They moved in so quietly at first that the Grand Islanders were scarcely aware of their coming.

"Many, many mens," Maxim said, "and many differen' colors, *Mam'selle*, and *they* knew *how* to run a business, them."

The men were Cubans, Santo Domingans, Orientals, Malays, Portuguese, Slovaks, and of course French, German, English, American. They bore the scars of their business with them— wooden legs, armless sleeves, eyes covered with patches. They were dark and silent on their working days, gone from the harbor for days or weeks at a time. But when they returned— *mon dieu*, what parties! Roaring and rioting, drunk with stolen wines and liquors of a dozen nations, they danced for nights on end with the island girls.

The gangs were loosely organized, brawling and quarreling among themselves, dividing their riches after fierce fights which often diminished their numbers. Then one day a suave Frenchman took them over.

Jean Lafitte, with his elder brother Pierre operating a blacksmith shop as a blind in New Orleans, became the king of the corsairs. Their New Orleans location enabled the brothers Lafitte to meet and do business with the city's best merchants and the biggest Louisiana planters. Silks and satins, gold and silver, all the merchandise captured off ships of the Spanish Main—plus black slaves forbidden legal entrance since America had taken over Louisiana in 1803—these were sold by the brothers from their blacksmith shop on Bourbon Street. Jean was an elegant gentleman, a dandy, a man of the world whose charms were appreciated by ladies as much as his business ability was admired by men. Pierre was a sturdy, dependable partner, serious, silent and efficient.

Their enterprises were widespread. Down on Grand Terre

Island, across Bay Rigaud from Grand Isle, they established an expansive base of operations. A huge, rambling storehouse held riches of untold value. A heavy stockade confined hundreds of slaves, captured off the sunken slaveships and waiting their turn to be sold to plantations throughout the South.

Ships of every description, boats large and small, crowded the placid waters of Bay Rigaud. Luggers and schooners sailed in and out, replenishing the storehouse, and on one shore of the little bay a special marine ways did a booming business in remodeling captured vessels.

Outlaws from all over the world heard of the bonanza, came to join forces with Lafitte's men. The conglomerate crew was capably handled by Lafitte's lieutenants. Fierce, heartless men, they led their reckless gangs in the most highly organized piratery the world has yet seen. Dominique You, Louis Chighizola, Nez Coupé (Split Nose), Johnny Gambi—their names became almost as famous as Lafitte's and were passwords to terror.

For a decade the pirates ruled the Gulf from their protected strongholds on Grand Isle and Grand Terre, with polished, elegant Captain Jean representing them in the commerce halls and ballrooms of New Orleans.

Finally, their bold thievery could no longer be ignored by the Government. Something must be done!

The pirates entered politics. In 1814 they were courted by the British who hoped to pluck the rich plum, New Orleans, away from gauche Americans. Lafitte and his men heard the Britishers' offer—$30,000 in gold and a naval captaincy for Jean Lafitte—if the gang would agree to guide them through the treacherous water passages to the Crescent City.

Lafitte delayed his decision, contacted high-positioned Americans and offered his help for the defense of New Orleans. His offer was refused. Ungrateful Americans put a price on his head. They stormed his stronghold on Grande Terre, destroyed his defenses, took a bountiful harvest of goods and ships.

Then the picture changed. Americans were hard pressed to

defend themselves against the British. Spanish fishermen along the marshy coast were aiding the enemy, revealing to them the water paths which led to the city. The Battle of New Orleans loomed inevitable. General Andrew Jackson needed help, anybody's help he could get. From a hidden retreat Lafitte sent word that he would still lead his men to an American defense. This time his offer was accepted.

The buccaneers, fighting boldly, proved a decisive factor in the battle. The city saved, General Jackson saw that the nation pardoned Lafitte and his men. For a while the pirates were heroes.

The men reveled in respectability, enjoying it as flamboyantly—for a while—as they had loved their former piracy. But this kind of glory proved too dull, and too unprofitable, for their adventurous leader.

It is said that no one knows exactly what became of Captain Jean Lafitte. After his kingdom on Grand Terre was destroyed, after Baratarian waters were cleared and calmed, the scene was spoiled for him. His lustrous character called for a more dramatic stage to play upon. Though some of the lesser members of his troupe could settle peacefully in cottages of Grand Isle and Chênière Caminada, the hero could not content himself with such mediocrity. So he must sail west again, for Texas coasts and the unknown theatres of history which awaited him there.

He tried to stage a comeback on Galveston Island. For a time the waters along the Texas coast echoed the name of the corsair king. Then, mysteriously, he disappeared.

There are many tales of his denouement and death. The one which Grand Islanders like best claims that Captain Jean's body was returned by faithful followers to the Baratarian waters he loved so well and that he was buried here where he had lived so boldly.

"They's halfa dozen graves where you'll fin' him buried, *Mam'selle*," concluded Maxim smilingly. "You jus' go to any cemetery in the village of Lafitte, an' you can see his unmarked grave."

Maxim told me now of the Island's fourth strong man, the one who had come in recent years to take the title of "da bos" that had been Captain Jean Lafitte's.

A native of the island, his name was John Ludvig—"Vic" Ludvig to his fellows. His enterprises and imagination had done much to restore prosperity to Grand Isle's drooping economy.

At the turn of this century, long after the sugar planters had withdrawn, unable to cope with the Island's soil and weather conditions, Vic Ludvig devised a way to build a successful vegetable market on Grand Isle's shallow, sandy earth. Using the refuse from shrimp factories to fertilize the weak soil, Vic directed the islanders in a unique agricultural method. He had them build long rows, two feet high and four feet apart, then plant the rows to vegetable crops. Between the rows they fed the crops "shrimp bran" twice during the short season. What emerged was a vegetable market which beat the Florida crop by several weeks and thus proved a lucrative business to the islanders.

A second enterprise showed Vic Ludvig's ability to adapt to his homeland's strict necessities. For many years the islanders had used dogs to hunt big diamondback terrapins on the *prairie tremblante* of the nearby marshes. From these their wives concocted a terrapin stew that was a gourmet's dream. Now Vic Ludvig set about to establish here the world's largest terrapin farm, a source from which restaurants of New Orleans and all America might draw the basis for this delicious delicacy. He built great pens to enclose bull and cow terrapins which were brought to him by trappers and hunters from the whole Gulf region around. Breeding hosts of young in his pens, he produced some 50,000 terrapins a year for the market, shipping them out in barrels filled with grass for keeping them cool.

For many years "da bos"—who was hotel owner, postmaster, storekeeper, shrimp fleet owner and promoter—ruled Grand Isle's economy with a paternal autocracy much like that which Captain Jean had maintained on Grand Terre. But with his death there had been no one to take his mantle of leadership.

His businesses had fallen on hard times, and with them had vanished the source of many an islander's fortune.

Today, concluded Maxim sadly, the islanders must rely on unpredictable "inside swimps" for their main livelihood. And this would be so until another "bós" appeared to lead the natives in some new and unexplored field of action.

It had grown late, as we sat talking on the cottage *galerie*, and so I bid a swift *bonne nuit* to my hosts. Walking down the narrow lanes with me on the way back to Hotel Victor, Maxim said that we would leave *early-early* on our fishing trip tomorrow.

"Da swimps don' know no more sleepin' than a Cajun on Sat'day night," he said.

The next morning, in the dim light of early dawn, I joined Maxim at the shrimp docks and climbed aboard his trim white lugger. In a matter of moments he and his mate, working silently and efficiently, had cleared the docks and were leading the fleet of trawlers out toward the shrimping grounds.

Across Bay Rigaud and through Rigaud Pass our white lugger strode to the sea. On our right, Grand Isle and her long, pale beach; on our left, Grand Terre Island with the ruins of old Fort Livingston musing moodily in the mist, dreaming of the glory it had known so long ago.

Through the Pass we reached "the outside" waters at last. The waves were high, blue-green and capped with white. Behind us raced the fleet of two hundred trawlers, looking like white feathers blowing across the billowy blue coverlet of the sea. Suddenly our noisy motor slowed and Maxim and the mate lowered the big black trawl net over the gunwale. Splashing, crashing, pounding through the waves behind us, the other luggers let down their own huge black nets.

Then it was drag, drag, drag through the sea—the waves thundering over and the sturdy little boats bobbing through, the crews shouting back and forth as they passed around us, and the boats' flags flying red, blue, green and yellow against the pale grey sky.

Maxim was singing a wild, high song, waiting for the nets to fill. Excitement twanged the air. Clinging to the mast, I felt the sweep of wind, the beat of wave, the thrill of flying spray. It was this, I shouted to Maxim, that made the shrimpers' life!

"Non," shouted Maxim practically. "It is de swimps, and we ain't gettin' any!"

That was the sad truth. It was testified by all the other boats who soon began drawing in their trawl nets and heading back inside to try their luck in the quiet bay.

Inside Bay Rigaud, Maxim and his mate, a grinning Baratarian who knew just half a dozen words of English, let down our net again and we took a long trawl. The net dragged heavy in the water. They drew it in finally, using a mechanical winch on the long hard pull. My eyes bugged out with excitement—my first shrimp haul, coming slowly, surely in in the great black net!

Then, anticlimax . . . crabs, crabs, crabs!

Maxim cursed and cut the ropes and cursed again and emptied the sterile trawl.

"C'est fini!" he muttered. I hovered cautiously on the fore-deck, hoping the Baratarian did not believe that superstition about a woman aboard a man's boat.

It was soon all right again, though. Maxim brought the gallon of wine out of the cabin, the mate set to work cooking the spaghetti-with-shrimp that we were to eat with crusty French bread for lunch, and Maxim told me tales of other, better days and bigger catches of "swimps."

Lunch over, we headed for the fish dock on Grand Isle. Here Maxim joined his business partner in buying the shrimp that other boats of his fleet of fifteen had succeeded in netting.

All afternoon we spent at the dock. Shouts of "Maxim . . . Maxim . . ." kept my host racing from one boat to another, unloading catches into the tall wicker baskets, loading them again and again into the ice trucks. There were luggers of all sizes, all states of repair, all colors, all kinds, flying their myriad flags. I sat on deck listening to the French and to the pidgin English being shouted from boat to boat.

The fishermen seemed glad of a vistor on the boats. Pretty soon they were bringing me all kinds of gifts, telling me about their strange catches.

"She be a sea-bean, Miss," said one, handing me a pretty, rounded little button. "All da way from Sout' Ameriky she wash."

And another, bringing a soft-shelled crab, "It eat like no other taste, *Mam'selle.*"

And, best of all, an eager voiced lad carrying the four-foot bill of a swordfish.

"Twenty feet long she be! She rip my net, wham! To piece she rip my net, yes—the devil! But I got 'er bill, yes, and now I give heem to you."

They were a gracious crew.

Yet these were not Evangeline's people. There was a wild-ness and a fierceness about them that was not of peasant blood. These people met adventure and danger with a joyous deviltry. Here was little of stolid Acadian fortitude, more of the fiery defiance of buccaneers. "Benoques" the outsiders called these natives. Like the origin of the name, the origin of the people themselves was obscure.

There were French and Acadian among the Benoques and Baratarians, but there were also all the different bloods that had been Morgan's men and the men of Lafitte the gentleman-pirate.

Maxim said he had heard of the Cajuns.

"Ah yes, the Cajun, *Mam'selle.* The Cajun, he a trapper. You find heem on da marsh. You go look for heem on da coast below Berwick. My *p'père*, he got a frien' what trap there. We gonna sen' you a letter to dis man—Monsieur Boud-reaux on Little Bayou Black in Berwick. You gonna see *some* trappers, them Boudreaux mens!"

Campboat Caravan to

Palmetto Bayou

viii

The wet marshlands of South Louisiana are like a lush green and gold carpet that is frayed at the edges, jagged, and full of holes.

From New Orleans to Texas the carpet of green and golden grass stretches along the Gulf Coast for four hundred miles, reaches inland sometimes for ten, sometimes for thirty miles. Its frayed edges are hundreds of small peninsulas, islands, and points of land cut by little and big bayous, lagoons and lakes.

This is the youngest land in America. Geologically speaking it belongs to the immediate present—a great alluvial plain, made by silt-carrying floods from the Mississippi and Atchafalaya Rivers. The soil of thirty-one states and two Canadian provinces is washed down each spring to add new islands and new peninsulas to this ever-changing world.

The grassy waterlands are strange, misty, mysterious.

As if some ancient hand had flung a giant fish net across the grasses, and each thread of the net had cut a watery streak through the carpet, the great coastal grassland is split by thousands of tiny threads. These are the rivers and sloughs, the channels, chutes and bayous of a strange realm.

And these are the pathways for its people.

For into this weird waterland go the Louisiana muskrat trappers every winter, intent on harvesting a crop that places their state first among the fur-bearing regions of America. With the coming of winter thousands of families leave their homes in town and go out into the watery prairies in America's greatest mass exodus of people. Theirs is a voluntary exile. It has its own rich reward.

For nine months of the year these people are shrimp fishermen, crab fishermen, frog hunters, moss gatherers. Oftentimes they are carpenters, lumberjacks, shipyard workers; and sometimes they are lawyers, engineers, merchants, businessmen and

students. They live in cities, towns, villages, and in small five- and six-family houseboat communities along bayou and river banks of the inland swamps.

But with the coming of every fall, each of them feels the same overpowering urge, a yearning that will not be denied— the strong and irresistible necessity of "going into the marsh." If ever a man has walked the green and gold marshlands as a boy, following the trap lines with his father, that man will forever feel a restlessness in the cool October days.

"Comme ça, mon ami?" he will say to his neighbor. "It will soon be the time, yes?" And they both will know that he is thinking of how the wind feels as it blows across the salty marshes, and how the little bayous look as he push-poles his boat toward the trap lines, and how the early sun glints on the steel of his newly-set muskrat traps.

All these things I heard before Maxim's father introduced me to the Boudreaux clan. Now I was to see for myself. For *Grandpère* Boudreaux had promised I could go with his family to their trapping grounds on the marshlands that lay beyond the mouth of the Atchafalaya, on the vast grassy prairie where hundreds of trappers' camps would soon come alive. We would trap in a section where Palmetto Bayou cuts a thin blue path through the golden roseau-cane to the Gulf's rough waters.

Today I sat on the porch of a small, neat houseboat— "campboat" as I learned to call it—in Little Bayou Black. Beside me was *Grandmère* Boudreaux, a tiny, wizened little lady with an almost elfish air of gayety. She knitted busily on a throw net, trying to finish it before dark. We waited for *Grandpère,* patriarch of the clan, to appear.

Before us, rocking gently in the languid bayou waters, lay four other campboats, tied by ropes to tremendously large, moss-laden trees. The cluster of floating homes belonged to other Boudreaux, sons and grandsons of the old couple who were to be my hosts.

Little Bayou Black, in which the colony was anchored, was a narrow bayou paralleling the broad Atchafalaya River, with only a two-hundred-foot strip of land separating the two. Boudreaux campboats were tied here for protection against the rolling swells and wild winds of the big river.

From the galleries of their campboats, the Boudreaux wives could look across the narrow strip of land and watch the activity on the river—big shrimp boats with their black nets swinging from white masts, smaller luggers of their bayou neighbors, cruisers of the oil men and big tugboats pushing barges loaded with oil.

During the long summer days it was like a never-ending water pageant passing by the door, always with something new to stir gay gossipers who sat on shady galleries or leaned out the campboat windows.

But it was late autumn now, and dusk. As we sat on the foredeck, waiting for *Grandpère's* return, we saw a lamp lighted in the forwardmost campboat. Its rays splashed a golden path through the window onto the muted twilight water of the little bayou. The Boudreaux wives poked up the coals in their woodstoves and began to ready their suppers. Husbands, weary from their long days of preparation for tomorrow's exodus to the marshlands, rested on campboat galleries, smoked their pipes, and scolded the children good-naturedly.

Tomorrow was the Big Day. Everybody in the Boudreaux camp felt this deep in their bones, a kind of tingling excitement that came every year on the night before breaking camp and leaving for the marshlands.

Just before dark we saw the old man come round a far bend in the bayou, a dim silhouette, tall and angular, standing in his narrow pirogue and push-poling his way toward us. The silhouette grew larger as he came out of the shadows, letting the pirogue glide quietly, barely rippling the water.

Grandpère Boudreaux was strong-muscled, with a lean grace in his movements. Instinctively I felt him to be a man of dignity, and of wisdom in the ways of the marshlands. He had been a muskrat trapper since boyhood, but he was old now for so strenuous a life. This was to be his last season as a full-time trapper. His family, and all the neighbors up and down the bayous, wanted it to be the best season of his whole life. *Grandmère*, who had trapped alongside him as a bride during their first season together in the marsh, fifty years ago, smiled as he gave a final long push on the pole and turned the pirogue toward the gallery.

With one hand he tied the tiny craft to the porch pillar, and with the other he held a string of fish in the air, laughing at our pleasure in his return. Others of the clan had been watching too, for immediately the shout went up from two of the closest campboats:

"*Non de dieu*, looka *Grandpère*'s catch! Whatta string he got!"

"*Mon dieu*, looka what *Grandpère* done brought for a good-bye catch! Y'all come over to *our* camp for da good-bye supper, *hein*, *P'père?*"

The old man grinned at his wife.

"Listen them lazy sons of yours, *ma chère*. Wanta let their old *père* keep feedin' them for always!"

As *Grandmère* took the long string of channel cat from him, he shouted, "Everybody eat with feets under his own table tonight, my children. An' when you finish, come over here, you lazy ones, and meet the lady what goes trappin' wit us tomorrow."

The old man reached for an enamel pan hanging from the deck post, filled it with water from a pitcher on a nearby table, washed his hands and face noisily. Then he tossed the water into the bayou and sat down beside me with a sigh.

"Been a long day, *Mam'selle*, and tomorrow be longer, *mais* sho!"

Inside the campboat, *Grandmère* Boudreaux bent over the woodstove and began to prepare the fish. When she called us in to the campboat kitchen, we sat down to a table holding fish, oysters, shrimp and squirrel. The variety was slightly

(On facing page) *Two "lil swimp" boats—of a Louisiana design adapted by Acadians from boats of Brittany and Normandy—tie up to a trapper's camp to wait out a storm.*

overwhelming, although I had heard that bayou dwellers often set tables of great richness.

"Ain' no Boudreaux ever starve yet, *Mam'selle!*" *Grandpère* beamed as he filled my plate. "An' if it ever happen, it won' be on da night 'fore we leave for trapping grounds! You'll see when we get to camp, *Mam'selle* . . . trappers needs plenty strength on their ribs."

Grandmère Boudreaux hovered over the table solicitously until *Grandpère* insisted she join us.

"Come eat wit us, *chère*, we don' need yo' help now, I guarantee you. Eat plenty . . . we got big day tomorrow."

The meal was one of the best I'd had in the bayou country. Later I must remember to get these recipes from *Grandmère* Boudreaux. For now it was enough to sit at the table by the campboat window, savor the splendid dishes and watch the darkening stream outside. As black night settled on the waters, lights gleamed in all the campboat windows.

When we had finished our feast, *Grandpère* rose, lifted the big Coleman lamp from its hook on the center rafter and beckoned us to follow him to the front gallery.

"Leave them dirty dish, *ma chère*," he said to *Grandmère*. "Ain' no need to wash till later. We mus' make our gues' acquaint' wit da family."

Outside, he hung the big lamp from a hook on one of the porch pillars and shouted, "Hey, you Baptiste, bring a light and show yo'self! Yo' whole family too . . . an' call them others. We got a new trapper here . . . *très jolie, aussi* . . . Tell 'Fayette to bring his guitar, him . . . might as well have some music, *mais* sho!"

It was as if the closed, quietly rocking campboats had been waiting for just this signal from the patriarch. Suddenly the camps became alive, began to sway, fall and rise in the bayou as their occupants poured out the doors, sometimes the windows, and as they leaped from decks onto bayou banks. The air came alive too, with shouts and laughs called from boat to boat.

"Come over to *Papa's*, you Jean and Camille. . . . You, too,

Adrian and Nanette, and bring yo' kids . . . hurry-hurry! *P'père* got a gues', him. You put on manners, you outlaw alligators."

Baptiste passed the word along, then herded his own brood toward our campboat. He stopped to hang his lamp to a low limb of a live oak tree, then strode up the gangplank to the campboat porch where we sat. He was followed by four stair-stepped children and his wife, carrying a baby in her arms.

Baptiste Boudreaux, *Grandpère's* oldest son, was tall for a Frenchman, lithe, graceful, dark-skinned, with straight black hair. His eyes were deep set, with a kind of fierce intensity. Seeing him so, and for the first time, I realized that he was a completely competent man in this outdoor community, that his personality and intelligence made him the leader of the Boudreaux clan, the one who carried out the judgments handed down by *Grandpère.*

As *Grandpère* introduced us, Baptiste looked at me intently for a moment, then gave a vigorous nod of his head.

"Oui, très bien, Mam'selle . . . We Boudreaux are honored . . . We make you the bes' lady trapper in St. Mary Parish if that what you wanta be!"

I was honored too, and pleased by his quick acceptance of me. Before I could say so, the tall fellow was introducing his family, naming each of them with pride in his voice and a pleased sort of chuckle.

Mimi Boudreaux was a slight, wispy-looking woman who might have been a beauty ten years ago. She bore her big jostling baby in her arms as if he were ten pounds too heavy for her, which he was, but her eyes moved proudly from him to Baptiste, rested on me the smallest moment as she gave a jerky little curtsy.

The oldest sons, Toto and Eddie, were awkward teen-agers who smiled at me and shook hands clumsily. Clotilde, a curly-headed blond of about ten, and Lizette, six, were shy like their mother and hung back behind her skirts as they were introduced.

Now the Baptiste Boudreaux were crowding to the far end of the deck in order for *Grandpère's* second son, Adrian, to come aboard with his fat, giggling wife, Nanette, and their four sons—Popo, Bootsie, Napoleon and Pierre. Adrian and Nanette, who seemed to carry some kind of exciting and jolly secret around with them, became solemn for just a moment as he said:

"Welcome, *Mam'selle,* and give thanks that you gonna see the bes' trappin' year that ever came to us on Palmetto Bayou. *Mon dieu,* I feels it in my bones, yes!"

Then he herded his giggling wife and laughing boys off the campboat, making room for others of the Boudreaux clan who kept coming in a sort of gay processional which *Grandpère* and *Grandmère* Boudreaux viewed with unconcealed pride and with some confusion.

Their only daughter, Fifi, seemed a bluff, aggressive, good-natured woman who looked like a youthful edition of *Grandmère.* She was married to Lafayette Thibodaux, a whimsical sort of man, evidently a favorite of the clan, who was nicknamed intermittently "Plunk" because of his prowess with a guitar and "Brudder'n'law" because of the relationship. Their eight children were all girls: Coco, Maria and Mercedes, twelve-year-old twins, Odalia, Ophelia, another set of twins, Octavia and Olivia, and a ten-months-old infant known simply as *Bébé.*

Jean Boudreaux, the youngest son, was a tall, lean man like *Grandpère* but with a less rugged manner. His wife, Camille, was a nervous, frustrated mother type who seemed to be continually cluck-clucking over the children because she and Jean had none of their own.

"*C'est triste,*" said *Grandmère* softly, as Jean and Camille left the boat to follow the children and some of the adults to the small clearing on the bayou bank before the grandparents' campboat.

(On facing page) "*P'père is a muskrat trapper, him.*"

By now there were half a dozen lamps hanging from trees that circled the little clearing, casting a golden glow against mossy draperies of the surrounding cypress. The swaying lights and shrouded trees made an eerie stage set in the Boudreaux clearing on Little Bayou Black. Among shadowy knees of broad-based cypresses the youngsters played their game of catch-me-if-you-can, or they chased giant lightning bugs which had lingered on through the warm autumn nights. Their elders sat on logs and stumps around the clearing, gossiping, completing the final plans for the morrow's exodus to the marshlands.

Baptiste went into his campboat and broke out a case of beer, bringing an iced tub of bottles to the center of the clearing shouting, *"Bien, mes amis,* no more'n two o' these around fer you scalawags. Don' forget, we break camp at 4:00 A.M. tomorrow . . . and all you sleepy ones got plenty work to do if we make Palmetto Bayou by first dark."

As his brothers and sisters crowded around the tub of beer, Baptiste sent bottles to us on *Grandpère's* boat deck. Pretty soon we heard them pleading with Baptiste.

"Aw, come on, brudder, how about jus' a *little* ole *fais-dodo!* If our feets jump tonight, our sperrits jump tomorrow, *hein?"*

Before anybody could refute this logic, Adrian shouted, "Whatcha waitin' on, Plunk? Strike them chords, man. And where at's *P'père's* accordeen, I wants to know?"

Beside me *Grandpère* rose and went into the campboat, came back with an old-time French accordion. He walked down the plank, beckoning us to follow, and went to the log where Plunk sat tuning his guitar.

From the accordion came a high-pitched, tremulous wail, ending in a quick, staccato chord. Then *Grandpère's* voice, good-humored but with the always-present note of authority:

"Awright, my chil'ren, we make a good-bye *fais-dodo* . . . but a very leetle one . . . No more'n half an hour of this . . . Then off to bed, you silly ones . . . Have you forgot what is tomorrow? The Big Day, it is, and you gonna need your plenty strengt'. Now . . . *Dansé, Calinda, Dansé! . . ."*

Grandpère struck up the joyous tune, and Plunk joined him loudly, plucking the guitar with loving fingers, singing the old "Gumbo-French" song with a dramatic gayety:

> *"Dansé, Calinda, dansé . . .*
> *Dansé, Calinda, din, sin, boum, BOUM!*
> *Missieu Tremoulet*
> *Gagné plien milets*
> *Fais so nègre sué*
> *Quand ye volé poulets!"*

Baptiste grabbed me round the waist. "Come, *Mam'selle,* you do the honor to me?"

He swung me off with such sprightly steps that I was breathless before we had danced once around the little clearing. There seemed no pause in the swift rhythm of the old tune. We danced with concentration, no talk, with an intensity that matched the zeal of *Grandpère*'s accordion and Plunk's guitar.

> *"Dansé, Calinda, dansé,*
> *Dansé, Calinda, din, sin, boum, BOUM!"*

Three times around the clearing and I was dizzy with the rhythm. There were shouts and laughter from other dancing couples. Baptiste danced faster than anybody, and could still throw back his head and laugh his great, rough laughter. I could not laugh, nor speak either, for trying to match his huge steps, his swift-paced path among the other dancers. There was a sort of frenzy in the last bars of the tune, then finally it ended. I sank to a log on the edge of the clearing, and was surrounded by a laughing group of Baptiste's kinsmen to whom this kind of dancing seemed the order of the day.

"*Très bon, Mam'selle, très bon!* You dance lak a Boudreaux, for true, *Mam'selle.* That Baptiste! You keep up wit dat fas'-feeted raccoon, you gonna lose your breath every time!"

As the music started again, they left me sitting there. I

watched the swiftly whirling couples, saw Baptiste pass by
with his wife, almost lifting her off the ground with his big,
fast steps, I smiled wanly at Adrian, who sat waiting for me
to recover.

"That Baptiste! He dance lak he walk," Adrian chuckled
fondly, "and he walk like what he is, da bes' Goddam trapper
on the whole marsh . . . 'Scuse for language, *Mam'selle*, but it's
the Goddam truth, I guarantee you!"

Adrian, bringing me a second bottle of beer, grinned as I
gulped it down.

"You get winded here, *Mam'selle*, you oughta take in that
Trappers' Ball in Abbéville nex' year! *Mon dieu*, you ain'
never seen such broad steppin' at no *fais-dodo* in the worl' like
them trappers carryin' on at Abbéville. And the folks over
there say there ain' never been such a dancin' man as that
Baptiste Boudreaux!"

Watching Baptiste lift Mimi off her feet in a magnificent
swirl of skirts and petticoats, I found it easy to believe—
and was grateful to Adrian and later to Jean for their more
subdued steps.

By now the children had joined the crowd and the lamp-
lighted clearing in the cypress brake was awhirl with dancing
couples, young and old spinning round in circles within circles,
while the guitar and the accordion sped the rhythm to a feverish pitch.

Then, just as it reached a pace I could not follow, the music
stopped abruptly. The dancers, brought to a sudden stop,
spent a final blast of energy in a wild kind of shout that
echoed through the encircling trees and down the hidden bayou.

Grandpère, his face glowing with excitement, shouted,
"*Allons*, my chil'ren, that's *fini* to it! Now get yo'selfs home
and to bed . . . And don' forget this kind of strengt' you got,
tomorrow when you needs it bad."

But the *'ti fais-dodo* was hard to bring to an end. The whole
clan begged for more music.

"*S'il plaît, P'père!* Jus' one more, *s'il te plaît!* Let Plunk
tell *Mam'selle* about *Les Maringouins!*"

The old man laughed and gestured to Lafayette who had not yet laid his guitar aside. Then the two of them—Plunk on his guitar and *Grandpère* on the accordion—struck up that amusing song which tells of the vicious mosquitoes of the bayou country. After the opening chords all the Boudreaux joined in together to sing:

> *"Les maringouins ont tout mangé ma belle,*
> *Et y ont laissé juste les deux gros orteils;*
> *Y les ont pris pou' faire des bouchons d'bouteilles.*
>
> *Ton papa 'semb'é ein éléphant,*
> *Et ta maman 'semb'é ein automobile,*
> *Ton 'ti frère 'semb'é ein bullfrog."*

Then, laughing and singing with gestures, they repeated the song in English, to be sure I did not miss the words:

> *"The maringouins have eaten up my sweetheart,*
> *They have only left the two big toes;*
> *They took them to make corks for bottles.*
>
> *Your papa looks like an elephant,*
> *And your mama like an automobile,*
> *Your little brother looks like a bullfrog."*

Grandpère and Plunk ended the music with a flourish, then the old man gestured commandingly toward his frolicking clan, motioning them toward their homes.

"Allons, mes enfants! C'est fini! Bonne nuit! Bonne nuit!"

A chorus of *bonne nuit*'s ran through the departing Boudreaux, and the clan dispersed so quickly that it seemed just an instant until the clearing was empty and quiet.

The last lamp was lifted out of the trees by a sleepy Adrian, who walked slowly away toward his camp, calling good night softly as he passed each campboat. From *Grandpère's* gallery his lamp bobbled down the path like a languid glowworm and faded finally into the black night.

In a matter of moments I had said good night to my hosts

and was comfortably settled in my bunk in the small store-room behind the kitchen. Through the window I could see lights from other campboats painting their wavering golden streaks down the black bayou waters. One by one the lamps went out and finally the bayou was an ebony ribbon seen dimly and as a mirror for millions of stars that hung above us.

Later, around midnight when a bird's shrill scream from the swamps awakened me for a moment, I could not see the bayou at all. But I could feel its presence, a deep slow-moving bed upon which our campboat floated as on a liquid earth.

Even before dawn the next morning the community was a cyclone of activity. Lanterns swung from porch roofs to light men and boys as they busied themselves at breaking up homes and casting campboats free of their moorings. Women scurried around their stoves, making coffee which the men swallowed greedily as they worked. Children dressed themselves and each other, then rushed to help their mothers prepare big breakfasts which were eaten hurriedly, in gulps.

Finally, dawn of the Big Day burst like an explosion along Little Bayou Black—loud with sputterings of gasboats, of anchor chains clanking along campboat hulls, furious with wails of animals and pets being tied in their cages, raucous with shouts and yells of the Boudreaux clan as they rushed nervously to last-minute tasks which must be finished before the water-borne caravan could get underway. As the sun came up most of the smaller gasboats, skiffs and pirogues were tied together and lashed to the stern of the campboats. Each campboat had its own towboat in position, ready to start the long pull downriver and out into the marsh.

There was a last minute rush among women and older children who had the responsibility of getting livestock crated and aboard. Chickens, pigs, and the cow that belonged to Adrian and Nanette joined in the swelling chorus of human shoutings, laughter, cursing and general confusion.

Just as Adrian drove his cow into her tiny floating barge with the high, fenced sides, she bowed her head, bellowed frantically and broke loose in a full run into the swamp. Adrian cursed, gave chase and finally brought her back into the fold, prodding her with a boat hook as he loaded her onto the barge.

Lafayette crouched in the stern of his small gasboat, the *Three Brothers*, and hovered dramatically over his muchly-patched old motor. He had equipped her for the season with a new generator. The motor was, next to Fifi and his eight daughters, his special pride in life and he talked to it with feeling.

"Sweet lil kicker, come see, come show us how you can go. Kick off like a Goddam Diesel, my little one! Show 'em you can pull this whole dang outfit, you."

And then, as the motor failed to start, *"Mon dieu, mon dieu,* looka what you done to us now! Have pity, you gas-eatin' lil bastard!"

Fifi and the girls paused long enough to look with anguish at each other, shrug their shoulders and lift their eyes heavenward.

At last the motor started its furious sputter, then hummed into action. Smiles spread over the anxious faces and they nodded to each other with satisfaction.

"Papa done it again, him. *Le bon dieu* bless that new generator!"

Finally all the campboats were cast free from their moorings and the group grew quiet as word passed from boat to boat that all was ready. Everybody looked toward *Grandpère's* camp, which was second in line, following Baptiste's lead boat. *Grandpère* stood on the aft deck of his campboat, pointed his shotgun in the air, paused for a moment. He bared his head and looked, open-eyed, toward the sky, saying:

"St. Christopher, go wit us and proteck us again in the marsh. And, Mother Mary, bring us a good season."

Then he fired the shotgun into the air.

Bedlam broke loose again as the boat engines sputtered and roared into action. Baptiste's campboat, in the lead, was towed by his twenty-foot lugger *Sea Dream*, neat and shining with a new coat of paint. *Grandpère's* camp was also pulled by a lugger, the *Half Fathom,* more delapidated, but sturdy and rugged. The other camps were towed by a various assortment of gasboats. Each camp had its own accompanying boats —skiffs and pirogues of all sizes and shapes.

Lafayette and Fifi were barely underway with their outfit when Fifi, collapsed with exhaustion and leaning against the deckpost of the camp, suddenly screamed:

"My chil'ren! . . . Ah, *nom de dieu,* my pore *bébés* . . . where dey at? . . . Is not one lil *bébé* los' dis time in dat dirty bayou?"

As she wrung her hands in despair, Coco, the oldest daughter, ran out of the camp carrying the baby.

"*Non, Maman,*" she soothed. "We are all of us here, yes."

But Fifi cried, "Out wit you, ever las' one o' you, and let yo'self be counted!"

As the children gathered on the front porch of the campboat, she counted nervously, pointing to each girl as she spoke:

"One, Coco, *deux,* Odalia, *tres,* Ophelia, *quatre,* Maria, *cinq,* Mercedes, *ses,* 'Tavie, *sept,* 'Livvy, and *octo,* my sweet *Bébé!*"

Satisfied at last, Fifi frowned roughly on the whole crew and cried, "Wal, *allons* with you! Don jus' stand there gaping. This is Big Day, yes, but ain' all just *fais-dodo!*"

The Boudreaux boats carried a bulging, madcap kind of cargo. Crowded to its full capacity and seemingly beyond, each boat bore a part of the collected gear which represented the full possessions of six families.

Their household goods were crowded inside and out. Extra crates of groceries, canned goods, cases of beer and wine bottles were stowed among fishing tackle, large piles of muskrat traps, clothes wringers for the camp, carpenter's tools, extra boots and other regalia. Chickens in crates rode gaily on rooftops, squawking in dismay at the whole procedure. Baptiste's pigs grunted angrily from their pens inside his

(On facing page) *The trapper's maman is a competent woman.*

large skiff. And Adrian's cow continued to bawl her protests all the way down the narrow bayou.

One at a time the campboats proceeded in line down Little Bayou Black. They came at last to the broad waters of the Atchafalaya River and here they encountered new problems as currents and waves of the big river tossed skiffs and pirogues around.

Maintaining more or less of a line one behind the other, the campboats passed other trappers engaged also in towing their own outfits down the big river. Some of these families did not tow campboats but carried on the decks of their luggers all the gear they needed to construct small cabins on their trapping land. Mattresses, bedsprings, rolls of blankets, kitchen pots and pans, household necessities were stacked ludicrously together atop the lugger, along with trapping gear of all kinds, lumber, tool chests, nail kegs, rolls of tar paper. Women and children, somehow hanging on amidst these mad collections, were gay, laughing, shouting to each other, exchanging bons mots.

The trip downriver into the marsh was the season's first adventure for the trappers. The work and planning of many weeks was culminating in this proud day when trappers' families set out for their annual trek. They shouted and teased with their neighbors, every man happy and expecting the best of this new season.

A passing lugger, loaded with a wild assortment of gear and a laughing family, slowed its motor as it passed the Boudreaux clan, in the usual courtesy of river traffic.

"So, *mon ami*," the man shouted. "You go again to that pore Palmetto Bayou, *hein?* Can' no Boudreaux never learn nuttin', *hein?*"

Grandpère laughed and replied, "*Mon dieu*, Vic Vidar, is it you again wit dat flea-bitten rig of a lugger? An' you not afraid she will lan' you and the lil ones in da river, dat pore boat wit such a plum outsize load she got?"

As the lugger moved on, Madame Vidar slapped her fat thigh, clutched the newest baby tighter to her breast and leaned out to shout to *Grandmère* Boudreaux, who sat in her rocking chair on the front of her campboat.

"An' what for you trap dis year, *ma chère?* You get dat new livin' room suit' dis year, maybe, yes? And what for the other Boudreaux trap, *hein?*"

Grandmère reported news of the clan, for this interchange of confidences and hopes was part of the enjoyment of the trapping season.

"*Oui*, Camille and me get new living room suit' after dis season, wit' the help of da Blessed Virgin. And le's see . . . My ole man think he want a new shot*gun* an' a lil Diesel for his *Half Fathom*. An' Baptiste, of course, inten' to buy dat beautiful campboat off'n the rich Widow Clement. An' also a bigger lugger, him, so he can go swimping further outside nex' summer.

"Nanette want a washing machine and Mimi want a set o' blue paint' dish. An' Plunk want a new electric guitar and a V-8, the crazy mans, to ride all his kids to town on Sat'days."

She finished with a flourish:

"*Oui*, all us Boudreaux got us *some* big plans, I guarantee you, if *Monsieur* Mus'rat just give us dis year a break on Palmetto Bayou."

The Vidar lugger passed, increased its speed and soon drew out of sight on the long, broad river ahead. The Boudreaux entourage proceeded slowly downriver with several such exchanges between neighbors and friends who passed in faster boats, pulling smaller camps behind them.

By late afternoon we came to the mouth of the big river, saw it broaden subtly as it poured its currents into Atchafalaya Bay.

We must cross a wide section of this bay, actually the inland-most part of the Gulf of Mexico, before we could enter the narrow protected waters of Palmetto Bayou.

This was the tensest part of the whole trip, the most dangerous passage to be maneuvered by the campboat caravan. If the winds were high, piling treacherous waves against the marshy shores of Atchafalaya Bay, we would have to anchor in the river mouth and wait till the pitching waters quieted.

I felt the gay mood of the Boudreaux fade, saw their faces grow solemn, watched *Grandpère* and Baptiste exchange grim looks—each standing apprehensively at his pilot wheel as they traveled side by side toward the river's mouth. Even the children ceased their screaming frolics as they were ordered off the campboat galleries and forced inside. They crowded to windows and watched nervously as their mothers went about the decks checking lines, seeing that all was securely tied down and ready to meet the rough waves' onslaught if it should come.

Grandmère Boudreaux, still rocking on the campboat gallery where we sat, looked out searchingly toward the great bay, then ducked her head briefly, made the sign of the cross, and murmured:

"St. Christopher, be wit us yet . . ."

Then, as we crossed the point where the brown river currents met the bluer waters of the bay, a shout went up from Baptiste, followed by a loud hoarse echo from *Grandpère*, and from Adrian and Jean.

"Mother of God, looka da flat water!" was Baptiste's profane cry of relief. And "Sonafabitch!" yelled Adrian, "she flatter'n a turtle's backside, from here to Big Carencro!"

It was true. Once across the riptide separating river from bay, the surface was smooth, blue as a mariner's sweetest dream.

Relief surged like a full-running tide through the waterborne caravan. The men, standing alert at the tillers of their towing craft, waved happily to camps of their kinsmen. Women and children poured out of campboat interiors, calling to each other, pointing eagerly toward the receding shoreline and toward open waters which lay ahead. *Grandmère* started her rocker to racing again, then paused contritely, remembering to cross herself again and mutter a cheerful *"Merci* . . . sweet saint . . . *bien merci* for crossing us over again."

Straight ahead lay the Gulf of Mexico, breeder of hurricanes and quick tropical cloudbursts. Yet the winds that swept

over us now were gentle, spicy, fragrant to a sailor's taste.
The little waves that chuckled against the hulls of our campboats were teasing, playful. There was no sharply biting spray
to chill our faces and our hearts, only an occasional sting of
salty wash from the lead lugger's churning wakes ahead.

Far behind, sweeping in a long, slow curve to the east of
us, lay the flat golden sea marsh—miles upon miles of it,
stretching a green and gold carpet along the curving shores
of the whole Gulf of Mexico. Too small for us to see, but
good to think about, were the tiny bayous that cut their
limpid paths through towering roseau-cane and "three-
cornered grass"—paths that trappers might follow, making
their sets in the marsh grasses, trails just wide enough for
the slimmest pirogue to follow.

Somewhere on that distant shore far ahead and far to the
east there were four larger bayous cutting wide avenues
through the grassy carpet.

Palmetto and Plum Bayous, Creole Bayou and Big Carencro
—each of these watery boulevards would support dozens of
trappers' families, bearing their campboats, their gasboats
and luggers, skiffs and pirogues, giving the floating communities a limpid main street for the winter season ahead.

Palmetto Bayou—somewhere out there, far away on that
"trembling prairie" of muck and marsh grass, it lay waiting
to welcome us, its deep, clear water winding invitingly through
swaying grasses, its banks lined with broad palmetto sprays,
offering us beauty and safety, a haven against winds that
could whip these Gulf waters to foaming frenzies. Though it
was no more than a name to me now—Palmetto Bayou—it
held a kind of special magic in its syllables, a promise of
happy days to come, of good fortune, of riches, perhaps, for
my trapper friends.

In what distant dip of far horizon would we find the haven?
By what magic of navigation would these water-borne house-
keepers locate the mouth of their special bayou, in all the
vast sea of marsh grasses that swayed and swelled against
the sky's low rim?

"Chênière de Willow, she'll mark their way," said *Grandmère* Boudreaux laconically, and pointed to Baptiste and *Grandpère*, both leaning out of pilot house windows, shielding their eyes from the sun's brilliant last rays, and searching the dim coast to the east.

Suddenly Baptiste shouted to his fellow trappers:

"Heh, my brothers! There she stands . . . Chênière de Willow!"

I looked forward toward where he pointed, far ahead to the distant marshy coastline and saw nothing. But I heard Adrian's excited yell and his children's eager screaming.

"Sonafabitch, if she ain't," he shouted. "And time enough too, to be showing herself!"

Still I could see no change in the flat golden shores ahead.

"What is it . . . a *chênière?*" I asked of *Grandmère* Boudreaux.

"Jus' a lil hill rising in da marsh . . . sometime with trees . . ." And she leaned far out from the porch pillar and cupped her eyes with her hands, like the men in the pilothouses.

"See, *chère*, it is there . . . Look closely . . . that blue hill yonder . . ."

Yes, there it was—a slight rise in the horizon—Chênière de Willow. First, I saw it as a sea mirage, a dim blue bulk standing like a cloud's shadow against that flat horizon. Slowly it grew clearer, more believable, then stood forth in clean, noble lines—a small, true hill rising from the green-gold marsh floor, topped with a crest of giant willows which even at this distance could be seen to stretch their limbs defiantly toward the sky.

Our caravan turned eastward and as we grew nearer, I saw the ghostly *chênière* stand out in reality, an inverted bowl, a salt dome formation peculiar to the coastal marshes, a mark for mariners, a pleasant homelike island in the strange wilderness of the grassy plains.

Baptiste led the four campboats, with their accompanying fleet of smaller boats and barges, in a single line now, advancing to the south of the *chênière* by twenty degrees. From where

I sat on the campboat gallery beside *Grandmère,* I could see him leaning out of his pilot cabin again, with the same searching look toward the coast line.

Then he saw it, and shouted, "Palmetto Bayou . . . Praise Mary!"

A shout went up from all the assorted crew of Boudreaux, men, women and children, as each in his turn caught a first glimpse of the bayou's mouth.

Still I could see nothing, no single break in the marshy shore which lay so close to us now. It was all one long prairie of grasses, rippling in the Gulf breeze like the bay's watery surface. Until we were almost in the bayou itself, I could not see it. Then, in a quick instant, I felt the change, felt the bay behind us, the shore close on—and in the next moment we were inside the sea of canes, riding on a narrow ribbon of water through the towering roseau-cane that made a trappers' paradise.

Dusk was settling fast. Brilliant colors of the Gulf sky's afterglow mirrored in the bayou, turning it to a ribbon of silken *moiré.*

We had to hurry if we were to make camp by nightfall. Looming ahead in the deepening dusk, we saw the silhouette of two large campboats, anchored on the right bank of Palmetto Bayou.

"Auguste Grenoir's and Jacques Fizette . . . they done beat us out dis year," said *Grandmère* Boudreaux.

There were shouts of greeting from the campboat decks to our caravan, and many calls of caution to our lugger pilots.

"Watch yo'self, Baptiste, man, and don' be scrapin' no paint off us," yelled a tall giant of a man who stood on the first camp's aft deck.

Baptiste waved genially but gave no answering repartee.

"Our mens is tired-tired," commented *Grandmère.* "We gonna be there soon and it's a blessing."

She rose and went inside to start the wood fire and begin preparations for supper. I noticed that the other wives had already disappeared into their kitchens. As the last dim after-

"Bes' part of a trapper's day . . . causerie 'round Grandpère's stove at night."

glow faded on the bayou waters and first dark settled like a curtain dropped from the sky, lights shone from campboat windows ahead and behind us. From Baptiste's camp came wonderful fragrance of new-made coffee. From *Grandmère's* kitchen there was the subtler smell of catfish court bouillon being warmed and stirred.

At last there was a shout from Baptiste's lead lugger:

"Ah, my brothers, I see her now! Boudreaux Landing straight ahead!"

Grandpère, weary at his wheel, echoed his son's welcome shout and it was picked up and repeated down the wavering line of our campboat fleet.

"Boudreaux Landing! Praise Mary!"

Baptiste slowed his lugger and let his camp float in. The

others did the same, each finding his place along the bayou bank. The fathers and oldest boys tossed their lines ashore, made them fast to stakes which they drove quickly into the soft earth.

"Enough for now," shouted *Grandpère* to the whole clan. "Res' yo'self, my chil'ren! Tomorrow we make ourself secure for the season. Now give thanks for a safe trip . . . and catch yo'self some supper an' sleep!"

The old man, anchoring our camp to its stake on the bank, paused for a moment and looked heavenward, made the sign of the cross and muttered:

"Mother of God, *bien merci.*"

Then he stepped lightly upon the campboat deck, smiled at me and called to his wife.

"*Allons, ma chère,* where at's dat *coobyawn* what smell lak a breath of heaven? Let me put my feets under dat table fast-fast."

We were all of the same mind. Never has food tasted like that to me before. Perhaps never again.

"It lak dis alway," murmured *Grandpère* as he gave me another helping of rice and court bouillon.

"We make da good trip an' we make da fine feast. Tomorrow we make da camp and eat again a feast. That's the *firs'* thing you learn about trapping, *Mam'selle* . . . Part of trappin' is workin' hard and eatin' good."

He pushed back his chair and smiled at *Grandmère*, "So, *ma petite*, we make another season, *hein?*"

She smiled back and gave him a gentle push on the shoulder, "*Oui*, ole man, and may the las' be the bes' for us, yes."

We did not linger long around the table. Looking out the window, I saw that the lights were beginning to go out in all the campboats. The Boudreaux had earned their sleep that night. Silence, thick and impenetrable, settled like a blanket over the campboat community anchored in the marsh. In my bunk I felt the boat sway gently back and forth, yielding to the rising wind from the Gulf, and felt no fear of what the winds might bring.

Trappers of the
Golden·Marshlands

ix

Next morning, long before the trailing mists had lifted from the marshes around Boudreaux Landing, the clatter of pots and pans mixed with excited screams of children to announce that the first day of trapping season was here.

Dressing hurriedly, I looked out the window to see our camp floating as in a grey shroud, a tiny island in the vast swirling mists of the marshlands.

A spindly-legged heron, perched tentatively on the gunwale of Baptiste's lugger, rose and flew down Palmetto Bayou, disappearing into its own strange, grey world.

Grandpère stood beside his pirogue, looked to the east hopefully, then called out, "*Allons, allons, mes garçons* . . . In half a hour the ole sun gonna shine t'rough and make fools of us all . . . Baptiste! Adrian! Jean! Come see! *M'sieu* Mus'rat does not wait for lazy mens, him."

From the doors and windows of the campboats sleepy faces appeared. Lafayette, still with his pajama tops above his trousers, stood in his doorway, yawning enormously, drinking coffee. Then he leaped into action just in time to grab his youngest daughter as she started to slip over the side of the boat into the bayou.

"You, Ophelia, what crazy t'ing you got in yo' haid? Wanna scare yo' ole *papa* to his grave so early in da mornin'?"

Fifi, balancing *Bébé* on her hip, passed a comb through the tousled heads of her other six daughters as they hung over the railing, screaming to their boy cousins in the next camp.

Camille, splashing dishwater out the window of her campboat, shook her head and sighed.

"Another season!"

When I came out on deck of our camp, *Grandpère* stood there in long hip boots and leather jacket, a corduroy cap perched jautily on his white mop of hair. He held his shotgun in hand. As he raised it and pointed it skyward, he winked gaily at me. Then the blast nearly knocked me off the boat.

Grandpère lowered his gun, smacked his lips with satisfaction, and called to Camille.

"*Oui, bien merci* . . . another season!"

The whole camp sprang into concerted action, like a well-trained and extremely versatile circus troupe. For three days they worked with a dedicated kind of fury, stopping only for meals, and three or four times a day, to answer that pleasant call from one of the wives:

"Heh, you mens! Coffee's ready!"

Adrian and Baptiste, with the help of Toto and Eddie, dug slips for the luggers and for the larger gasboats. Dressed in hip boots, they shoveled the slushy, shallow earth of the bayou bank and carved out openings as easily as a child makes ditches in a sand pile. Along the shore they drove heavy stakes and fastened the campboats securely with heavy tie lines. *Grandpère*'s camp was given the place of honor, tied to one lone, skeletal oak which somehow had resisted the Gulf's winds and tides and now stood gaunt and determined, like *Grandpère* himself.

Further back on the shore, Jean constructed a small tarpaper shack.

"Fifty baby chick peep-peein' in a brooder in the hull of my camp! For a whole season I couldn't stan' it . . . I buil' a house, me."

He was assisted by *Grandpère*, advised by Camille and harassed by more small children than there were mosquitoes on a warm night. When the shack was finished, he helped his brothers in constructing a series of chicken coops, a substantial pen for Mimi's lethargic hog, and a shed for Adrian's cow.

After the community effort was over, each man set up his own racks for drying muskrat hides. *Grandmère* went from camp to camp, offering pertinent advice as to the placing of nails on the racks. The stretching of skins is woman's work, she said. There wasn't a man alive who knew exactly how to make the racks.

She offered advice also on the placing of wringers on platforms over the water, and told the best method of using the battered clothes wringers to squeeze out the skins.

"*Bien,* this is da time!" She kept saying to herself, happily. Only for this, the trapping season, would she neglect her hobby, the making of wax flowers for cemeteries on All Saints' Day.

Further back beyond the pens, Adrian hammered together a rough outhouse. He worked rapidly, for once, cursing all the while that such an inglorious job had fallen to him.

Every so often *Grandpère* stopped to rest. He sat with his back to the sun, testing and inspecting the row of steel traps in front of him.

"Work, work and more work," he said. "Work yesterday, today and tomorrow. Give it all your back muscles!"

"Mother of God," screamed Fifi. "They finally done it, them two!"

She tossed *Bébé* to Camille and ran to where the twins, 'Tavia and 'Livia, were howling, their hands caught in one of the wringers. Fifi, grimacing and praying, twisted the wringer and removed their hands, miraculously unharmed. Nanette, panting, came rushing out of her campboat to help.

"*Regardez Tante* Nanette," shrilled one of the twins, "she wears still her corset, but no shoes."

"Hush, you two," screamed Fifi, "or I'll slap yo' backsides. You have, both of you, the head of a duck."

"Bah," snorted Nanette, "you have too many girl chil'ren, you Fifi."

By the end of the third day, most of the construction work was completed. Now the men must consider that important work known as "preparing the land."

As *Grandpère* put it, "The lan' she must be made sweet for da lil 'rats . . . Then she work good for da trapper."

So they spent several days digging *traînasses,* tiny water ditches which were just wide enough to carry a narrow pirogue. On these narrow liquid paths they would travel "into the back" and set their trap lines where the roseau-cane stood highest.

Part of the land needed to be drained where there was too

much water. So they dug drainage ditches through the muck. Another part was too dry and they built a small levee to hold the water in. The brothers grumbled over this tiresome work, but *Grandpère* kept them at it.

"*Oui*, good trappers are good engineers," he kept telling them, "an' the lan' she must be made sweet."

After supper on the third day, the four older boys paddled downstream to where the palmettos grew thickest along the bayou banks. They brought back great sheaves of palmettos to thatch Jean's roof. The smaller children helped to fill smudge buckets. *Grandpère* showed them how to string pots on drying racks and how to keep fires burning in them, "to scare away dem hongry mosquit', by dam' . . . 'scuse please, *Mam'selle*."

A fading sun had turned the tall grasses from gold to pale sienna before the last of the hammering died away. Most of the men, pleasantly tired, stretched full length on their campboat decks, shaded their eyes from the low-slanting sun. From Plunk's campboat came a few tentative chords from his guitar, but even the children seemed too weary to pick up the music's promise.

Grandmère sat in her rocking chair, shucking oysters with the skill of many years. To get these, *Grandpère* had pulled his battered old oyster tongs from the hull of the campboat and had dug the oysters from a nearby bed which the Boudreaux cultivated from year to year to furnish table oysters during trapping season.

Now *Grandpère* moved from the boat deck and took his favorite seat, in an old cane chair which leaned against the scraggly trunk of the one lone oak tree still growing along the bayou bank. He sat there smoking his pipe, watching the children tend the moss buckets.

It seemed a good time to talk, to ask *Grandpère* some of the questions which kept chasing around in my head. Already I had heard enough conflicting stories about Louisiana trapping to leave me thoroughly confused. Two more days and the season would open officially. My trip with the Boudreaux had revealed many things, but there was much, much more, that

A trapper needs plenty of boats, of all sizes and shapes, to work in the marshlands.

I must learn. I knew that there were many city folks who believed the muskrat trapper to be an outlaw, even a thief. I could not reconcile this with the hospitable, laughter-loving Boudreaux clan. Neither could I understand the resentments I had heard expressed by Baptiste and the others, toward "the company men" and "the system."

"What do you mean by 'the system'?" I asked *Grandpère*.

The old man looked at me quizzically, pulled a long draw on his pipe, stared dreamily across the darkening marsh. He spoke finally in a slow soft tone as if choosing each word with care:

"That takes a lot of talkin', *ma chère* . . . an' a lot of livin' too. You hav' to be an ole boot like me to unnerstan' it for true."

He paused, knocked the ashes from his pipe bowl and flung his arm toward the encircling prairies of grass.

"Why I can remember no more'n fifty years ago when dis whole marsh was nuttin' but wasteland . . . left to da 'rats and otters and snakes and 'gators . . . wit maybe a pore shrimper's shack here and there. My *p'père*'s camp was down at da mouth of Palmetto Bayou and we made good livin' wit our lil lugger goin' shrimpin' in summer, catchin' us a few minks and 'rats in winter. We made good livin' . . . and we felt da land was ours awright . . . *mon dieu*, we couldn't felt no better if da whole earth was ours, *mais* sho! There ain' no system in them days, *ma chère* . . . an' that make plenty difference."

He paused again, and shook his head regretfully.

"Then some big fool discover *Monsieur* Mus'rat's pelts was made of gold . . . or dat's what they say for awhile. Seem lak they caught all da rats out up north an' had start lookin' somewhere else. So somebody say '*regardez la Louisiane* marsh 'rats.' Pretty soon all the marsh men went wild, I guarantee you. Pelts what was two cents one day rose up to a dime, then a dollar, then as high as two-fi'ty.

"*Mon dieu,* we went wild! In them days it was a pore trapper for sure who didn't come out da marsh at end of season wit eight or ten thousand dollar. Ah, dem was the days, *Mam'selle,* when a trapper had his own heaven right here on his own bayou."

"But what about the 'system'?"

"*Oui,* it all start when men who really own the lan' decide they lak the looks of this propity after all. Mostly they claim they got da land in oldtime grants from French Crown. Us trappers was plenty surprise when they butt in. Here we was . . . and our *papas* before us . . . been trappin' this lan' and fishin' these water widout ever payin' 'tention to who own it . . . we jus' thought we own it, I guess, and nobody ever told us diffrent. Then all a sudden here come a company man ridin' up the bayou in one them big cabin cruisers and he tell us plenty straight who own the lan'. If we can't unnerstan' his talk, he gotta shotgun hangin' on da foredeck what speak a language any pore Frenchmans can unnderstan' . . ."

"And is that what is called 'the system'?" I asked, persistently.

The old man sighed. "Dat's a good part of it, *chère*, if you listen to a trapper's side da story . . . and if that's what you asked me for. You see, big mens in the city what own da lan', they lease it to other big mens who make up companies what handles da lan' and everythin' on it . . . all the mus'rat and mink too . . . and all us pore trappers too, *mais* sho. So now we gotta pay for da priv'lege of trappin' what we thought was our own lan' . . . and gotta pay t'rough da nose," he ended abruptly.

"How much do you pay for trapping on Palmetto Bayou?" I asked.

"It is not in lump cash we pay, *Mam'selle*, and that is da shame . . . It's in a percentage, a big percentage, of what our season's catch turn out to be."

"Is that so bad?"

Grandpère's answer was a bitter smile and a shrug of his shoulders. While we talked, Baptiste and Jean had joined us, sitting silently on the bank beside *Grandpère* and listening. Now both of them spoke together, gesticulating:

"Nom de dieu, Mam'selle . . . Is it bad?"

"Is it bad that a mans must give the bes' of his catch, the bes' of a year's hard work, for the priv'lege of making a pore livin' for his family. *Is it bad* that I mus' stan' by and watch da dirty buyer claim my bes' skins for 'the company,' then set his own price on the res'?"

Jean interrupted him, frowning and vehement. *"Is it bad* when I know I get twice that price in town but if I leave camp and go there to sell, he kick me off da lan' and that is finish me for a trapper? *Oui, Mam'selle,* it is plenty bad, I guarantee you!"

Before I could speak, Jean added:

"And how you lak da 'no visiting' law, *Mam'selle?* We ain' got it here, *bien merci*, but lots of pore trappers suffers it. Like a dam slave it makes a man," he grimaced.

"And some company buyers forbid they trappers go to town for anyt'ing at all, even to a doctor!"

"Remember Étienne Ducet," Jean said, "who was afraid to take his boy to town that time he was bite by dat Congo? Before Étienne could bring the doc from town in his gasboat, the pore *bébé* had died, *mon dieu!*"

Baptiste and *Grandpère* nodded sadly and the old man spoke again:

"The system is a bad thing, *chère*. It does not give a mans a chance. We would pay . . . be glad to . . . if we could be independent trappers and pay in cash for whole year's lease, lak them lucky mens on the Gov'mint lands on Marsh Island. You go see the fur auction at Abbéville, *Mam'selle*, where them independent trappers on state-owned lands can get a bid from half a dozen free-wheelin' fur buyers. It is a beautiful t'ing to watch, I guarantee you. At them Abbéville auctions a man can take the highes' price he's offered and sell to whoever he Goddam please, instead of handing over his full catch to a company man, like we mus' do."

Jean interrupted, "Lak *who* say we do, ole man?"

Baptiste joined him in loud laughter, as if enjoying some secret joke, but *Grandpère* only smiled and shook his head.

"It is not good that a man mus' cheat and mus' bootleg fur to feed his wife and lil ones. A man should not be force' to steal."

His sons nodded, agreeing, and I got that feeling again that they shared some secret withheld from me. Perhaps I would share it later. For now, I saw clearly that the talk was finished. Baptiste and Jean, saying good-bye, walked wearily toward their campboats.

"*Bonne nuit, Mam'selle . . . mon père.* Today is gone and tomorrow come another day, *hein?*"

Dusk had turned to first dark as we talked and silence settled over the bayou banks as women and children gathered inside around the kitchen tables.

Grandpère smiled at me as we stepped up the plank and went inside to another of *Grandmère's* delicious suppers.

For a week the men worked from misty dawn through the heavy blue shadows of half dark. All of them began to show the first sproutings of beards, said to be a sure sign that trapping season was underway. To my surprise there was no special recognition given to the official opening day of the season. The routine of work activities around the camps began to change gradually and nobody remarked on the fact that the men stayed longer and longer in the marsh these days, and that their shoulder sacks were not empty when they came out, and that an increasing number of skins were beginning to appear on the drying racks. I had expected something more dramatic for the opening day—had thought that *Grandpère* would blast forth with a louder than usual explosion from his old shotgun.

There must be a reason for this quiet transition from preparation to actual trapping, I thought. Later, as I came to know the trappers better, it seemed less mysterious. For the Louisiana muskrat trapper is not man for laws, nor for official dates nor for artificial regulations not dictated by the more primeval legalities of the marsh itself. When his land is prepared for trapping, he traps . . . *"comme ci, comme ça . . . mais sho, it is simple, no?"*

And so I do not know whether or not I was a legal trapper on that memorable day when Baptiste took me into the marsh as he ran his lines. At the beginning, the day was like any other . . . grey swirling mists over the bayou settlement . . . the sun struggling through shrouded skies . . . muted mother-of-pearl colors on the gently rocking campboats along Palmetto Bayou. Yet before it ended, I had known a different world and seen something of the ways of the marshlands.

"Today you learn much," Baptiste said, as I checked my boot straps, pulled the earflaps down on my hunter's cap. The night had brought the season's first cold snap, and I was glad to have two sweaters under my leather jacket, glad to feel the warmth of the long hip boots whose tops I tied to my belt, like any well-dressed trapper.

Stepping cautiously into Baptiste's pirogue, I shivered to think how the freezing water would feel if the tiny craft should tip over. Baptiste stood in the stern, push-pole in hand, as steady and as perfectly balanced as though he stood on a paved sidewalk . . . and smiled as he read my thoughts.

"The pirogue, she ride on a dew, yes . . . an' have no fear, *Mam'selle*. We do not swim this morning."

As we poled past the camps of his brothers, we saw them through the campboat windows, hunched over their kitchen tables, drinking pungent French coffee which would give them strength in the cold marsh.

"We get an early start on *Monsieur* Mus'rat," said Baptiste, "and on my brothers too. I feel it in my bones, *mon ami*, this will be a good day with the 'rats."

Past the campboats, the bayou seemed to disappear, to fade into marsh and sky, leaving us floating on a misty stream of grey without beginning or end. Except for the small liquid drip from Baptiste's push pole, there was no sound. We rode through a shrouded world, impenetrable and silent.

The sun broke through just as we reached the spot where Baptiste's *traînasse* opened off the bayou, so that we could see the tiny man-made streak of water cutting like a pencil line through the marsh. Turning into it, I saw gold and green grasses soar high above us on either side. It was as if our tiny craft wallowed in a trough of gold sea-waves. At any moment we might be lifted by the swaying roseau and carried across the grassy sea! Frost lay like spray upon the marsh grass, glistening in the early sun, and the air's cold freshness was of the sea.

Our enchantment was not broken until Baptiste poled the pirogue into a ditch along the bank and motioned me to step ashore. We had crossed some invisible line, lost to me in the engulfing beauty of the marsh, known and recognized only by the trapper and his brothers.

"My lan', she is here," Baptiste said, stepping ashore, shouldering his empty pack sack. In one hand he carried a few long cane poles, each one bearing a small cloth flag which seemed to be torn from an old red shirt. In the other he carried a bunch of glittering new steel traps. Their shiny teeth glinted cruelly in the sun. To me they looked deadly indeed, but Baptiste held them proudly.

"We make some new sets today, *Mam'selle*, and *M'sieu* Mus'rat bes' watch hisself this night. These new traps won' take no flirtin' wit."

Trappers pole their way easily through the waterways of the marsh, in slim pirogues that an outsider would capsize in an instant.

When we had walked just a little way into the roseau-cane, Baptiste stopped, bending over to examine the earth carefully.

"*Regardez*," he said, "come see. Look like *M'sieu* Mus'rat highway intersection."

Looking closely, I saw a tiny inch-wide trail running along the mucky earth, and then a second one, and then a spot where the two crossed each other. It was a highway intersection all right, one of the millions of crisscrossing trails made on the marsh floor by furry animals who roamed ceaselessly by night.

Baptiste grinned as I put my finger at the exact spot where the trails met, then said, "*Regardez, Mam'selle* . . . more signs." He pointed to bits of chewed-off grass which lay close by the small watery trails.

"*Oui, mais* sho, we lay a good set here."

He bent down, dug a small hole about four inches below the surface, placed one of the new traps in the intersection and covered the spot with grass. Carefully he opened the jaws of the trap. Then he stepped a foot away and planted one of the tall cane poles firmly into the soft marsh floor.

"*Bon, Mam'selle*, it is a fine set. You'll see. Tomorrow, I bring in one fat sassy 'rat from this set here."

I followed him as he walked further into the towering grasses of the marsh. He walked easily, with the springy, high-stepping gait of the born trapper. I stumbled awkwardly, seeking vainly for a foothold, feeling the marsh floor tremble and sway beneath me in a disconcerting, sometimes frightening way. When we had gone about fifty feet, Baptiste stopped to look for more signs.

In a moment he motioned me to the spot where a circular mound rose some three feet above the ground.

"*Regardez* da mus'rat palace, *Mam'selle*." He walked around the hill and looked closely at the ground. "Ah, and come see . . . His Highness' dive hole, *aussi*."

Plainly visible, leading from the nest, was a trail broader than the little water trail where we had made our first set. At the point where it entered the hill was the dive hole, a subterranean entrance fashioned with skill by the muskrat dwellers whose home we were invading.

Baptiste dug into the dive hole, placed his trap, then covered the surface with bits of broken grasses.

"*Bien, mon ami*, I teach you to make a good set, no?" He planted another of the tall cane poles, and we watched as the rising wind caught the little red flag and made it ripple.

Walking further into the marsh, we set half a dozen more traps, watching always for the signs of muskrat activity and being careful to make a good set each time. This was a big part of the trappers' skill—for in his guessing game with the muskrat, the trapper must understand and predict all the animal's activities, must know which of the tiny water trails are in use and which have been abandoned, must know a new dive hole from an old one, must develop an instinctive insight into the animal's habits of living and a keen prediction of his dying.

As we finished making the new sets and walked across the slippery marsh floor toward Baptiste's old trap line, he talked to me of the muskrat's habits. The animal is second only to the beaver in building canals and intricate apartment houses in the mud. He is an ardent and careless soul in the dark of the moon. Out hunting for food or fun, he stumbles into one of the unbaited traps, feels the tight steel jaws clamp down ". . . an' he got his start to being some city lady's fur coat."

Reaching the first of the older sets, we paused for a moment while Baptiste opened his small thermos and poured a sip of coffee for each of us. I was grateful for the moment's rest and for the strong hot savor of the Creole coffee. At our feet lay the first catch of the day, a large 'rat which Baptiste held up admiringly before he dropped it into his sack.

"*Bien, Mam'selle*, you bring me luck . . . Firs' trap and firs' 'rat . . . This will be a good day, yes."

He reset the trap carefully, shouldered his sack and motioned me toward the second trap, set fifty feet away and marked by its cane pole and tiny flag.

By noon we had covered half of his line and had swung back to the *traînasse* where our pirogue was banked. Baptiste

carried thirty-six muskrats and four mink in his sack. He was
happy. I was completely, utterly, through-and-through ex-
hausted. My hip boots, which had felt so cozy and comfortable at the start, were covered with muck, damp inside, and
seemed to weigh a thousand pounds each. Several times I had
sprawled headlong in them, and felt the sharp bite of cold
water enter over their tops. Now I felt as though I walked on a
floor of ice, dragging my lifeless feet along by will power only.
The last half hour was a misery of freezing numbness in every
cell. I was too tired to hear, too tired to see . . . and yet I knew
I must somehow pull myself over that last hundred feet and
crawl into the waiting pirogue.

Baptiste was talking to me but I could not understand what
he said. Gratefully, in the bow of the pirogue, I gulped the
remainder of the coffee and felt it warm my brain into life.
I heard the trapper say:

"We already covered the bes' land, *Mam'selle* . . . I mean
the bes' walking land. We'll catch some lunch at the camp and
I'll finish my line this evening. You better not go this evening,
mon amie. The res' of my land is plenty rough . . . and not so
easy like this morning."

I could see that Baptiste did not know how close I had come
to going out on him, and was glad. "So easy like this morning . . ." I shivered and tried not to think of what the "plenty
rough" marsh would be like.

Baptiste continued to talk as he poled the pirogue along with
long slow strokes.

"You gotta practice your marsh-walkin' some, *Mam'selle*,
before you cover rough land. You gotta walk wit your knees
drawn up, steppin' high like, and shift your weight wit every
step. Watch me and my brudders, how we lift our knees. In
town peoples say they can tell a trapper by way he lift his
knees : . . it's lak pavemints burn his feet . . . but they don'
know how there's no pavemints at all in the marsh and no firm
place at all."

I asked him about the "trembling prairie" I had heard about.

"*Oui*, my land this afternoon, she is some trembling prairie," he said. "You mus' not go this afternoon, *non* . . . Even the bes' trapper can go down on trembling prairie."

He suddenly became quite serious, and poled the pirogue along in silence. "I think about my *Nonc Télèsphore*. He was lost las' year on Plum Bayou, suck down in trembling prairie before my cousins could throw a line 'round his shoulders."

Baptiste shuddered at the thought and I felt my own shoulders jerk too.

"It happens, *Mam'selle*," he said, soberly, "and jus' lak alligator holes, *aussi*. A man gotta watch for them too. A man falls into an alligator hole on a cold day, he can freeze hisself 'fore he get back to camp."

Such talk was not designed to warm the bones nor the heart of one who had just pulled through her first half-day in the marsh. Something bleak in my face must have told this to Baptiste. He spoke no more until we sighted the huddle of campboats at Boudreaux Landing.

"*Bien, Mam'selle*, we is home. *C'est très joli*, yes?"

The camp was very pretty indeed, and very warm to look at and very friendly too. Smoke curled from the crooked stovepipes protruding through campboat roofs, children played along bayou banks, women worked at clotheslines or inside their kitchens. From a far distance I could see the silhouette of *Grandmère* Boudreaux sitting on her porch deck in the sun, rocking and working at her paper flowers. I too felt that I was coming home, and *très jolie, aussi*.

At sight of us the children set up a great cry and the women stopped their work, standing on the campboat decks to call out their welcome. The reception was a royal one. As Baptiste pulled the pirogue into his camp and tied to a deckpost, we were besieged. And when he lifted his heavy 'rat sack and swung it up onto the *galerie*, there were cries of delight from the whole clan.

Toto and Eddie grabbed the sack, pulled it onto the bayou bank and emptied it dramatically near the camp chair where their mother would sit and skin the 'rats. It was a good catch for a single morning and the stack of 'rats looked impressively large to me.

But nothing at the moment seemed as good as the coffee pot that *Grandmère* held in her hand, motioning me inside our camp. She had welcomed home many a trapper in her day but never one more weary than I. When I dragged numb feet up the gangplank and put them under the kitchen table, it seemed that I could go not a single step further. With strong hot coffee inside me, though, I managed to pull off my dead-weight boots and clothes and to slip gratefully into the bunk.

A couple of hours later I awoke with a pleasantly languorous ache through all my bones.

"I shall live again . . . but not to walk the marsh," I thought.

From the bunk I could look out the window and watch the activity around all the camps. The Boudreaux wives were busy skinning muskrats, wringing skins in clothes wringers on the docks over the bayou, stretching them on wire hangers. Children ran back and forth, carrying stretched skins to wooden racks where they hung them in rows from long nails.

Several of the men were back early from the marsh, not being as industrious as Baptiste. They lolled lazily on the boat decks, soaking in the warm sun. *Grandpère* leaned back in his chair beside his tree, carving a toy pirogue for *Bébé*. These days he spent only the mornings in the marsh, and on land that was close to the camp.

Baptiste's twin boys were climbing the mast of his lugger, swinging from the sheets, playing Tarzan. Suddenly I saw one of them stiffen, look far down the bayou and point as he shouted:

"*P'père* . . . *P'père!* The grocery boat . . . she comes!"

He shinnied down the mast pole and joined the crowd of other children who dropped their tasks instantly and waited in a huddle for the approaching boat, wriggling and jumping about like excited terriers.

I flung on my clothes, pulled on short rubber knee boots, and joined them. This must not be missed.

Rounding a turn in the bayou came a sturdy full-cabin

lugger, with a small figure standing stolidly at the helm. As he raised his hand to salute, a great hoarse whistle sounded. This was the official greeting from Monsieur Alcée Hebert, owner and proprietor of the grocery boat *Jambalaya*.

While children screamed excitably to the hoarse tune of this water-borne Pied Piper, their elders quietly began to take down a good part of the skins which hung from the drying racks.

I heard *Grandmère* say scoldingly to Camille, "Don' get so full of jump and tremble." And to her daughter, "You, Fifi, take care to put away the skins. This Hebert has the quick eye and the busy tongue. Don' do no good to have such bayou trash making talk-talk about our catch."

Jean winked at Camille and said, "Ah, *chère M'mère*. She is so wise. You young ones . . . jus' good for love and to spen' da money."

Nanette, *Grandmère* and Camille came aboard their camp-boats with arms loaded with pelts. I saw *Grandmère* put away her bounty in a delapidated old wooden chest which sat always on the aft deck. This business of hiding the skins was a bit mystifying, but I had been warned not to ask too many questions around the trapping camps.

Now everybody hurried to the bayou, joined the children in welcoming the grocery-boat operator.

Grandmère said, "There is much we need . . . Seem lak ever' week my forget-list is longer . . . Les' see . . . red beans, sausage, garlic . . . flour for the ole man's biscuits, and no wonder wit him eatin' like a marsh hog . . ."

Plunk nudged Fifi, "Don' forget my wine this time, *ma petite* . . . and cherries for the cherry flips."

Fifi murmured quietly, "Ah, my *jeunes filles*, how happy they will be! Their new dresses come at last . . . what a poke-slow is that Monsieur Hebert! He do not know the heart of a *jeune fille*, no."

Grandmère replied, "Ah, Fifi, you have still the head of a duck. Always, always, dresses for your girls. With you there will never be no cash under the mattress."

"*Mais* sho, *Grandmère*, they must have dresses to make da marriage some day!"

"What foolishments. You marry 'Fayette when you have only flour sacks."

The grocery boat was close to *Grandpère's* landing now, and the children's screams of joy increased. Just before throwing his motor into reverse, Monsieur Hebert pulled again on his whistle, sounding a blast that almost lifted us off our feet.

Grandpère fumed sourly. "*Mon dieu*, that circus whistle! Some day he'll blow up a hurricane."

Grandmère added, "He scare the whiskers right off a mus'rat."

On the bow of the brightly-painted lugger stood Monsieur Hebert's deck-hand, a buck-toothed youth who held the tow lines lightly over his shoulder and searched the crowd of Boudreaux hungrily, looking for the prettiest of Fifi's daughters. In an instant he had thrown the line to Plunk who tied it securely to the dock, and had jumped to the bank, saying in one breath:

" 'Aye, sir . . . where at's that Coco?"

The next instant the lugger was invaded by the Boudreaux clan, laughing and calling jokes to the captain while waiting for him to open shop.

The grocery boat was a sight to see. Its decks were stacked with a wild disarray of goods, for the storekeeper had not re-packed his merchandise since leaving the camp below us. The *Jambalaya* looked somewhat like a miniature market after a bargain sale, with groceries mixed companionably with the lugger's seagoing necessities. The mast was festooned with sausages. A huge bunch of bananas hung from the wheelhouse roof. On deck, fore of the hatch, three cases of beer rested on the fifty-gallon gasoline and kerosene drums. Atop the pilot cabin was a large rectangular icebox which *Grandpère* said contained steaks, roasts, pork chops and fresh milk. I got a fleeting glimpse inside the cabin behind the wheelhouse, enough to understand that it was a thrilling sight for the isolated families. Along the walls were rows of shelves wearing brightly-labeled canned goods, great baskets of oranges, potatoes, fruit. Further aft were crates of soap, piles of fishing tackle, jugs of wine, boxes of ammunition.

Protecting this beautiful bounty from the eager invaders, Monsieur Hebert stood stolidly in the wheelhouse door. He knew he was a man of distinction during his brief stay at the camp and he made the most of it.

The owner and proprietor of the grocery boat was a neat little man who wore garters on his shirt sleeves and looked too much like a small-town storekeeper to be pilot of a seagoing lugger. Besides serving as purveyor of foodstuffs, he functioned as bringer of messages, carrier of the mail, general advisor and link with the outside world. It was difficult to tell which of the roles he liked best, for it was obvious that *M'sieu* Alcée found life in general very much to his liking. A good part of his *joie de vivre* was in the lively battles he carried on with housewives. As soon as the lugger was safely tied to the dock, he killed the motor and stepped out on the foredeck, grinning and ready for the fray.

"*Mon dieu, M'sieu*, what keep you so long?" shouted Mimi as she lifted her skirts and rushed aboard, surrounded by a surging stream of children. "Ever since he got his new boat, this one is lak an ole woman . . . afraid maybe he'll scratch the paint on a piling, *hein?*"

"*Allons, allons, ma chère*. Don' waste my time wit yo' foolishments . . . I'm a busy man, me, wit other customers to serve besides the hongry Boudreaux. Watch them kids now, *mon ami*, and keep them bayed till I can wait upon their betters."

He turned toward the other wives, who came in single file up the landing plank, and bowed to them with exaggerated courtesy.

"*Bonjour, chères Mam'selles*. Dispose yo'selves, *s'il vous plaît*."

Grandmère sniffed disgustedly. "*Chères Mam'selles*, pooh . . . me wit my t'ree sons."

Fifi added, "An' me wit my eight lil flowers!"

Monsieur Hebert's eyebrows lifted in mock horror: "*C'est impossibl'!*"

Grandmère cautioned, "You young ones, watch out for dese mens from town. They have the words of da Black One his-self."

The storekeeper pretended to change his tone to one of deepest respect and solemnity: "*Bonjour, mes amis,* come aboard, *s'il vous plaît.*"

Grandmère, still caustic, said, "*Bonjour,* you seller of soft bananas and hard bread."

"Ah, *Madame,* what a pity to waste such loveliness on the mosquit'. Your words as ever caress my ears." He turned to caution the children again.

"*Mon dieu,* you busy raccoons . . . Avast now! Quieten down an' keep in sight here on da foredeck or I put you overboard. There be no *tac-tac* for nobody till the lovely ladies is served."

He stepped toward the wheelhouse and entered, motioning the wives to follow. "*Attendez,* please, *Mesdames.* We will now commence. Beans is aft of the onions . . . and the price is still eighty-five cents for potatoes . . ."

Grandmère snorted, leading the group. "Robber! For potate, eighty-five cent? *M'sieu* is still a crook . . . He wishes to retire at end of one trip . . . an' all at expense of da Boudreaux."

Camille added righteously: "In the city store they are much cheaper."

Hebert, overhearing as he was supposed to, said, "Then get them at the city store, *chère.* Does the great one, Mr. Alidore, bring his store to you? Maybe my gas costs me nuttin', *hein?* Maybe I risk my stock in hurricane for fun, *hein?*"

Grandmère continued to grumble. "Then potate we do not eat. You could buy a gas station wit yo' profits."

Monsieur Hebert made a sour face, then looked specula-tively at the old lady. "You Boudreaux is so cheap. You make much, much money cheatin' the company, but eighty-five cent is too much for fine potatoes."

Grandmère looked seriously shocked and said, "I regret such talk, Monsieur Hebert. You know da 'rats have lef' Palmetto Bayou . . . and maybe we leave too next season, and where at is your bes' customers, *hein?*"

Plunk hastened to add, *"M'mère* is right. Floods last year washed the 'rats right out to sea. All the time it gets harder to find da 'rats on Palmetto Bayou."

The storekeeper shook his head wisely. "Alla time it the same story, but the Boudreaux keep comin' back. It is maybe for da duck shootin', *hein?"*

Fifi was tugging impatiently at his sleeve. *"Mon dieu,* M'sieu Hebert, will you ever quit talk-talk and fin' those dress for my lil butterflies? They goin' grow an inch taller all 'round just waitin' here on this foredeck!"

To her waiting daughters she shouted, "Girls . . . girls . . . Coco, Marie, Mercedes, Odalia . . . you slow one, Ophelia . . . 'Tavie, 'Livie . . . Hurry-hurry . . . Maybe Monsieur Alcée bring yo' new dress from da catalogue, yes?"

She lined her daughters up in a row, counting noses. They clutched eagerly at the big package which Monsieur Hebert dug out from behind sacks of potatoes. Everybody stopped arguing and watched Fifi hand a paper bag to each girl, gesturing eagerly:

"Regardez, mes petites filles! Très jolie . . . très jolie!"

Then, as the girls held the dresses up to their shoulders proudly, Fifi's face changed and she cried in despair.

"Mais non, mon dieu! It cannot be! St. Cecilia, help us! Nuttin' fit nobody! That catalogue she is nuttin' but a Goddam slowpoke . . ."

Grandmère clucked solicitously. ". . . an' o' course your *jeunes filles* is growed too, shootin' up like young roseau-canes."

The girls were beginning to cry, but Monsieur Hebert stepped forward like the master of ceremonies that he was.

"Non, non, *mes petites!* Dry yo' eyes . . . *M'sieu* Alcée fix for you. It is a simple thing, *n'est-ce pas?* Give to each girl the next bigges' dress, and for the largest I have something special . . . a big box from Breaux's Sweet Shop in town!"

As he handed the box of candy to Coco, the other girls began exchanging dresses, holding them up to their shoulders and arguing among themselves importantly. "But I wanted the red

one!" . . . "Mine mus' be green to match da new feather hat,
mais sho!" . . . "But, Mercedes, she cannot wear da blue, no?
And 'Livie, she would look so bad in red?" . . . "Ah, *Maman*, .
what we gonna do?"

Hebert had the answer for that one too.

"Well, come now, you silly girls. Give them all back to me
quick. Lemme get away from dis troublesome camp . . . I got
other fish to fry down da bayou. *Allons, allons,* giv' the dresses
back! An' the sweets *aussi!*"

He reached out for the dresses and for the box of candy.
Screams of protest answered this maneuver, and the girls
gripped their dresses closer to them.

"Maman! Help us! Nasty ole *M'sieu* Alcée! Don' let him
take our dress away!"

It was settled now to everybody's satisfaction. Hebert
shrugged, lifted his arms resignedly and let them fall.

"Womens! Womens! Da pullets is wors' dan da hens . . .
Allons, let us get away from here . . . on with business! I have
not all day to spend with da noisy Boudreaux!"

The wives turned to shopping, studying their grocery lists,
serving themselves from cabin shelves. Monsieur Hebert
beamed as he saw the piles of supplies grow larger, turning to
his scales to weigh sack after sack of potatoes and beans. He
smiled and winked at Nanette as she picked up four more
loaves of bread and added it to the six she already had taken.

Plunk held up a jug of wine before placing it beside his
stack of groceries. "Is it any good this trip . . . or is it taste
lak color punch at da church fair?"

"Oui, it is da bes'. It is import from . . . California. I sell it
las' trip to Chevalier's when they make a *fais-dodo* to honor
their new boat. Ev'body dance and sing like crazy all t'rough
da night . . . They don't go to traps for t'ree days . . . Sure,
it is da bes'."

Camille was studying her list. "Syrup, beans, olive oil . . .
motor oil . . . no red peppers. Alla time you forget red peppers,
ole man. You want my gumbo should taste lak no-good?"

One by one the Boudreaux wives settled their accounts with

the storekeeper, motioned their husbands or bigger boys to shoulder the sacks of groceries. Monsieur Hebert, stuffing bills into the money belt which bulged around his waist, dispatched gossip with each sale.

"*Oui*, that Annette Guidroz, she marry her second cousin from Petit Caillou . . . an' her brudder, Achilles, he had a bad-bad accident, him . . . *Oui, Madame*, the coffee is up two cents . . . Sorry . . . *Mais* sho, one dollar . . . Achilles, he smash his laig 'tween his boat and da dock . . . The Guidroz, they have a very bad season . . . The company man fin' dem sellin' to night buyer and it does not do well wit dem . . ."

Plunk picked this up quickly, as Alcée expected.

"The company man . . . he already been to Big Carencro?"

"*Oui, mon ami*, an' you can look for him here in Palmetto tomorrow." He watched Plunk's face carefully and added:

"An' when he fin' them measly half-filled racks of yours, what he gonna say to da Boudreaux, *hein?*"

"Come along, ole alligator-face," *Grandmère* called, "yo' coffee's waitin'. Better drink fast-fast if you expec' to tie up tonight at the Billiots' landing."

"And that what I expect to do," said Alcée, leaping to her campboat deck. "If I don' get dem boots to Noogie Billiot, he won' be able to run his lines . . . and dat make plenty trouble, *mais* sho."

He took a gulp of hot coffee from the table and pecked *Grandmère* on the cheek. "Still the bes' dam' coffee this side of Morgan City," he said, "and jus' what I needs to help me beat the moon up the bayou."

In another moment he stepped aboard the *Jambalaya*, yelled lustily for his buck-toothed young deck hand, and prepared to cast off his lines.

It was dusk as he pulled away from the landing, blowing his horn for a farewell salute to the campboat colony.

We stood in the doorway to wave good-bye.

Grandpère said, "The ole goat . . . He better be careful pulling into Plum Bayou in the night. He hit a snag 'round them ole pilings an' the *Jambalaya* will deliver groceries to da frogs and fishes."

Fur Buyers

Day and Night

X

All the next day, late into the afternoon, the children were excited with their new purchases from the grocery boat. César fell twice into the bayou chasing his new top. Clotilde and 'Livia stuck chewing gum in each other's hair and 'Tavia tried to cut it out with a penknife. Screaming her annoyance, Fifi banished all three to the shed room behind the camp.

It was a busy day, with no time to be lost with such "foolishments." The men were home early from the marsh, each bragging about his extra-fine catch. All hands were busy, skinning 'rats, hanging them on racks, separating the dried furs before storing them in cartons.

Skinning the 'rats was women's work. I watched as *Grandmère* flashed her sharp knife, split an animal swiftly between the legs and across the tail. With one dextrous movement she turned the muskrat inside out and cut the skin away from eyes, nose and mouth.

"Look at *Grandmère* go," sighed Camille. "Me, I can't skin no more'n one mus'rat a minute, not even for the Angel Gabriel.

182

That one, she can do two a minute without a half-try. She go so fast she don' have time to bless herself. What a womans!"

Mimi and Nanette were busy taking dried hides off the stretchers, placing them in a pile for the men to look over. Baptiste took over the sorting of furs, grading them swiftly with one quick expert glance at each pelt. As he worked, he hummed a little tune, off-key but oddly fitting his words: "One for the buyer, one for the mattress . . . this one good . . . this one bad . . . So much for this, so much for that . . . *Comme ci, comme ça . . . Eh bien.*"

The words made little sense to me but seemed to amuse his wife. She murmured, "It is too bad your beat-up shell of a pirogue burned in the marsh fire. Now we must hide in the old way."

"It is still the bes' way," *Grandmère* said, wiping her knife free of blood and reaching out for the armload of dried skins that little Napoléon handed her. "Come see . . ."

She turned to a faded, patched mattress which hung limply across the top of her chicken coop, and ripped open a seam with her skinning knife. Quickly she drew out the grey moss stuffing, stacked the armload of skins carefully inside and replaced some of the moss.

With a sly grin she said, "And now, Mr. Fur Buyer, when you come tomorrow you see nuttin' but my beat-up ole moss mattress."

Baptiste and Mimi laughed at my startled expression and said to *Grandmère*, "Look at yo' guest, *Mam'selle* Pop-eyes. You wanta scare her plum to death, *hein?*"

But *Grandmère* was busy with her own affairs, ignoring me. Now I understood what was going on and why Baptiste said to me softly, "She make you one of us now, *Mam'selle*. If *she* got no secrets, *we* got no secrets . . . *Bien*, it make us close-close friends, for sure."

I was flattered to be so fully in their confidence but saved my thanks in order to listen to more of *Grandmère*'s musings. She was sewing the mattress up swiftly, nodding her grey head as she spoke.

"My cousin Minette, she always lak to keep her furs in loaves of bread, and that Nanette do too . . . but that is a lot of waste to me. *Oui,* the mattress is the bes' way."

Jean looked carefully at the pile of skins which he was sorting for the fur buyer.

"Here's a poor one," he said. "No gloss. Come, Camille, give dis ole 'rat a pretty coat with da stove black."

The other women giggled as Camille picked up the skin. ·With the proud air of an expert, she went inside the campboat.

Jean continued his sorting and the pile of fine pelts grew higher. "Not for five-six year have I seen such pelts," he said.

"It is because of starry nights. When nights are cold, ole mus'rat feels hisself frisky. He come out his dive hole to chase *Mam'selle* Mus'rat. He runs into our traps, and *voilà!*" With his bearded jaws Jean made a sound like a steel trap closing.

"*Non, non,* my brudder," said Adrian, "That is not all. Part of it is we is become smarter than *M'sieu* Mus'rat. We have learn to cover traps so dey do not shine in moonlight or catch flash from the stars. The mus'rat get smarter . . . we get smarter too, *n'est-ce pas?*"

He finished his sorting of skins, placed them carefully in a large apple crate and shouldered the crate toward his camp.

Camille stood in the doorway, holding a fine dark pelt in her outstretched hand.

"Come see, *mon cher* . . . Looka what a pretty black coat has *Monsieur* Mus'rat now!"

"*Eh bien, Madame,* what a top grade 'rat he is now!" Jean laughed and placed the skin on his stack of best pelts.

Like Jean, the other brothers and their wives were finishing work, turning toward their camps. *Grandmère* had gone inside some time before, and now she stood in her doorway and called.

"Coffee's ready, my chil'ren. Come for one lil cup 'fore supper."

We sat at *Grandmère's* table, gossiping and drinking from the tiny demitasse cups, until shouts of the children and the distant purring of a motor called our attention outside.

"*Allo, allo* . . . *Grandpère!* Here come Mr. Émil . . ."

Grandpère padded to the door in his stocking feet, and said disgustedly, "That fur buyer! Why he always come at such a time? An' not due till tomorrow either. I t'ink he want to catch us nappin', *hein?*"

Immediately the gang broke up, brothers and wives scattering to their various camps with sighs, groans and sharp, rich curses.

I stood beside *Grandpère* in the doorway and watched as an immaculately white lugger, with handsome full cabin and shining brass fittings, cruised slowly up the bayou.

The old man spoke quietly, as though thinking to himself. "Ah, Mother of God, how many times I watch that Émil come up dis bayou . . . How many times I see him take our 'rats away . . ."

Grandmère spoke curtly, interrupting his reverie. "Get the lead from yo' britches, ole man, or Monsieur Émil take *all* da rats dis time for sure!"

Tidying up the camp with quick efficient movements, she included *Grandpère* in her work, giving him a gentle push out to the porch deck. I saw him step ashore, pick up a rusty abandoned wash tub and toss it carelessly on top of the mattress which lay over the chicken coop. He turned to the other camps and called:

"What you say, you womens? All is well wit yo' mattresses? Everything is ship-shape for our old friend Émil?"

Mimi shouted from the nearest campboat, "*Oui, P'père.* All is well wit ever'thing . . . don' you mind."

The lugger approached slowly, a crewman standing by with bowline ready to tie up to *Grandpère*'s camp. Inside at the wheel Émil Bourgeois, the fur buyer, leaned toward the window, waving to the various campboats as he passed. The trappers waved back genially and shouted their greetings.

It was almost dark when the lugger nosed into *Grandpère*'s camp and tied to a deck post. Émil Bourgeois was fat, barely five feet tall, greasy-skinned, with small furtive, pig-like eyes which darted restlessly over us and every detail of the camp. For a fat man he seemed possessed of a rare vitality. He bounded off the boat with a grunt, shook hands violently with *Grandpère* and me, pinched *Grandmère*'s cheek familiarly. Shouting a loud greeting to Baptiste and the other trappers, he walked inside the campboat with an air of authority and pulled a chair up to the table.

"*Eh bien* . . . here at last . . . And how about that famous Boudreaux coffee, *hein?* I guess you got some on the stove for ole Émil?"

He roared with laughter as if he had said something clever and lolled back in the chair with a comfortable groan, while his restless eyes roamed the rafters of the campboat. Waiting for *Grandmère* to pour from the small drip pot which never had a chance to grow cold, he finally brought his eyes to rest on me. He did not seem to like what he saw.

"You're the strange lady I hear about on the marsh, *hein?*"

From the corner of my eye I saw *Grandmère* make a face. Before I could answer *Grandpère* said measuredly:

"*Mam'selle* is no strange lady . . . She is our frien' . . . She is the guest of the Boudreaux on the marsh."

Émil nodded and gave me a sly smile. "The trappers' friend, *hein?* Out to make a duck shoot on the marsh, maybe? *Eh bien,* I bid you welcome to the company land, *Mam'selle. Bonne chance* with your hunting."

His laugh had an insincere ring that made me uncomfortable. Suddenly I remembered what Baptiste had said about the "no visitin' law." So that was it! In the fur buyer's book I rated as a suspicious character. The thought amused me and I looked to see if *Grandmère* shared my enjoyment of it. She did not. Nor did *Grandpère*. Both of them were silent, with fixed stubborn frowns of their faces.

I was glad when Baptiste and Camille interrupted this unpleasant conversation and when the other brothers and their wives drifted in to sit at the table or lean their chairs against the walls, shooting questions at Émil.

A kerosene lamp hung on a low rafter overhead, swaying gently with the boat and casting long shadows around the plainly furnished room. Hanging on nails about the walls were half a dozen coonskin hides, stretched on square frames for drying, and two mink skins in long narrow frames. From the rafters of one corner hung several dozen muskrat skins, sending their pungent acrid odor throughout the campboat. An alligator hide hung against one wall, and leaning against other corners were dip nets on long poles, push poles, long hip boots, battered leather jackets and other paraphenalia. On two racks above the door rested a long double-barreled shotgun and a powerful rifle.

Strange, I thought, how much at home I had come to feel in

this simple, functional room. Part of that lay in the warmth
and graciousness of my hosts, who gathered now in the lamp's
circle of light and prodded the fur buyer with questions. Émil
parried them with uncertain answers.

"Ah . . . the price? Wal, it's the same old story, Boudreaux.
The price is poor, *mon dieu* . . . off four cents from last
week . . . It is very poor, yes . . . as always . . . A bad year,
yes, for the trapper and the company too."

The men exchanged glances. Émil shrugged his shoulders
and changed the subject.

"What about some supper, you trappers? Is it not true that
the Boudreaux feed better than any family on the marsh? My
pore ole chops been droolin' all day, just thinkin' about *Grandmère* Boudreaux's jambalaya."

Unable to get any news out of Émil, the brothers and wives
gulped their remaining coffee and began to disperse. Émil had
the parting shot.

"Tomorrow we grade fur early. You mens can get into the
marsh after sun-up for once. Ole Émil is too tired and hungry
for tonight."

Grandmère set the table for four and we sat in silence
through most of the meal. Émil was right about one thing, I
thought—*Grandmère*'s jambalaya must surely have no peers
anywhere in the marshlands.

Next morning, activity centered around the fur buyer's boat.
Each of the trappers stood around with a heavy sack of dried
pelts at his feet, waiting for Émil to finish first with *Grandpère*.
When Émil had graded *Grandpère*'s fur, paying him in cash,
each of the sons took his turn and leapt upon the deck of the
lugger with his heavy sack of pelts dragging behind.

Émil worked silently, automatically, with concentration.
They knew that he was thinking many things as he graded
the fur. Separating the pelts into grades, he soon covered the
deck with four stacks—tops, mediums, shorts, kits and pieces.
Occasionally he found an especially large, glossy pelt, broke
into a smile as he held it high for all to admire. Mostly he was

glum, serious. This was not a time of jollity for anybody.

As Émil finished with each man's skins, he grunted, reached for a pencil and paper, figured in a little brown notebook. Then he gave each man a record of his pelts and announced, "I pay by the round as always . . . sixty cents this week. Fell off four cents since jus' last week, *mes amis*."

The trappers grumbled among themselves, their wives looking peevish and angry. Émil, accustomed to this routine reaction at every trapper's camp along the bayous, was little concerned. He completed the grading finally, sighed and shrugged his shoulders.

"Wal, it's a bad year for us all, *mais* sho. And where, I wonder, is those beautiful rat we use' to fin' on Palmetto Bayou and Plum Bayou and Big Carencro and Belle Isle? They run off into the sea, maybe, no?" He forced a laugh, then looked speculatively at the trappers. The Boudreaux, men and women and children, returned his look with closed faces.

Émil put his cash box in its niche inside the cabin, then jumped off the deck for one more cup of coffee.

In a moment he was back aboard his lugger, signaling his crewman to cast off. "Must get on back to town wit dis stuff," he shouted and waved to the sullen trappers standing around their camps.

The lugger reversed slowly, turned around and headed up the bayou. Soon it was only a small white spot in the immensity of green-gold marsh grasses.

As the trappers watched Émil's boat disappear around a bend in the bayou, each man fingered his handful of bills, recounted them and handed them to his wife.

Almost immediately their faces brightened. Soon there was an air of gayety around all the camps, as though the atmosphere had been cleared of some contamination. The wives, shouting to each other happily, put the cash away in their various safekeeping spots. The men picked up their marsh sticks and 'rat sacks, headed into the marsh with shouts of encouragement and good wishes to each.

"Papa, *he's some trapper, him, and we help him dry the 'rats on the racks.*"

(On facing page) *A fine string of muskrat pelts means a happy season for these trappers.*

I noticed that *Grandpère* still stood in the doorway, making no preparation for going into the marsh. Baptiste yelled to him as he passed.

"Ay, *P'père,* don' forget . . . this is da night for pore *Tante* Cloe's funeral, yes! Jean and me run yo' traps for you today, while you build da coffin, *hein?*"

By this time I was accustomed to mysteries around the trapping camps, but this talk of coffins and funerals topped anything I had encountered so far. By keeping a discreet

silence and concealing my curiosity about many of their
affairs, I had been accepted by the Boudreaux clan as a trust-
worthy friend and ally. What was about to transpire I could
not fathom. Again in my mind I blessed Maxim Terrebonne's
father who had introduced me to the Boudreaux with such an
enthusiastic recommendation that they never doubted my
friendship and loyalty. As indeed they had no reason to.
Already I knew more about the trappers' life on the marsh
than I had hoped to learn in a whole season, more than most
outsiders ever learned. So *Grandmère* assured me. I believed
her and was touched by the family's acceptance. Now, it appeared, I was to learn still more. I took a chair on the porch
deck and tried to look as inconspicuous and non-existent as
possible.

Inside the camp I heard *Grandpère* and *Grandmère* mur-
muring to each other. Then they emerged, *Grandpère* carrying
the first of two large wooden crates which he placed carefully
in his skiff, covering them with two armfuls of moss from
his straggly tree. While he shoved off into the bayou, rowing
toward the other campboats, *Grandmère* motioned me to follow her to the camp of Baptiste and Mimi. Seeing us coming,
Mimi shooed all the children out of the campboat. "You,
'Tavie . . . you, 'Livia . . . all you big-ears, run now . . . This
is not time for house-play, no. You build that bamboo pirogue
for yo' dolls, what you talk about for a week now, *hein?*"
Shoving the last wide-eyed daughter out onto the bayou bank,
Mimi beckoned us in. We watched while she dug energetically
under a stack of quilts in one corner of the cabin and finally
uncovered what appeared to be an ordinary moss mattress.
It turned out to be no more ordinary than *Grandmère*'s moss
mattress of the day before.

When Camille split one side open, a mass of muskrat pelts
fell out on the floor. The women handled the pelts fondly,
smiling as they saw how neatly Baptiste had graded and
stacked them. Mimi gave a little mock kiss to the record book
in which her husband had recorded the contents of the mattress, then shoved it into the bosom of her dress.

"*Très bon, Grandmère . . . très bon.* Nice catch for da firs' month, *hein?* My man Baptiste, he one fine trapper, him!"

Her face was all smiles as she placed the packages of pelts into a large wooden crate and motioned for *Grandpère* to load it into his skiff.

We stood on the porch deck and watched as *Grandpère* went from one campboat to another, knowing that the scene was being repeated in each camp. The women handled the pelts fondly, smiling as they took them from their hiding places and added them to the collection in *Grandpère's* skiff. Each family's catch was recorded in a little record book and kept in its own place in the skiff. As *Grandpère* left each camp, he covered his load carefully with moss. A stranger passing along the bayou by the Boudreaux camps would see nothing suspicious in the old man's loaded boat, for trappers used moss to keep sun and water off all kinds of things.

By the time *Grandpère* had visited every campboat, his skiff was heavy with its valuable load. It floated low in the water with the gunwales barely clearing the surface of the bayou. When he returned to our camp, *Grandmère* and I helped him pull the boat up on the shallow shore. Carefully *Grandpère* rearranged the moss, threw an old canvas over the top, leaned a broken push-pole against the loaded skiff. As a final note in his artistic design of concealment, he tossed a broken dip net against it.

We stood back to admire his handiwork and *Grandmère* whispered, "*Mon dieu,* it is beautiful, yes!"

Then she said to *Grandpère* fondly, "Sit here and res', *cher,* and I will get yo' tools from the shed."

Going into the palmetto-roofed tool shed, *Grandmère* returned with hammer, saw and a canvas bag full of nails. Then she went back for an armful of new lumber. Some of the girls from Mimi's camp came out to help her, each one carrying a single board in her arms and placing it carefully on the stack of lumber.

Finally, *Grandpère* began his work. As women and children looked on he laid out the skeleton of a wooden coffin. It was a day-long task, building the coffin, and it called for many stops for coffee, much gayety and laughter from the onlookers as the coffin took shape and finish under *Grandpère's* skilled hands.

By late afternoon, he had finished. As a final touch, working with the true artist's pride and care, he fashioned two handles from rope and attached them to each end of the coffin and to the top and bottom of the lid.

When the trappers returned from the marsh there was loud laughter among them. Each man came by, pulled along by his children or wife to see *Grandpère's* handiwork and congratulate the old man on his artistry.

Grandpère, enjoying the attention, tried to conceal his pleasure by urging them in a gruff voice, "*Allons*, my sons, we mus' make time this night. Get your suppers early and eat plenty. We hav' many miles to go and *Tante* Cloe must have her funeral before midnight."

Still mystified, I joined the two old people at the supper table. *Grandmère* had cooked a chicken gumbo "in honor to *Tante* Cloe," she said with a grin. *Grandpère* ate silently, tired from his long day's work, and left the table soon.

Just before dark his sons gathered on the bayou bank. *Grandpère* gave directions as they uncovered the crates in his skiff, loaded boxes of pelts into the coffin, and lifted the coffin into Baptiste's larger skiff. One of the older boys was posted as lookout although *Grandpère* said:

"That Émil, he far gone from here by now. By dis time he over in Creole Pass eatin' up da groceries of the Brunay gang."

When the coffin was filled completely, they placed the lid on, covered it with *Grandmère's* crepe-paper flowers and stood around to admire it.

The children laughed loudly and the wives giggled.

"Pore old *Tante* Cloe, she die ever' year."

"But look how pretty her coffin look. She get prettier ever year, *hein?*"

Grandpère said modestly, "She is a beautiful corpse o' treasure, *mais* sho. An' it is a blessed miracle, yes, that nobody ain' never see her coffin but us."

Grandmère added, "She is so *très jolie*, sometime I wish ole Émil and the others could see her."

"Hush, *ma chère*," said *Grandpère*. "Don' wish a thing lak that on us. *Mon dieu*, you ruin us, for sure."

It was dark by now and lamps were going on in all the campboats. Women were calling children inside, shouting admonitions to their husbands.

"Hurry now, you mens, or you never get her to that place in time. You wanta waste all yo' trouble by bein' late to the burying grounds, *hein?*"

The men gathered around the loaded skiff as *Grandpère* placed a final touch on his creation. They chuckled as he nailed the base of a crude kerosene lamp into the top of the coffin, and lifted the globe to light the wick.

"Now, my sons, your *Tante* Cloe be ready," he said with a little laugh. "Watch yo'selfs on the way. If a wind come off the Gulf, you better kill the lamp."

Toto, Baptiste's oldest boy, took his place proudly in the skiff behind the coffin.

"You watch her good, you Toto," said *Grandpère*, then smiled at the boy, "Your firs' funeral, *hein, cher!* You watch close now."

Baptiste tied the skiff to his own boat and the other brothers took places in pirogues behind the coffin-laden skiff. Baptiste stood with a push-pole in the bow and leaned on it heavily. The boats moved slowly away from the bank, with barely a ripple and barely a sound. It did indeed look like a small funeral procession.

As the line of boats passed each camp, women and children poured out on porch decks to call out laughing comments and encouragement.

"Poor *Tante* Cloe, it is for the third time she die," said Fifi to Coco. "But that Émil he never once run into her funeral procession. Me, I t'ink the mens make too much care of it."

Coco said, "But, *Maman*, she do look so pretty, the coffin wit flowers and da lamp. *Grandpère* like it this way, like in da ole days, *mais* sho. I think it better this way."

I sat in the stern of Jean's pirogue, silent, knowing that the men would regret their generosity to me if I murmured a single word. Gripping my heavy mackinaw tighter against the cold night, I hunched my shoulders in the darkness.

The procession wound slowly down the bayou, with the lantern atop the coffin casting long slants of yellow light on the still water. We traveled in deep silence for two hours. The black night fit around us like a velvet glove.

Once we passed two large skiffs, each with a man rowing in standing position. The men hailed us as they passed.

"*Allo,* Boudreaux. What goes on wit you mens?"

"*Allo,* Sylvester. You come from Montaigne's boat, *hein?*"

"*Oui, mon ami,*" the first man said to Baptiste. "He jus' aroun' the next bend."

The other man said, "But yo' pore Cloe, she die again like las' year, *hein?*" He laughed and the other chuckled appreciatively as they drew away from us and pulled on up the bayou.

Baptiste and the other Boudreaux continued to row silently and with care, slowly now, for the loaded skiff grew heavier and Baptiste breathed with a sort of sigh in his chest. Adrian called softly to him, offering to spell him in the lead boat, but Baptiste refused.

Finally we rounded a bend in the bayou and saw a streak of yellow light streaming like a ribbon down the dark water. I heard Jean curse softly under his breath, then whisper:

"That devil Montaigne . . . He's a chance-taker, I guarantee you. He get us all in trouble bein' so proud o' his big cruiser he got to beam it like a lighthouse on the marsh."

At the head of the streamer of light I saw the black silhouette of a sleek cabin cruiser. It floated without a sound on the darkened waters, but a light below decks indicated that there was life aboard.

As the glow from *Tante* Cloe's coffin joined the yellow light from the big cruiser, Baptiste slowed, motioned Toto to blow out the lantern. At the same moment, someone stepped on deck

from inside the cruiser, closing the cabin door and cutting off
the boat's light. The night suddenly became dark as the inside
of a tomb, and was silent. I shivered. Then the soft rustling
of wind in the grasses gave a voice to the encircling marshlands.

I heard Baptiste give a low whistle, like a pelican's cry, and
from the deck of the cruiser came an answering whistle. We
eased alongside the cruiser, the men glad to rest with one hand
on the boat's gunwales and wait.

The man on the cruiser spoke softly,

"Ah, Baptiste, you Boudreaux are the last to come. What
kep' you, man?"

"We hav' to build the coffin again like new," said Baptiste.
"And we mus' proceed slowly for the funeral, *mais non*?
Don' forget we gotta pass t'ree of Émil's pet camps to get here,
an' that call for care."

The man Montaigne nodded sympathetically. He held a
flashlight in his hand and used it to examine the coffin. His
lips gave an appreciative sucking sound as he noted its size.
It took three of the brothers to lift it from the skiff and put it
on the boat deck. Montaigne chuckled happily as he lighted
their work. Baptiste, panting as they finished, rested on the
deck. The others ringed around the coffin and urged Montaigne
to proceed quickly with the business.

Deftly they opened the coffin and each man laid his pelts
on the deck before him. I saw the eyes of Montaigne, the night
buyer, glisten in the reflected light from his torch. He graded
the pelts swiftly, while the brothers looked on outside the
circle of light.

"What price you give this trip, Montaigne?" Baptiste
whispered.

"I give dollar ten per round dis trip," the bootleg fur buyer
said quietly. "It is four bits a round more that you got this
morning from that pig Émil, *hein*?"

The brothers looked at each other and smiled with satisfaction.

"It is worth a good funeral," said Jean. "You are a good

man, Montaigne, and the trappers' friend."

Adrian cautioned him, "You be careful in town, man, and don' get yo'self tangled up wit them company spies. We don't wanta lose you on dis bayou, *mon dieu*."

Montaigne nodded, kept on with his grading, making notes in a shabby black notebook. Finally, he went into the cabin and returned with a bulging bag of bank notes. He pealed off a bunch of bills for each man, pointing to the totals in his notebook as he paid.

"Twelve hundred betweens you," he said. "Not bad for a couple week's extra fur, *eh, mes cousins*?"

Little Toto let out a shout and it cut across the still marsh like a lion's roar. His father grabbed him and popped a big hand over his mouth. Startled and frightened, the men became motionless, looked at each other with apprehension. No other sound broke the heavy silence of the marsh, and finally they broke their frozen positions and began moving quietly to their skiffs and pirogues.

Montaigne muttered, "Get along now . . . Me, I mus' be in town by midnight. They wait at the ole warehouse."

As we pulled away from the cruiser, the night buyer went into his cabin, started his smoothly purring motor. When we were a hundred yards down the bayou we heard him reverse the boat slowly, with muffled motor, and turn toward the bay and town.

Our procession made more time on the way home, without the weight and forced solemnity of *Tante* Cloe's coffin. There was a feeling of gayety in all the men. When we sighted the camps, with a tiny spot of light in each to tell that the wives were waiting up for their arrival, they let out shouts and piercing rebel yells.

By the time we tied to porch decks, the wives and older children were there, shouting and calling to us, laughing, reaching for the tie lines. *Grandmère* had fixed coffee in a huge pot saved especially for such occasions, and the clan moved automatically toward her camp. Soon the porch deck, the living room and the bayou bank before the campboat was crowded

with her sons, daughters, and grandchildren—rubbing their
sleepy eyes and not wanting to miss the celebration.

The crowd proved almost too much for *Grandmère's* coffee
pot and as it began to run low, *Grandpère* disappeared into the
kitchen. In a moment he was back, bearing a fifth of bourbon
which he set down triumphantly in the middle of the table.

"Now, ole woman, how about some cherry flips for these
mens and womens? Coffee ain' strong enuf for us mens with
big city money in our pants, no!"

Jean shouted, "Wait and I'll get some of ole Émil's ice to
cool them cherry flips." He bounded out of the cabin toward
his own camp. Returning in a moment, he carried a twenty-
five-pound cake of ice in his arms.

"Ole Émil gotta right to be represent' in dis party, even if
it just in a cake o' ice, *mais* sho. He mighty gen'rous yesterday
with his ice for my tea. He know how I loves my ice tea!"

"*Oui*, you love yo' ice tea flavored with whiskey and cherry
and you loves it plenty!" affirmed Camille.

Mimi and *Grandmère* were busy getting down the glasses
and the cans of cherry juice. Baptiste cut the ice for the drinks,
filled the tall glasses, added a big jigger of bourbon and
topped it with a portion of cherry juice.

When all the grownups had a cherry flip in front of them,
Grandpère raised his glass and made a toast:

"*Bonne chance* to Montaigne, better funerals to *Tante* Cloe
and happiness to all my chil'ren!" He beamed at us round the
table, then took a long gulp of his drink and smacked his lips
appreciatively.

The cherry flip, made on the marsh by the Boudreaux,
seemed to me then the most satisfying drink I had ever had.
Still a little chilled from the long ride on the cold marsh, my
bones seemed to have been calling for this strong, warm bite
of bourbon and cherry.

Baptiste, mixing a second drink for the men, proposed another toast. "To Émil, ole skinflint, and to ice he bring fer
our drinks!"

Adrian lifted his glass to me. "To *Mam'selle la* Trapper,

and her pleasure with us this season!"

The toast brought a cheer from the trappers' families and more laughter when Baptiste described again my awkwardness on the marsh.

Soon the drinks and the gayety began to grow weaker. It had been a long day, a successful night, but there was tomorrow and the trap lines waiting. The brothers and their wives drifted out in pairs. The children had already slipped away. Soon we were left alone. Sleep had seldom been as good to me as it was that night in my bunk in *Grandpère's* camp. My only sorrow was the thought which came to me just as I lost consciousness—the remembrance that tomorrow I must leave the Boudreaux and go back to town.

It seemed less than an hour till I was awakened by the sound of a motor coughing and spitting along the bayou. It was Jacques Thibodaux—my ride to town!

I dressed in a moment and joined *Grandmère* and *Grandpère* in the kitchen. Outside the dawn was breaking with soft, muted colors creeping lazily over the marsh. My bag was packed. All I had to do was follow Jacques to his boat and step aboard. I wished there were some way to delay my going, but could think of nothing. It was hard to part with the Boudreaux. They had made me feel like one of them and now it was as if I were leaving my own people.

We had agreed that there would be no formal farewells, for I had given my promise to return for another visit before the season closed. A quick embrace for *Grandpère* and *Grandmère* and I was ready to go.

As I stepped aboard Jacques' gasboat and looked back toward the other camps, I saw that the brothers and their wives, with a goodly sprinkling of children, were standing on their porch decks to wave good-bye.

Jacques' motor sputtered in protest. But it moved into action, and we broke the still bayou water ahead with our bow. The calls and waves of the Boudreaux followed until we rounded the first nearby bend, and then they were gone. We were engulfed by towering marsh grass, traveling a grey-blue line through the roseau-cane. Ahead of us a white crane left its perch on a log and led us straight down the blue bayou. The rising sun began to warm us, turning the marsh into bright gold. Town seemed a far way off, but I knew we would be there by early afternoon, with the world of the marshlands behind us.

Jacques was not a talkative fellow and I kept my thoughts to myself for a couple of hours or so. The brown, brawny man with bushy black brows and heavy scowl seemed strangely foreign after the open-faced heartiness of the Boudreaux. Yet I knew he was their friend and therefore felt kindly toward me.

Finally, I asked him the question.

"Would you say that the Boudreaux are Cajuns?"

"Cajuns, *Mam'selle?* Why, ever'body know the Boudreaux is French, *Mam'selle,* with a little German mix. But they's insult if you think them Cajuns. They's peoples come firs' from da ole country—*oui*, Brittany, it was. And they great-*grandpère* come from one dem islands, Santo Domingo, I think. *Grandmère* Boudreaux say her *p'père* settle early in Bayou des Allemands—he wuz a German soldier once. Wal, you can say it for yo'self, *Mam'selle,* but I do not call the Boudreaux Cajuns, me."

Jacques paused and looked thoughtfully over the water prairies. "You want to see some real Cajuns, *Mam'selle?* They's swamp people, them. You know who can show you? Cap'n Dew Robert Vuillemont! That fishboat captain know dem peoples plenty."

The name sounded strangely familiar. Then I remembered Cap'n Brown Blakeman and the tone of his voice as he said, "Me, there's jes' one man in the whole worl' I envy—that Dew Robert Vuillemont what skippers the fishboat *Elaine.*"

With Jacques Thibodaux to introduce me, maybe I could see for myself what he meant.

Cap'n Dew Robert

and the Fishboat "Elaine"

xi

From atop the mighty arch of the Highway 90 bridge at Morgan City the fishboat *Elaine* looked like an undersize water bug as she pointed her bow against surging currents of the great Atchafalaya. She seemed a tiny midget of a water bug, bucking the red anger of a river captured at last from its upstream spreadings, twistings and meanderings, and forced to act like any other decent river, to hold a steady course between two substantial and strongly outlined banks.

The *Elaine* made a thin and wavering wake against the glistening sun-streaked surface of the big stream. And from the looks of her she would have need of courage as she set out into the mysterious, broad and sprawling waters of the Atchafalaya Basin.

For, as Captain Brown Blakeman had told me, this was a river and a region still unknown, not fully explored, still spoken of with awe by rivermen from Pittsburgh to St. Joe, and gossiped about by oldsters on levee banks above and below New Orleans.

Into this weird, wild region Captain Dew Robert Vuillemont took his sturdy little forty-foot lugger on two three-day trips every week. At Jacques Thibodaux's request he agreed to take me on as "crew" for a trip. It was a thrilling thing to anticipate, for surely there was not a better way to explore the remote recesses of the Atchafalaya's Great Basin, nor a more likely way to find my elusive bayou Cajun.

To Captain Dew Robert the *Elaine* was home. And the devious waterways of the Great Basin of the Atchafalaya into which he piloted her, was home. And the many strange people who inhabit these waterways were Captain Dew Robert's people, for he was born among them, a swamper himself, born on a tiny island in the midst of this bewildering land-and-water country.

From my vantage point on the highway bridge I saw that the *Elaine* had taken on her ice and gasoline and was heading into the dock, ready for leave-taking. I hurried down to board her.

As the fishboat left her Morgan City moorings, Cap'n Dew Robert was in high spirits. Standing at the wheel in his crowded pilothouse, clad in khakis and bright plaid jacket, he was a jaunty figure. He wore his battered hunting cap as if it were an admiral's decorated headgear.

I felt the strong affinity between this red-haired riverman and his cheery little vessel. Both of them had the lilting manner of the Louisiana French. Both fit to perfection the life they led in the treacherous Atchafalaya Basin swamps, where a boat and a man needed strength—and cleverness, initiative and imagination—if they were to meet the swamp's hard tests of valor.

Built on a design brought many years ago from Brittany and Normandy by French émigrés, the *Elaine* was a forty-foot, half-cabin lugger powered efficiently with a sixty-horsepower Diesel. Her cabin was cozy and comfortable, her twelve-foot decks broad, warm and bright in the sunlight, her hold built fat and big to bring in a bountiful fisheries harvest. Although she carried a wildly assorted cargo, the *Elaine* was primarily a fishboat into whose hold her captain would load a great variety of finny products bought from fishermen of the interior waters.

To dozens of families on her route the *Elaine* also served as general store and mail deliverer, the main connecting link with the world beyond the bayous. Through her and her doughty captain they caught a glimpse of how life moved on "the outside," as the swampers called the landlubber's world beyond their own watery universe. On the lugger which he named for his thirteen-year-old daughter, Cap'n Dew Robert brought messages from town, papers, books, and the mail-order catalogue which was often the swampers' complete library. Also fishing tackle, twine, hip boots, oil slickers, shotgun shells, new clothes, medicine, toys for children, candy, gum, liquor— everything.

Before the *Elaine* had traveled far from her dock, loquacious Cap'n Dew Robert was launched on his favorite subject —the Great Basin of the Atchafalaya and his life among its devious water trails.

"Morgan City's jumbo men tell me the sea she like a woman. Wal, I t'ink the Basin like dat too. She a wench, though, dat's for sure . . . A changeable, cheatin', hard-to-handle slut . . . She drive a man crazy tryin' to figure her out."

The skipper ran a gnarled hand through his shock of red hair and struggled to describe his watery homeland.

"Can't make up 'er mind if she river or lake! Or maybe a mess of bayous and sloughs . . . I t'ink she really one awful big lake, by dam'! She Grand Lake, you know . . . and dozen, maybe two dozen littler lakes. God knows how many islands . . ."

His last phrase gave me a shock, for I had heard almost the same words from Cap'n Brown Blakeman and had seen enough of the Great Basin from the high, white decks of the *Kursweg* to understand something of the captain's frustration. Surely in his forty-five years of living among meandering bayous of the

Atchafalaya's diverse water system, Captain Dew Robert had seen as many mysteries as any riverman in America.

We were making good headway against the swift currents. Behind us the great highway span at Morgan City began to lose its grandeur, to take on the diminutive look that had been the *Elaine*'s when I first glimpsed her from its soaring height.

Now we passed the big houseboat community called the Borrow Pit, just over the levee. Digging beneath crowded shelves of the pilot cabin, Cap'n Dew Robert came up with a pair of fine German glasses. Training them on a campboat which lay at the very end of the little canal, he waved to his wife who stood on the deck of their home.

He told me that his wife, like himself, had grown up in the Atchafalaya Basin, but she preferred to live in town in order to keep their two youngest children in school and to be nearer their oldest son, married now and living in a town close by.

"My younges' boy love da swamps like I do," said the captain. "Pore lil thing . . . his *maman* she dead set for him to finish school in Morgan City, and many time he cry and cry, he want to come wit me so bad."

As he spoke he turned the wheel deftly and pointed the *Elaine*'s bow straight into the broad waters ahead.

There was a sudden change of tempo. Tremors ran through the lugger's timbers. A look at the captain's face told me that we were now well on our way into the river's Great Basin.

To Cap'n Dew Robert each voyage was a new adventure.

"*Le bon dieu* hisself is the onlyest one who know what we bring in this trip," he said. "Me, I hope it's two thousand pounds of blue cat and not so much *goujon* . . . ah, and plenty of *gaspergou*, and not so many little crayfish, by dam' . . . a good trip I betcha!"

Turning to his chart, glued to the side of the crowded pilot cabin, he pointed out our course. This chart by which he navigated the Atchafalaya's intricate water system was a collector's item. Enough to turn an ordinary river captain blue with fear, it was nothing more than a battered, weather-beaten Louisiana highway map.

"Looka dat chart," he said, taking some pride in the wide area representing the river's Great Basin.

"They's nothing but emptiness on da chart from the source of the river to Morgan City. That's lengthwises. And crosswises they's just as much emptiness. Grand Lake she colored blue on da map. The res' she just green emptiness wit bayous running through like snakes. Ah, that is Great Basin awright, and a by-dam' lot of it, if anyone aks you."

Like sailors everywhere, Cap'n Dew Robert loves, and hates, the waters he navigates. From him I learned many things about this strange waterway.

It was evident that he agreed with river engineers who

This is a typical trading post on the Atchafalaya, where fishboats and fur boats unload their rich harvests from the Big Basin and from marsh country around and below Morgan City.

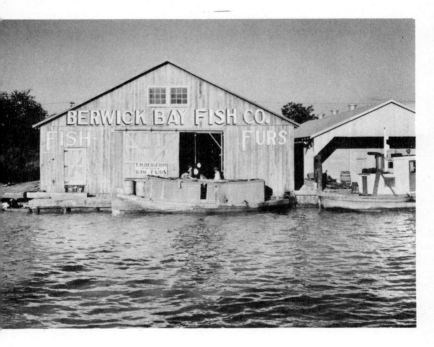

thought of the Atchafalaya as America's River of Doubt, for
at its very beginning the Atchafalaya was a peculiar thing in
rivers, more unpredictable than the Mississippi. Its source
was at a point three hundred miles above New Orleans, where
the Mississippi forked to the west to form a short channel
known as Old River or "The Gut." This channel, just eight
miles long, met the Red River of the South, flowing down out
of Oklahoma and North Louisiana, and the two streams
merged to form the beginning of the Atchafalaya.

Actually the mysterious river was spawned by two different
mothers. In the fall its mother was the Red which sent long,
copper-colored streaks curling down the swamps. In the spring
the Mississippi was its mother and sent a great flood of water
down the Upper Atchafalaya. For thirty miles this made a
swift, deep river flowing between well-contained banks; then
it burst into the myriad bayous, cuts and bays of the Lower
Atchafalaya Basin.

"From there on out, she crazies' river any boatman ever
seen, I guarantee you. You gonna watch her good now. Maybe
when you see the Basin for yo'self, you tell me if she angel
or devil . . ."

We had passed from the flat reaches of Six Mile Lake
through a bayou that led into bigger, sprawling Grand Lake.
Now, abruptly, as we approached Grand Lake's northern exit,
Cap'n Dew Robert clamped my hands over the *Elaine*'s pilot
wheel.

Bounding out of the cabin, he grabbed a long grapple iron
and hauled aboard a five-gallon gasoline can which swift
currents had borne down upon us. He stached the gas can away
on the crowded deck and, grinning sheepishly, returned to take
the wheel.

"My oldes' boy, when he use to make trips wit me, say he
had the coocoo-iest dad that ever ran a fishboat, the way I was
alla time latching onto funniest things when they floated by.

"But me, I say you watch me sell this driftin' can to some
swamper fer enough to buy the wife a pair of fancy stockings.
Ah, you be surprised how much stuff I pick up floatin' in

bayous and sell right back to swampers themselves. I study the waters and read 'em for information. Many time when we well up into the littler bayous, I look at driftin' water and mostly tell you who's visiting whose camp ahead of us, by the brand of empty tobacco can I see drift by . . . and whose wife she want to buy coffee, by the brand of empty coffee tin . . . and all kinds of funny stuff, if you know the peop' and all. We come to the firs' camp soon and you see what I mean . . . Bet you two can of beer that I can sell that gas can . . . and that Mrs. Alcide St. Martin buy a can o' coffee . . ."

From out of Grand Lake's choppy waters the *Elaine* entered Bayou Boutte, first of several tree-bordered, sparsely inhabitated bayous where she plied her trade. We were now deep in the interior swamps of the Great Basin. Around a bend we came in sight of Bayou Boutte Landing.

With a stinging suddenness the air came alive. The *Elaine* seemed to quiver through her hull, her Diesel motor roared and she bounded forward like a race horse.

Gradually she slowed as we neared four or five campboats lying cozily alongside each other, tied to giant cypress trees in the grey-blue water of the bayou.

Everywhere there were people—oldsters, youngsters and babies—all busy, laughing, shouting to each other in gumbo-French. Boats were all over the place, of all kinds and sizes. Everybody seemed to have his own water craft and know exactly how to handle it.

There was swiftness and deftness in these water-dwellers. They were completely at home in their floating homes, their gasboats, rowboats, "plankboats" and pirogues, and even on the bouncing logs which made up their walks and pathways.

To us, coming out of the still atmosphere at the bayou's mouth, this activity seemed rapid, intense, even feverish. Fishermen families worked furiously at tarring their nets, knitting new nets, repairing boat motors, building pirogues.

From limbs of cypresses hung long black hoop nets. Fifty-gallon oil drums, black and filled with tar, floated on platforms among the three trunks. Smoke and fumes rose from the drums. One group of men was busy "tarring up"—dipping huge hoop nets in coal tar to make them withstand the rigors of underwater service. Young men were best for this job. It took strong muscles to struggle with the windlass and pull big nets, heavy with tar, out of their tubs and high into the air to dry.

Children enjoyed the sight and hung out of campboat windows, shouting encouragement. Old men sat in pirogues, held a quiet paddle, and gave advice.

This was the camp of a single family, three branches living on five separate "flatboats," as they called their campboats in this region, and all working together at the common task of fishing.

At the sound of the *Elaine's* pert horn, all work stopped, suddenly and completely. Everybody, young and old, hailed the approaching fishboat. Almost before we docked, swampers poured over the *Elaine's* decks, making her lurch giddily. Those who couldn't get a footing on deck tied their pirogues alongside. They all laughed loudly, shouted jokes to the captain.

"*Comme ça*, ole alligator-face, you gotta nerve keeping me waitin' for dat twine, *hein?* How you t'ink dis pore fisherman gone to win dat bet wit my new brudder-'n-law Bootsy, if I can't get my nets in them catfish holes?"

The women, impatient to trade with the fishboat captain, piled aboard first to bargin for groceries or mail-order clothes he was delivering.

Although the tiny cabin held only one shopper at a time and the stock was limited to what could be crammed into half a dozen shelves hanging from the five- by ten-foot walls, these wives seemed to get the same thrill from their shopping as their city cousins did in a supermarket.

As one wizened old lady searched through the shelves of canned goods, Cap'n Dew Robert said, "Ah, Mrs. Alcide, you lookin' for your special coffee, yes? I got it right here for you."

She counted out her change and the captain added, "Mrs. Alcide, she know a good coffee when she see it, *hein?*"

He winked at me and murmured, "One can of beer for me!"

Crab fishermen leave the dock in Morgan City and head across the Atchafalaya on their way to the Great Basin swamps.

Finally, when all women and children were cleared off the the deck, the captain began his real work—buying fish from the swampers.

Men and boys of the camp opened floating fishcars, tied to stakes in shallow water, and dipped up bulging nets. One car held all blue cat, some weighing up to a hundred and fifteen pounds. Another held *goujon,* the yellow or mud cat which sometimes is bigger than the blue. In another fishcar there was a great splashing and thrashing that the captain said was *gaspergou,* or drum, or buffalo.

A couple of young boys, teen-aged and toothy with grins, brought aboard two loads of frogs which they had gigged with grappling poles during the long, dark swamp night.

One man brought in three snapping turtles as big as wash tubs. The captain did not relish having these aboard as they must be kept alive—and snapping—until the *Elaine*'s return to Morgan City. But he bought them nevertheless, for the same fisherman might have a carload of fat blue cat on the fishboat's next trip.

A tall, bearded fellow pulled his pirogue alongside and unloaded three hundred-pound sacks of monstrously big crayfish. Almost as large as California lobsters, these red crayfish, known as "crawfish" to the swampers, were a delicacy in New Orleans' swank restaurants where French chefs prepared delicious crayfish bisque.

Cap'n Dew Robert weighed all the catches on big scales which hung over the forward deck, then turned the heavy baskets toward *Elaine*'s ice-lined open hold. Catfish, scalefish, crayfish, frogs—hundreds upon hundreds of pounds, basket after basket of them—slithered and slid in a silvery mass into the ice. As each man's product was weighed, Cap'n Dew Robert paid him off in cash. He shoveled white layers of crushed ice over his load, battened down the hatch and paused for a moment's conversation with his customers who, like fishermen everywhere, find theirs the most exciting trade in the world.

I had a chance to look closely at the swampers. The men wore a wide assortment of costumes, all with a strong marine flavor. Belts of their bluejeans held up olive-green hip boots. Neatly patched khakis were covered with heavy, black oilcloth overalls. Long hip boots, whether tied to their belts or crumpled below their knees, gave them a swashbuckling, piratical look. The women, especially those youthful ones whose dark French beauty had not faded with the difficult swamp life, wore brightly colored cheap cottons. Most of the children wore very little and, like the majority of the womenfolk, were barefoot.

Cap'n Dew Robert spoke to one tall, booted fisherman. "Alphonse, my friend, you need another gas can like I sold you las' trip? I had you in mind for another one, and got it right here wit me!"

Alphonse reached for his wallet gratefully, then rolled the gas can off the deck. The captain grinned broadly at me, and smacked his lips over an imaginary can of beer.

Then the fishermen's talk was interrupted by Bootsy, a shy, handsome youth, coming aboard holding the hand of his beautiful tawny-skinned bride.

When they asked us to dinner, Cap'n Dew Robert and I followed to their tiny ten- by fifteen-foot floating home.

Bootsy grinned proudly as he seated us at the table.

"My 'Ti Bébé, she some good cook, her."

We found it true, for 'Ti Bébé's stewed chicken and her catfish court bouillon were pure magic, even in that country of exquisite cooking.

I asked for the recipe, of course. Like all good recipes of South Louisiana, they begin with "first you take the *roux.*" Anybody knows what the *roux* is—a Yankee's gravy gone to Heaven.

The stewed chicken recipe I took down as she gave it to me.

"First you take the *roux.* To make it you need half a teacup of oil, good and hot, in a skillet. Then you jus' stir in a large cookspoon of flour, stirring fast-fast, so to keep it from burning. Some folks like a dark *roux* and some like a light *roux,* but when you got yours just like you want it, sort of medium brown, you add your chopped-up onions, about two cupfuls, and let them get brown too. Already you have fried the chicken, so now you jus' put the *roux* into the big black stewpot, add the chicken to it, add enough water to cover it, and let it cook a long-long time; keep addin' water and stirrin' till the chicken is tender, depending on how ole the chicken is, about one and a half hours, I guess."

'Ti Bébé's recipe for catfish court bouillon which she pronounced "coobyawn" was one of the finest I ever heard:

"Supposin' you want to serve four folks, like us now," she said, "and supposin' you can get Dew Robert to bring you some celery and green peppers on the boat, well, you cut up two medium-size onions, real fine, and one green pepper and six stalks of celery. You fry these in four level tablespoons of bacon grease and on a slow fire till they're barely brown, and be sure to put in the onions last. Then you add one large can of tomatoes, chopped up, two cans of tomato paste, one can of water, one quarter lemon sliced thin and includin' the rind, one clove of garlic chipped up fine, and a good lot of salt. You stew this for a long time, real slow, about two hours, in the big black stewpot. When it's ready, you cut your fish bite-size and put into the stew and cook it—without stirring, of course—for about twenty minutes. About two pounds of catfish for this amount of stew.

"So that's your court bouillon and when it's ready you jus' put it on da table and serve it, always of course on *top* of your rice. If you cook rice *with* court bouillon instead of extry, that would make it lak a jambalaya."

Before I could get details of 'Ti Bébé's jambalaya, the captain rose and announced that we must get the *Elaine* underway.

Back aboard the lugger, we cast off and pulled away from Bayou Boutte Landing, heading into another of the quiet bayous of the Great Basin. The captain lighted a cigarette, leaned against the pilot wheel and began to talk about the people of this swampy wilderness.

In the old days, he said, Great Basin swampers were a wild and Godless crew, second cousins to the turtle and the alligator. Strange and mysterious in all their ways, they were held in deadly fear by those few people of "the Outside" who dared venture into the interior.

Swampers were mostly outlaws who drifted in on flatboats or jumped cargo vessels on the big Mississippi River. Frenchmen living in bayou towns nearer the Gulf did not understand them, for they hailed from such far north places as Tennessee, Kentucky, and Ohio—and they were tall like Texans and had yellow hair and blue eyes. A fierce breed of men, for sure, and it was not safe to ask one of them exactly *where* he hailed from or why he had come to the big swamp.

For many years there were no churches and no schools at all in the settlements which slowly grew up around fishermen's camps. Social life was rowdy and wild. At big dances, known as King and Queen Balls, the chief excitement was not dancing but a deadly kind of gang war. Victims were sometimes cut and stabbed with long Bowie knives and forced to swim the bayou under gunfire.

But gradually the outlaw swamp communities felt the softening influences of civilization. The coming of "putt-putt" motors allowed children and grandchildren to have closer contact with "the Outside". The boorish strangers began to marry with fun-loving French and to fall into their slow, pleasant rhythms of life.

Schools were still scarce, but these people were unusually grateful for what educational chances they had. It was a fine

Maman *will cook this fine catch in a court bouillon better than anything you'll ever eat in New Orleans.*

sight to see a loaded school "bus," a long gasboat crowded
with brightly clothed, laughing children, go rushing past the
slow-moving fishboat, or to see the school boat tied up before
one of the tiny one-room schools on a bayou bank.

Cap'n Dew Robert told me how he had helped one fishing
community get a school simply by speaking to the parish
superintendent. And how the swampers expressed their thanks,
saying "Dew Robert done pass us a miracle, him!" And they
proved their gratitude by keeping a near-perfect attendance
record, second highest in the whole parish, in spite of rains,
floods, and icy winds that made a bitter thing of winter in
the swamps.

On our three-day trip through the Great Basin we saw as
wide a variety of poverty and prosperity as could be seen in
any similar set of communities on "the Outside." For here
as elsewhere, men varied widely in talents, skill, and indus-
triousness.

We saw cabins built on bayou banks with no floors at all
and with splits in the wallboards letting cruel winds surge
through. Some swampers lived in almost unbelievable filth
and their children knew nothing at all of the use of a toilet,
not even a primitive Chick Sales.

A few families enjoyed comparative prosperity, with well-
furnished flatboats, many conveniences of town life, and a fleet
of cabin boats, gasboats, and outboard motorboats.

The swampers' investment in property, while not as high
as a home-owner's in town, represented considerable cash for
one whose income was so variable. An average flatboat home
cost about eight hundred dollars, one gasboat (most families
had two or three) cost about five hundred. Additional equipment included several plankboats or pirogues averaging about
fifty dollars each. Several families had factory-built cruisers
which cost several thousand dollars.

Fishing rig was expensive. A fisherman usually worked from
twenty-five to one hundred big hoop nets at a time—at fifteen
dollars each—and these were easily worn, had to be replaced
often. In hoop nets alone, his basic equipment cost from three

hundred and seventy-five to fifteen hundred dollars. A cray-fish rig, for one month of springtime fishing, added another three hundred.

Good swamp fishermen could clear about one hundred and fifty dollars per week during the best seasons, about forty during bad times. Poor fishermen sometimes earned nothing at all. Spring fishing "in the woods," more thrilling but not as lucrative as in the winter season, averaged for a good many about seventy-five dollars a week.

Like their friends the muskrat trappers of the Gulf marsh-lands, these fishermen were inclined to blow their cash with extravagant living in good seasons, only to scrimp to the point of starvation at others.

In the spring, with fish running thick "in the woods" of flooded swamplands, the air sang with the good life. You could almost hear the echoes of cash jingling along the bayous. Swampers felt a sort of fishing fever, similar to that irresistible fever that trappers felt with the first frosty days of winter. Fishermen pulled alongside each other in the bayous, talked eagerly of lines and nets they were preparing, looked long at pale skies and shivered a little in the spring wind.

"The big 'uns will be running soon," they would say, "I got my nets ashinin' like black diamonds out dere."

"Me, I gonna snag more cat out of dem woods than ever rode for free in the *Elaine*'s forward hold."

But often before the season was over, their hopes were lost, for the river was a strange, mad wench indeed and sometimes the spring floods did not come at all. Then what few fish there were to seek were gasping and fighting for life as the waters fell away from the woods.

Watching the life of the great swamp unfold from my safe seat on the *Elaine*'s forward deck, I began to understand the perplexity of Cap'n Dew Robert when he was asked to describe this country.

It was the third day out, our swamp journey was nearing its end . . . and my own confusion had grown, not lessened. I could not say if she were angel or devil.

There *was* something sinister about the watery wilderness.

The Great Basin *was* a kind of flippant, unpredictable mistress, giving her favors to some, withholding them from others, inviting some to a warm sunlit intimacy, banishing others to the cruelly wailing swamp winds and the bitter leafless woods.

Now the *Elaine* glided by shores that were not shores, water going back into woods that were not woods, far back into the weird, impenetrable reaches of the swamps. It was a world of water, willows and cottonwoods, grey and green and black —of white cranes standing silently in the water, keeping their timeless watch on these deep woods—of bullfrogs and crickets singing their swelling chorus while far back in the forests a screech owl sent out its ghoulish, frightening call.

Just as the captain had prophesied, this had been a good, rich trip. He was happy with the cargo in the hold—fifteen hundred pounds of blue channel catfish, half a dozen alligator hides, four hundred pounds of *gaspergou* and buffalo, enough big crayfish to supply a New Orleans restaurant for a month, ten sacks of long-legged frogs—all the exotic harvest of the great Atchafalaya swamp.

He made a quick calculation of our trip. From the Morgan City fish dealers he would collect three cents per pound commission on nineteen hundred pounds of fish, making fifty-seven dollars. Commissions on the crayfish, frogs and alligators would bring the total to about seventy dollars. On the groceries and clothes he would make about the same amount.

"Ole Blum and Casso will give me a han' tomorrow." He spoke of the fishdock operators to whom he would deliver his cargo.

"They ship these cat and scalefish everywhere from Denver to New York. In a couple of days peoples all over the country will be settin' down to eat these cat. An' fancy folks in N'Awlins will be asighin' over dem dam' ugly crayfish."

As he hunched over the wheel, steering his *Elaine* through the swamps toward "the Outside," Captain Dew Robert was content.

Jumbo Men in the Shrimp

Capital of the World

xii

It was a few days later that I sat near a stack of newly-cut pilings on the dockside at Morgan City—"Shrimp Capital of the World"—and watched the feverish activity along a half-mile section of river front. Beside me was Harvey Lewis, president of the Fishermen and Trappers Union, said to be the one man who knew all the complexities of the booming offshore shrimp industry.

Lewis was a slight, sandy-haired man with freckles, keen blue eyes and sense of humor that had kept him laughing through countless hectic tribulations of the fast-changing world he thrived in. He was not a native of Morgan City . . . "But who is?" he asked with a chuckle. "At least none of the jumbo men," he added, "and they're only ones who really count."

Lewis had floated down the Mississippi and Arkansas Rivers in a small stern-wheel paddle boat fifteen years before, bringing his wife and baby boy. He was on a search for mussel shells for a Northern button factory. But he grew disgusted with the poor quality of Southern shells he found, traded his stern-wheeler and came in to Morgan City on a Louisiana lugger.

His arrival here had predated the jumbo-shrimp boom by a few short years—enough for him to become acquainted with the crab fishermen and "little swimp mens" who were natives, enough so that they had marked him for a man of superior intelligence and an ability to handle business affairs smoothly. Such a man stood out among the uneducated, sometimes illiterate swampers of the Atchafalaya Basin above Morgan City. Lewis trapped muskrats in the marshes and did fresh-water fishing and crab fishing in the bayous and rivers. Accustomed to comparatively more profitable fishing on the Illinois and Ohio Rivers, he was aghast at the backwardness of Louisiana fishermen who he said "were still just ten years this side of the Civil War."

This keen-eyed, alert Midwest riverman had a know-how in fisheries that caught the admiration of crab fishermen and "lil swimp" fishermen of inside coastal waters. When crab fishermen decided to organize a union, in 1936, Harvey Lewis was a natural for president. He had been president ever since. He had proved his ability to negotiate with the dealers who bought and resold the rich harvest from the waters that the Louisiana fishermen knew and loved.

"But all this gets ahead the story," said Harvey Lewis to me. "Let's look about here, if you want I should show you our Shrimp Capital at work. The fleet's due in. We got news on the ship-to-shore wire."

He turned toward the docks and toward the river where I could see the white hull of a big lugger approaching a lift bridge half a mile below. When he began to talk about the jumbo shrimp boom in Morgan City, his words painted a rich picture drawn as vividly from life as a Currier and Ives print. To listen to Harvey Lewis was to see the jumbo shrimp industry complete and in its entirety.

Flying the proud red flag that marked her high boat of the fleet, the *Mystery* came up the Atchafalaya slowly, majestically, her black-tarred nets swinging heavily in the rigging, her fat white sides sunk close to the water—and her hold bulging with a one-hundred-and-twenty-barrel cargo of jumbo shrimp out of the Gulf of Mexico.

Sirens started screaming and the Shrimp Capital of the World came alive. Other boats followed the *Mystery* up the big river, their crews shouting to each other as they came, laughing, making bets on the size of their catches. Coming in (but never, never in outside waters) they told the secrets of their catch:

"Shrimp are running off Ship Shoal Light . . ."

"They're runnin' off Trinity Shoal . . ."

"We found them in Southwest Pass . . ."

"At Grand Isle, at Raccoon Point, at Wine Island Pass . . ."

Sirens wailed louder still at the shrimp docks and women "pickers" all up and down the river hurriedly tucked their babies in cribs, shook admonishing fingers at the oldest girl-children, and rushed toward the waiting factories to put in a good day's work deheading and deveining shrimp. Behind docks and factories fifteen-ton refrigerator trucks and trailers waited, their sides bearing names that marked destinations to fish houses all over the country. In them the hundred-pound boxes of fresh, iced Gulf shrimp would be rushed to New York, Chicago, Washington, Philadelphia, Baltimore, Los Angeles, San Francisco—and some to Canada and Hawaii.

Excitement surged through Morgan City and through Berwick, its sister city across the wide, rough Atchafalaya. It spread to Greenwood, three miles up Bayou Boeuf and to Patterson, eight miles up Bayou Teche. For these towns shared Morgan City's name and her fame among fishery centers of the world.

In the four communities making up the Morgan City area, merchants dusted their shelves and added new gewgaws to their windows, bartenders cleared out their saloons, made ready for big business, night-club operators got on the phone and begged their suppliers for more beer, more beer. Ice houses piled on the steam, turning out carloads of ice to grind for the boats going back to the shrimping grounds. Gas and oil stations along the water front buzzed with the business of refueling the tanks of the big boats. Carpenters at The Greek's shipyard paused to listen to the whistles, then went quickly back to their hammers and saws, trying to turn out new boats faster and faster, to get them in the fleet in a hurry. All up and down Front Street people nodded at each other confidently, knowing "the shrimp are runnin' " and knowing that meant boom times for all.

Lewis, describing all this to me, paused long enough to light a cigarette and toss the match into the river below us. Then he continued:

On days like these old timers of Morgan City still rub their eyes and shake their heads in wonder. They find it hard to recognize their home town. They remember it as it was seven years ago, a slow-paced, leisurely village where crab fishermen and cat fishermen brought modest catches to the docks in skiffs and putt-putts. The big lakes up above, where the Atchafalaya spreads out and loses itself in swamps, had once produced a stupendous volume of these products. But now the fish seemed to be playing out.

A few twenty-six-foot and thirty-foot Louisiana luggers joined small boats out of Houma and other villages to the east of Morgan City and fished in shallow inshore waters for a small shrimp used by cannery plants. This shrimp-canning industry, and another product known as "platform dried shrimp," were old ones to Louisiana and ones in which the state led all other states in volume and value. They depended on a three- to five-inch shrimp, caught during summer and fall months just a few miles offshore in the bays and lagoons bordering the Gulf. But only a few fishermen went from Morgan City to join small luggers operating in this industry and there were no canning plants at the Atchafalaya river town. As a fishing port Morgan City seemed doomed.

That was in June of 1937.

In July of the same year came an event that was to revolutionize Morgan City's history and to leave its mark on the whole of U.S. fisheries. A school of giant shrimp—"jumbos" they soon were called in the trade—was discovered some forty miles off the Louisiana coast near the mouth of the Atchafalaya.

Biologists of the U.S. Fish and Wildlife Service had for some years been dragging the bottoms of the Gulf in search of a large shrimp they felt to be there. In 1937 trawl nets of their research boat, the *Pelican*, picked up big nine- to twelve-inch shrimp in seven fathoms of water between Trinity Shoals and Ship Shoals. About the same time a Florida shrimp dealer, sending two of his boats out on explorative tours in Louisiana waters because shrimp seemed to be migrating away from Florida, discovered the same school. Thus Louisiana's jumbo shrimp industry was born.

Today, barely a decade later, Morgan City has taken on the roaring spirit of any pioneer boom town. Fisheries people all over America were calling it the industry's fastest growing town. The boom town's jumbo industry—a sort of giant in swaddling clothes—had become one of the most amazing phenomena in the history of U.S. fisheries.

Lewis summarized the picture this way:

Fifteen dealers now operated shrimp factories in the Morgan City area, with an approximate investment of three hundred thousand dollars in buildings and plant equipment. About one hundred and seventy-five boats, of a new and much larger design than ever before used anywhere in the shrimp industry, operated out of here. With the minimum price of these boats set at thirteen thousand dollars, the investment in boats alone came to over three million dollars. Some two thousand people were employed, including fishermen, factory employees and truck drivers. About six hundred fishermen composed the Morgan City fleet. A hundred or more trucks, complete with modern refrigeration equipment, furnished transportation for the shrimp and represented an investment of almost a million dollars. Three ice plants, devoted exclusively to the shrimp industry, represented a quarter-million-dollar investment.

And the industry was still growing, so fast that people wondered where it would all end. In spite of its youth, it had had its own erratic history. The "jumbo men," pioneers in this business, are still young men today. They are mainly raw-shrimp dealers from Florida who began by bringing a few of their boats to Louisiana when the school of giant shrimp was discovered and they ended by bringing their whole fleet, building many more and bigger boats, and installing new factory equipment.

At first there was bitter rivalry between the two states over the giant shrimp. Louisiana attempted to forbid non-resident dealers from coming in, feeling that they would take the money they made here and return to Florida to spend it. "Residence" laws were passed but they had little teeth in them and several big suits fell through in the courts. This contention settled itself rather quietly when Florida packers moved their factories and their families to Morgan City and thus proved their good faith. Also the wiser of the Louisianians simply decided to call off the fight and get into the money themselves by building their own large shrimp boats and opening their own factories.

None could ever deny Morgan City's right as center of the Gulf's jumbo industry. Its big Atchafalaya Bay lay almost directly between Trinity Shoal and Ship Shoal where the original pool of jumbos was discovered and where the best fishing still takes place. Although the port itself was eighteen miles inland, the Atchafalaya River—one of the deepest in the world—provided a good channel and a safe anchorage for boats when hurricanes tore at Gulf waters. It was a good rail-shipping center and was on an east-west national highway.

These things, said Harvey Lewis, were of prime importance in handling a perishable product like shrimp.

Processing of shrimp was simple. In the packing houses women workers picked the heads off shrimp because its stomach is in this "head." With the head removed the shrimp was ready for shipping fresh, in ice. At least seventy percent of the jumbos were marketed as fresh, headless shrimp. The other thirty percent was sold cooked and peeled, quick-frozen raw in five-pound cartons, and a very few were canned for export. Jumbo shrimp is a high-priced product, sold to a fancy trade—to wealthy hotel consumers, to fine restaurants and apartment houses.

Everything was new in this youthful industry. Methods of fishing, methods of packing, of shipping, of marketing—all had been developed around the new school of jumbo shrimp.

"Fishing for the big 'uns is a special kind of business," Harvey Lewis told me. "The jumbo men are a different breed,

with every one having his own idea about the best way to
find and catch the big 'uns."

Before I could express the thought which leaped to my mind,
Lewis shook his head and grinned.

"Nope, the answer is nope. Ain't no woman ever made a trip
with the jumbo men yet, and I guess never will. You know, bad
luck."

He told me of other superstitions. With their livelihood depending on a creature of such erratic temperament as seagoing
shrimp, it was small wonder that the jumbo men were a superstitious bunch, much given to watching for signs and portents.
As with fishermen everywhere, weather was the leitmotiv of
their existence. Nor'westers could tie their boats to the docks
for days on end and sou'easters, coming one after another in a
wicked series, could lay them in port for weeks. To help stay
the elements' fury, shrimp fishermen never whistled aboard a
boat—that was a sure way to bring a nor'wester. When a single
porpoise followed their wake and "beat his tail on the water,"
then a school of porpoise gathered, that was another sure sign.
To keep these creatures away men never spoke the word "porpoise"; they referred to him, carefully, as a "fisherman." And
if "fishermen" gathered too close to the boat the captain headed
for port.

No shrimper would ever bring a black suitcase aboard his
boat. And of course it went without saying that taking a
woman aboard on a trip would be tempting the storm gods
beyond all reason and sense.

"Best you can do is to talk to the men," said Harvey Lewis.
"Some of them talk real sharp about the fishing. Preacher's a
good one—right civilized too. Wanta meet him?"

When I agreed, we left our perch on the dock and walked
down the wide, rough boardwalk beside the incoming shrimp
boats. By now there was an almost solid line of big luggers tied
to the dock's pilings, with more coming in. Moving slowly into
the wharves, they looked like mammoth water-borne white
geese gliding in to rest alongside their comrades. From short
mast poles hung great black nets, swinging rhythmically as

the boats moved slowly in for their landings. Crewmen stood on the bows, directed the captains in the pilothouses, and shouted excitedly to their fellow fishermen on the other boats. There was gayety in the air and a sense of well-being in the glowing, happy faces of offshoremen who had finished another trip in safety and success.

Shrill whistles of the shrimp factories added a piercing, triumphant kind of carousel tone to the men's shouting and laughter. This was a happy homecoming for every soul in the shrimp capital. Leaping off their boats, making the lines secure to the big black pilings, most of the men wasted no time in shouldering their bundles of clothes and moving away. A better welcome awaited them at their homes, where wives and children had heard the factory whistles and gathered in eager family groups to await the father's return.

Standing to one side, leaning comfortably against a great piling to which he had tied lines for a new net, stood a tall, slender fisherman. He had paused in his knitting to watch the incoming fleet. As we approached, I saw that Preacher Robichaux had a sensitive, almost aesthetic face which contrasted with the rough, sometimes scarred faces of his fellow fishermen. It was easy to see that he was a philosopher. Standing apart from his fellows, he studied the fishermen with an analytical eye. He seemed to enjoy the study of his trade and its workmen in the same way that a scholar enjoys his books.

He nodded pleasantly when Harvey Lewis introduced us, and smiled when I examined the fine work that he was doing with the net.

"We came in yesterday for repairs," said Robichaux, "and I took today to finish the new trawl. It will be a beauty, eh, Harvey?"

The big net lay in swirls of shining rope at his feet, with a part of it stretched between the two closest pilings. It was a peculiar amber color and would not match the black ones swinging in nearby rigging until it had been tarred with a protective coating.

Harvey Lewis told me, "Of course, you know this whole

business started with a single trawl net." He motioned dramatically down the half-mile' length of wharves, included the growing number of incoming shrimp luggers, and ended with a sweeping gesture toward the row of bustling business houses along Front Street.

"Preacher, I bet she like to know about Captain Jones Smith and how he invented the first trawl net."

Preacher told me how just a few years ago a fisherman in the little Florida village of Fernandina began to study experiments that he had seen conducted in Beaufort, North Carolina. Men of the Fisheries Service there were working with a new kind of try net used to catch minute fish for their analytical studies.

Captain Smith wondered if the same kind of net, made on a Gargantuan scale, would catch and hold small shrimp which were sought in inshore Gulf waters along the Florida coast. He began to build a giant net, modeled on the try net used in North Carolina. Other shrimpers laughed at him, an old man sitting on the dock all day fooling with mountains of strings and ropes and big wooden needles. But when the net was finished and when Captain Jones Smith tried it with his new and stronger mast poles and rigging lines—and especially when he returned from a short trip into the Gulf with his boat's hold filled with the swift takings of the big trawl net—fishermen of Fernandina stopped laughing and started to copy the captain's net.

It was a spectacular success from the first. Boats returned to port in half the time, with bigger and better catches. In a little while the new trawl net had revolutionized the whole shrimping industry. And scarcely had Captain Smith's net become accepted by all the Florida fishermen when the jumbo shrimp school was discovered at the mouth of the Atchafalaya River in Louisiana. The Florida shrimpers moved over en masse and became the jumbo men of Morgan City.

"That's history, Miss," said Preacher, "though it ain't so long-ago history."

The trawl net looked like nothing at all to me save a woven

mass of thread. Preacher picked up his long wooden needle from the piling post and pointed out the net's features, making me see how it worked in the water.

On either side there were trawl boards, which some called "doors" and others called "otter boards" because of the way they glided through the water. The boards were three by seven feet, designed in such a way that they would drag the net downward and pull it outward as it went down. When the big net reached the bottom of the sea it spread to ninety feet long but had only a tiny six-foot mouth. The mouth was kept open only by the power of the boat when it was moving forward at about three miles an hour.

Before the trawl net was let down, a fifteen-foot miniature of it, called a try net, was dropped overboard. When shrimp began to show up in the try net, the captain dropped his buoy to mark the spot and swung his boat in position to make a drag through the school of shrimp. Two crewmen threw the net overboard and let out tow lines until the net touched bottom. If the fishermen were right in their guess of location, the trawl net scooped thousands of pounds of silvery squirming shrimp into its mouth from the floor of the sea.

A single drag might last from forty minutes to three hours, with the second crewman or "rig man" testing regularly with the try net to estimate the amount of the catch. At the end of the drag the net was hauled in with a high-powered hoister —another important improvement in fast-changing shrimp fishery—and the shrimp were dumped on deck. From here on the fishermen worked fast, for shrimp cannot be left on deck more than two hours—and it takes a lot of shoveling to pack away eighty bushels of squirming creatures into the ice chambers of the boat's hold.

If the shrimp are running good, the captain swings his boat sharply for another drag. From then on captain and crew hurry with the work of picking "sea trash"—small fish, crabs, and so forth—out of the catch and stowing the shrimp away in ice chambers.

Sometimes a boat can fill its hold in eight good drags, sometimes she will make fifty drags and come back to port still carrying her ice, with no shrimp at all. So swiftly do the schools travel, and in so tight a formation, that one boat's trawl may fill completely in a drag while the trawl of a boat just thirty feet away may come up empty. Boats will sometimes fill to capacity in two days, sometimes they will stay out seven days and come back with nothing but melting ice in the hold.

If the try net shows no shrimp off Eugene Light, the lugger may run east for six or eight hours to fish off Ship Shoal, then on to the Mississippi River mouth. If the shrimp still eludes them, the captain turns his boat and cuts a zigzagging course across the Gulf towards Texas, working in and out in waters from three to twenty fathoms in depth. Sometimes he fishes sixty to eighty miles offshore and occasionally, as at Cameron and Pecan Island, he fishes within a quarter of a mile of the shore line.

This is one of the most unpredictable of all fisheries. It depends on many elements, but most of all on the shrimp itself—and therein lies the secret of its unpredictability.

"It takes one of them biologist fellows to tell you about that part of it and get it straight," concluded Preacher.

"Somebody calling my name?"

The man who spoke had been walking down the dockside a few moments back and had paused to stand beside Harvey, listening as Preacher described fishing methods. He was a short, stocky intelligent looking fellow, dressed neatly in khaki. He grinned amiably at Preacher as he said:

"I'm damned if it's not a relief to find a fisherman who'll take the lecture business away from me. It's the only part of my job I can't hanker to."

Harvey, introducing us, said, "Well, if it ain't Mr. Wildlife and Fisheries himself! Here's the man who knows more about shrimp than any other shrimp I know."

John Buchanan laughed, evidently accustomed to this kind of kidding. Then he became serious and began to talk about his favorite subject. As biologist with the State Game and Fish

Commission[1] for ten years, he had been in on many of the important findings.

His story of the research conducted by scientists, the gradual gathering of knowledge about the elusive shrimp over a period of years, matched Preacher's account for interest.

He told how until thirteen years before—when the U.S. Government and the State of Louisiana undertook their co-operative investigations—shrimp were the least known and the least understood of all fisheries. Today they have become more fully understood than any other important marine product, although there are still many unsolved mysteries about their habits. Biologists and practical fishermen still disagree on many important points about shrimp.

Fishermen sometimes claim they have seen old shrimp.

"Man, I seen great big fellows, ten-fifteen year old, I guarantee you!" John Buchanan imitated the patois of a Louisiana fisherman.

But he added, "We biologists have learned that shrimp live only one year."

Although this is the only important fishery that is dependent on a creature of one-year life cycle, shrimp exist in such astronomical numbers that scientists cannot conceive of any disaster so great ("this side of the complete destruction of the universe") as to wipe out all the shrimp.

This crustacean spawns throughout the spring and summer months, in open waters of the Gulf some fifteen miles offshore. A single female may produce as many as three hundred thousand eggs which, transparent as glass, measure only one one-hundredth of an inch in diameter. These young, hatching within twelve hours, become minute larvae which pass through a series of some fifteen rapid, remarkable changes, and assume a form resembling closely that of the adult shrimp, yet measuring only one quarter of an inch in length. While still in their larva stage, they begin the mysterious movements which are part of their life cycle. Biologists say that few animals have so strange, so complicated and so curious a history in their

[1] Now the Louisiana Wildlife and Fisheries Commission.

individual lives.

Helpless, adrift at sea, the young somehow cross wide
stretches of water and move into the warm, shallow waters of
bays, lagoons, lakes and bayous that cut the Louisiana shore
line. This is their nursery. As they grow older, they begin to
move offshore toward deeper water and to show up in offshore
fisheries. It is these immature shrimp that form the basis of
Louisiana's huge canning industry.

But countless millions of them escape the small luggers
which engage in fishing "on the inside." Colder weather sends
them further and further "on the outside," seeking the waters
of the Gulf stream. They live in deep Gulf waters, show a
marked growth rate, become adults and finally spawn.

It is these adult shrimp, the jumbos, which are the basis of
the Morgan City industry. There is actually nothing mysterious about their sudden appearance. They might have been
"discovered" many years sooner but for the fact that small
Louisiana luggers were not constructed or equipped to travel
many miles offshore into the deep and often stormy Gulf.
Their discovery is of great economic importance because this
harvest of twenty million pounds of shrimp in a single year
would die without again reaching the coast of Louisiana.

Another conclusion made by scientists working in the
Federal- and state-sponsored investigations is that ocean bottoms composed of sand, shell or coral do not provide suitable
habitat for shrimp. The crustacean lives on muddy bottoms of
the ocean floor. He feeds on tiny microorganisms that exist in
this mud. In stormy weather he buries himself in the mud and
digs billions upon billions of infinitesimal fox-holes on the
bottom of the Gulf.

When John Buchanan paused, Preacher said, "But you
didn't tell her the most curious part of it. The way you biologist fellows work is what always bugged my eyes."

"Oh, yes . . . the tagging. Well, I guess that *is* quite a deal."

He told how scientists working with the state's fisheries

commission had worked out a way to trace the migration of shrimp.

"Actually the study covered every unknown element about shrimp—the life cycle, migratory habits, growth rates, decrease through fishing, and fate of the adults.

"We placed small numbered discs on young shrimp, then released them to wander. We paid fishermen fifty cents for each tagged shrimp they found in their nets and reported to us. On each of these we recorded the approximate location of the catch and the date. Thus, over a period of several years, we have learned of their growth and traveling habits. Thousands have been released and returned. One appeared in an Indianapolis restaurant in someone's salad! We know that shrimp may travel as much as three hundred miles in one season."

He paused and Preacher said, "And if we have to go any three hunnerd miles to chase 'em, that's jus' what we will do. Harvey, whyn't you all go to The Greek's and have a good look at the boats what will carry us there?"

The four of us walked a few blocks up Front Street to the boatyard of E. Klonaris, known by all as "The Greek." Here I met a man who was considered the master builder, by a people and in a land where boatbuilding had for centuries been a fine art.

Fat, silent, impassive, The Greek gave no outward sign of the genius which lay in his mind and in his big slab-like hands which handled wood as delicately as a jeweler handles his springs and coils. Six years ago The Greek had come to Morgan City with a set of carpenter's tools and nothing else save the lines and planes and angles which were in his head. Since then he had built over a hundred shrimp boats from his own design, combining the best features of hulls from Florida and from Louisiana.

Now we stood in the cool shade of his giant boat shed and workshop—three hundred feet long and seventy-five wide—and watched him supervise the building of ten boats all at one time. There was a noise of electric saws, sparks of acetylene torches, shouts of workmen calling for The Greek's advice. The great hulls, in various stages of development, soared above us on their ways, with men working all over them at one time. This was an assembly line that The Greek had designed and built himself. It had revolutionized the whole boat-building business of South Louisiana.

His new type of lugger was called simply the "Florida boat," for its designer and most of the jumbo shrimpers themselves were Florida originals. This distinguished the jumbo lugger from the Louisiana lugger, a small shrimp and oyster boat whose patterns Frenchmen had brought from Brittany and Normandy centuries before and adapted for use in the bayous.

When The Greek first began to build shrimp boats, in Florida twenty years before, they were all thirty-footers. About 1925 the boats began to increase in size there, and he built forty-footers, then fifty-footers. From that length the Florida luggers grew to their present sixty- and seventy-five-foot lengths, for the shrimpers were going further and further out into the Gulf even before the jumbo school was discovered.

Proportioned to the greater length came some increase in beam, but in most cases the draft was kept to about six feet. That makes the Florida boat adaptable to Louisiana bayous. With larger capacity came other improvements. Pilothouses are larger today and are moved forward. Behind the wheelhouse is a roomy cabin for use by the craft's skipper. Harvey Lewis told me that a few of the newest boats have captain's cabins which rate the term "stateroom."

The Florida boats cost from fourteen to eighteen thousand dollars to build, whereas the smaller Louisiana luggers cost five thousand. If the present boom continues, said Lewis, if demand continues to outstride supply, and if the cost of lumber continues to soar, the price of all these boats may be doubled within a few years. Everybody in the industry, all Louisianians in the surrounding bayous know this and it creates a sort of fever that one feels at its highest pitch here in The Greek's boatyard. Boatbuilding is not limited these days to the big dealers. Fishermen are putting their savings into them, getting credit for the rest and paying out with their catches. Or they are building their own boats in back yards at home, copying The Greek's design as faithfully as possible. Thus they earn the boat owner's fifty percent of the catch as well as their share for fishing.

Nowhere was Morgan City's rampant boom spirit more in evidence than in the shadowed coolness of The Greek's great open-sided boat shed. Here I could feel the pulse of the boom— bigger boats, bigger profits, bigger catches of shrimp and bigger benefits for all.

"That's the good word in the Shrimp Capital of the World," concluded Harvey Lewis.

And when I asked his opinion of the next big horizon for jumbo shrimp, he seemed to speak for himself, for Preacher Robichaux and the men of the fleet, as well as for the state biologist and other scientists.

"Our next horizon is right at our front door, in the deeper waters of the Gulf. Our boats have not even tapped it yet. There will be bigger fishing, in deeper waters, and for still larger jumbos. Boats will fish in forty to a hundred fathoms. Buoys will be used to mark the coral reefs . . ."

He paused and as we said good-bye to The Greek, Preacher concluded, "An' wherever the Gulf has a mud bottom, we'll be scraping it for jumbo shrimp!"

A week later I strolled at dusk along the water front. It was quiet now all along the riverbank. The fleet was out. Against the hulls of a few lonely boats, the early evening breeze slapped gentle waves from across the river. Gone was all feeling of boom and bustle. Across the street from the mile-long docks, business houses had closed their doors early, leaving a few flickering night lights which would pick up strength as the night grew darker. It seemed hardly possible that this was the same dock where I had stood just a few days ago and watched two or three score boats sail proudly in, setting the factory whistles to screaming and stirring the town to a high excite-

ment. Yet I knew that before another week was out the boats
would turn in again from the treasure houses on the Gulf's
floor, bearing their rich bounties and bringing life again to the
old river town.

Since that first day when I had visited here with Harvey
Lewis, Preacher Robichaux and John Buchanan, I had met
many of the jumbo men, had heard their oft-told tales of the
fishery they loved best. Working continuously on the decks of
their sleek Florida boats, knitting or repairing nets on the
docks alongside, the men of the fleet had been willing enough
to talk. Among the jumbo men I had met Swedes, Norwegians,
Danes and Scotsmen, Italians, Germans and Greeks—"tar
heels" from the east coast, "square heads" from Scandinavia,
"sand snipes" from South Carolina, "crackers" from Georgia,
"conqs" from Florida. There was a camaraderie among them,
a teasing kind of laughter that caused them to give each other
such nicknames as Flying Fish Charlie, Big Nose Carl, Oscar
the Finn, Bluenose Bill, Salty Jim, King of Lapland, Limey,
Horse-Mackerel John, Bama the Greek and Pelican George.
Behind each of these colorful noms de plume lay a seaman's
story that the bearer could be persuaded to tell.

I had heard a Morgan City businessman sum up the city
like this: "The Jews own Morgan City, the Italians run
it . . . and the French don't give a damn!"

Perhaps this cryptic picture was the true one, for among
all the fishermen I found none who would call himself Cajun.

"The Cajun, he's a little swimp man, for sure. We got some
Frenchmen, yeh, but they is jumbo men like us. Look, Miss
I got it . . . You know them folks livin' in the Borrow Pit
under the levee, right alongside Tiger Island? Maybe you
oughta look there for Cajuns."

Scholarly Treasure Hunters

in a Shanty-boat Metropolis

xiii

"You'll find them in shanty boat and mansion . . ." *M'sieu*
André had said.

And just outside Morgan City was the biggest shanty-boat
town in all Louisiana, probably in all America!

I found it stretching along a spillway between Tiger Island
and the main east-bank levee of the Atchafalaya. It was called,
simply and unromantically "the Borrow Pit" because this
was what was left after the earth was borrowed to build the
sizable levee beside it.

Winds and waves off the big river beyond Tiger Island
scarcely rippled the surface of this fifty-foot, man-made canal,
so that campboats tied here were cozy and safe—let the
nor'westers blow, my friend!

There were all of two hundred campboats along the narrow

spillway. They were big and little, old and new, bright and dull, neat and filthy. Some rode the water merrily, flaunting radio aerials and showing new white refrigerators and washing machines through curtained windows. Others slumped despondently, their filthy ramshackle decks foretelling the state of dark and dank interiors.

Tied to deck posts of these camps or staked at anchor along crowded banks was as motley a collection of boats as I had ever seen. There were half-cabin "lil swimp" luggers, full-cabin luggers, fantailed old Biloxi luggers, dismasted double-ended sloops, discarded Navy "ducks," one-lung putt-putts, big and little skiffs, *péniches*, pirogues, and others which defied any known nomenclature or description. The luggers, old sloops and bigger skiffs were loaded with all sorts of miscellaneous nautical gear for inside and outside waters. Those belonging to crab fishermen carried stacks of wooden crates looking like chicken coops, so that when one of these left a dock and slowly surged through the crowded canal toward the big river it looked like a water-borne chick hatchery. Others were filled with big black hoop nets, freshly tarred in barrels under the oaks of Tiger Island and ready to go "back to the woods" of the Great Basin. Still others were loaded with trappers' gear—crumpled hip boots, cane poles, rusty worn-out steel traps, abandoned motors, anchors, chains, lines, ancient cookstoves—all the old plunder which might possibly be patched and repaired, come next season and time to head for the marsh.

During the week when I was talking with jumbo shrimp men of Morgan City, I spent most evenings walking along the Borrow Pit levee, enjoying the kaleidoscopic swirl of life among the water dwellers. Carrying a camera around my neck, stopping occasionally to photograph an infant or a four-year-old who was handling his *péniche* like a veteran, I got to be a familiar figure to the residents. Soon they lost the timidity and suspicion with which they met most strangers. Then they waved from campboat decks each evening, or motioned me to come over to their campboats to "snap a pix, *hein, Mam'selle?*"

of some child-mother's first baby or some doddering great-*grandpère*.

And that is the way I met Mr. Sterling and Mr. Chapman, two rare scholars of the Borrow Pit. They lived on a decrepit old full-cabin lugger which slumped precariously on the canal's edge. Its deck was on such a slant that Mr. Sterling stood gimp-legged, rather like a mountain goat, when he bowed to me. He opened the conversation in a rather startling way.

"Does the lady's camera record an image in the dark?"

"Well, not just exactly that," I replied, "but with a proper

attachment I can get enough light to photograph almost . . ."

"Ah, you mean the flash synchronizer?" he interrupted.
"Well, yes, that would do the deed, for true . . ."

He did not pursue the subject that first evening and, not
knowing Mr. Sterling as well as I grew to later, I supposed it
was an idle question.

Each evening after that Mr. Sterling bowed from his lugger
deck and we'exchanged a few words about picture-making and
other matters. I was surprised to, find that he knew quite a lot
about photography and could toss technical terms about in a
way that I could scarcely follow. Also I began to get the
impression that Mr. Sterling was not engaged in idle chatter,
that there was some purpose as yet unrevealed in his conver-
sations. It was puzzling. Especially when I realized that the
tables had been switched on me and that this interrogator was
finding out a good many more facts about me than I was about
him. In the background there was always Mr. Chapman, a
silent partner who nodded energetically at every wise and
learned statement that Mr. Sterling made.

The two gentlemen were so straight out of O. Henry that I
could almost see the ink smudges on them. By trade Mr. Chapman was a tinsmith and Mr. Sterling a piano tuner, which
vaguely explained his knowledge of things mechanical. They
plied their trades in the town behind the levee, but I found
that their real life went on mostly in the Borrow Pit which
fascinated them quite as much as it did me.

Mr. Sterling was Lord Chesterfield without a shirt. Standing
bare-armed and lank upon his weathered boat deck, he bowed
from the waist each evening and turned some graceful phrase
to open our conversation. He was, he told me, a Floridian by
birth, a man of the Florida coast . . . "an island man," he said
significantly, turning his head to one side and looking closely
to see if that held any special meaning for me. It did not, then.

Often he spoke of the Borrow Pit community and from him
I learned much about the life of this floating village. At first I
was careful to refer to the homes as "houseboats," "campboats," or "flats"—in the Louisiana manner. But to Mr.

Sterling, the Florida island man, this was his beloved "Shanty-boat Town."

"Ah," he said, in his courtly manner, "you should see this sight in the mist of an early dawn! We arise each morning, Mr. Chapman and I, and come topside the very first thing. There, with the sun gilding decks and roofs down a ribbon of gold and pearl, lies—our Shanty-boat Town!"

About his neighbors he told me quite a lot. Most of them were Acadians, but . . . "Beware the distinction, my lady, and do not call them Cajuns!"

Also there were enough outsiders to make this a most cosmopolitan community. There were those who had lived their lives out on trappers' campboats deep in the swamps and there were those who knew the sights of northern rivers and the bitter, bucking ways of Father Mississippi himself. Some anchored their homes here to one spot for life; others stopped here for only a brief year or so, then drifted on to other streams, forever seeking a watery Elysium of their dreams. Some were crab fishermen, cray fishermen, shrimp fishermen and moss gatherers; others were tinkers, tinsmiths, basket weavers or cobblers up in the town over the levee. And some made a living by staking out wax myrtle bushes in the river, letting the delicious little river shrimp feed on the leaves, lifting the bushes to shake shrimp into dip nets, and selling their catches on the levee top to neighbors who preferred river shrimp for their gumbos and jambalayas.

Visiting along the Borrow Pit for half a dozen enchanted dusks, I had talked as many times to Mr. Sterling before he revealed to me his true identity.

This was a dramatic moment and he made the most of it. Lowering his voice to a hoarse whisper, he clutched his ragged undershirt and pulled till he popped off a button, baring his bony chest and placing a clenched fist against his heart.

"My lady, I know you to be a friend . . . and I need your help. I tell you now . . . I am not just a ridiculous old piano tuner . . . I am a Treasure Hunter, the son and the grandson of Treasure Hunters of Amelia Island!"

The announcement seemed to give him the keenest satisfaction. Behind him, silent Mr. Chapman nodded his head more energetically than usual, beamed a proud smile toward his friend, clapped him on the shoulders heavily and laughed a great loud, prideful guffaw.

I had already learned that almost everybody in the Gulf Parishes was a treasure hunter, more or less, one way or another, *comme ci, comme ça,* some taking it more seriously than others.

Mr. Sterling and Mr. Chapman were dead serious.

Now the vocal one of the pair motioned me closer to the rotting deck of their old banked lugger and lowered his voice until I could barely hear.

"Our outfit is electricity," he told me, "but it is radio and radar too. A whole new concept! That's the best part. And can it find metal? My lady, you come see."

Inside the dark interior of their lugger home, Mr. Chapman played a flashlight around an odd looking contraption made of many tubes, looped wires, ground-glass screens, and a foot-long whistle which looked like a miniature of the whistle on top the *Kursweg's* smokestack.

"You know what we call her?" asked Mr. Sterling. "We named her the Gold Witch because she will surely 'witch' us whatever gold we seek!"

From here I could not tell whether the Witch was designed to announce the finding of gold by Morse code, radio wave, radar screen, or steamboat whistle. But what matter, if it worked?—and Mr. Sterling promised it would do just that.

"Magnificently, my dear, magnificently!"

With all this scientific apparatus at his command, it hardly seemed possible that Mr. Sterling could seek the aid of a humble photographer, but that is what he did.

So sure was he of his expedition's success, so unafraid of the inevitable heirs that hounded every triumphant treasure finder of history, that he wanted to tell the story of his great success in pictures . . . "so the whole danged world, 'scuse lady, can see how we broke Lafitte's richest treasure . . . and we can settle Captain Jean's wandering ghost for good and all!"

Once having revealed his secret to me, Mr. Sterling could talk of nothing else. His speech now rolled off his facile tongue in a sort of ecstasy of anticipation. He talked of nothing but pieces of eight, golden ingots, chests of crown jewels, king's ransoms, galleons of golden freight, shiploads of doubloons, Ali Baba's hoard, El Dorados of sea and land, and even the wonders of lost cities of the Incas, in unreachable heights of the lofty Andes. His eyes gleamed fiercely with reflections of all the lost treasure chests of history and glistened with shadows of golden bounties he would soon recover from Barataria waters.

Listening to him through the long autumn twilights, I learned more of pirate lore than I ever knew existed. In Mr. Sterling's mind the whole cavalcade of buccaneers from Sir Henry Morgan to Captain Jean Lafitte swarmed gorgeously and flamboyantly about, weaving their richly confused legends in a mad tapestry without time or pattern—but with a good solid core of historical fact, I was to find.

As was to be expected, Mr. Sterling showed marked preference for the polished gallants among pirates. Of such heathenish characters as bloody, boisterous Blackbeard—or Captain Teach, as he was properly named—he did not approve. With lifted eyebrow and troubled frown he talked of this Blackbeard who for many years had come to be pictured on stage and screen as the typical pirate and misled the public about some noble gentlemen of the profession. He told of Blackbeard's fourteen wives, his gory debacles, his torture of innocents, and his well-earned death at the hands of a British naval officer who cut off his head, mounted it on the prow of his own ship and sailed into Charleston harbor in a blaze of triumph.

"He deserved no better," said Mr. Sterling judiciously.

It was in the curious, less-known memorabilia of piracy that Mr. Sterling's scholarship really showed itself. He told me in detail about the Brethren of the Main, that seventeenth-century labor union for pirates which contained in its charter such worthwhile benefits as a proportionate sharing of profits, an insurance plan, a disability clause which provided set amounts for a lost leg, a chewed-off arm, a gouged-out eye, or a marlinspike's slash in the groin. There was, he said, little need for the Brethren to include an old-age and retirement plan, for life among the buccaneers was short, if jolly. Whole piratical careers, of which the world has spun tales of gore for two centuries, were actually born and finished in a matter of six weeks to two years. It was a long-lived, hoary old veteran indeed who survived as much as five years at the peak of his career.

To Mr. Sterling the pageantry of piracy had many heroes. He said the profession was among man's oldest and it encompassed the most daring and courageous souls among Phoenicians, Greeks, Romans, Norse Vikings, and Chinese. In his eye there were traditions of conquest, of gallantry, of knight-errantry which accomplished such historical *prima facti* (his term) as the sailing of Vikings to England, then to Greenland and our Atlantic shores, the invention of navigational instruments, the development of superior seamanship, the art of shipbuilding. Many historians, he said, thought of Columbus as a pirate, but he thought Drake and Hawkins were closer to it.

He was particularly enchanted with such colorful and romantic pirates as the Man with the Glove in His Hat, on whom Queen Elizabeth bestowed one of her bejeweled velvet gloves and who wore it through all his New World conquests, a glittering purple velvet adornment anchored to the front of his beplumed white satin hat.

He told me of Montbars, "The Exterminator," an idealist who had a most philanthropic and humane ambition to protect subjugated Indians and Negroes—and who liberated them from their Spanish oppressors by the direct method of slaughtering every Spaniard he could lay hands on.

He talked of young Red Legs Greaves who had begun life as a white slave of Cromwell's day, was freed by his owner in the Barbados and turned to piracy as a rewarding trade—but who was noted for his humanity and morality, never maltreating women nor torturing non-combatants, often endowing charitable institutions with huge sums, and finally ending his days as a sober, happy sugar planter.

It was such ironic quirks among the corsairs that appealed to the romantic in Mr. Sterling. He seemed especially interested also in two women pirates whom his readings had revealed. He spoke of them as petticoat pirates. Both these swashbuckling lady corsairs had been brought up as boys by their disappointed fathers but had turned to piracy only after their hearts were turned by youthful buccaneers. They had followed their lads to sea and indeed had out-buccaneered them until both ladies were captured by a British man-o'-war, ironically while they were tête-à-tête in one of their few womanly gossip sessions on deck of Calico Jack's pirate schooner. While Mary Reed languished and died of fever in an English jail, awaiting execution, Anne Bonny was retrieved and pardoned, only to disappear forever from the world of fellow pirates and from her husband, Calico Jack.

But of all the gentlemen pirates whom Mr. Sterling admired, none interested him so much as Captain Jean Lafitte. Here was a buccaneer with a true flair for romance, one who could make the most of his flamboyant adventures in a world of danger and intrigue. Most of all Mr. Sterling loved the stories that concerned Lafitte's fling in the high society of New Orleans. Vividly he pictured balls at which Lafitte appeared in fashionable attire and danced with the city's belles. He told of occasions on which the gallant pirate captain entertained New Orleans businessmen at his headquarters fortifications on Grand Terre; and how he, in return, sipped wines and fine liqueurs in the drawing rooms of the city's greatest bankers, charming their wives and daughters after having won spirited business battles with the gentlemen themselves. Here was a pirate after Mr. Sterling's heart!

From talk of personalities Mr. Sterling always came back to exciting recountals of the richest treasure troves of history. Here he would lose himself in dreams of splendor. In a sonorous, theatrical voice he would describe legendary Sargasso Seas—the rotting hulks of pirate ships, the littered riches of golden cargoes, the ghosts of doomed seamen, the incalculable wealth of a thousand sunken treasure ships.

And more than once, just as the sun dipped over the horizon of Tiger Island and slid behind the glowing waters of the Atchafalaya, Mr. Sterling raised his hand and pointed solemnly with a crooked forefinger as he recited a favorite verse:

> ". . . And so I saw a thousand fearful wrecks,
> Ten thousand men that fishes gnawed upon;
> Wedges of gold, great anchors, heaps of pearl,
> Inestimable stones, unvalued jewels,
> All scattered on the bottom of the sea . . ."

This was invariably my cue to leave. It got to be a sort of ritual which all of us enjoyed. After such a consummate performance, poems sung in such a Shakespearean style withal, there was little I could do but nod appreciatively to my friends, murmur a soft *"bonne nuit, Messieurs,"* and wander off down the levee road with my head filled with dreams of pirate gold unlimited.

Each evening that I listened to his tales and legendry, I felt that I grew closer to Mr. Sterling and to silent Mr. Chapman too. Particularly during the reciting of the scholar's favorite poem did I feel a bond growing tighter between us.

Finally came the memorable twilight when Mr. Sterling motioned me to look again inside his cluttered lugger cabin.

Beside the complicated treasure-hunting machine Mr. Chapman sat hunkered up on an old seaman's trunk. In his hands he held a small, battered and very rusty chest. He looked expectantly toward Mr. Sterling, as if awaiting a signal for opening it.

Again this was a big moment and Mr. Sterling was not to be cheated.

"My lady," he began, "I told you I was born on Amelia Island, adjoining Blackbeard Island, off the coast of Florida. My father and his father's father made this their home. Some claim that Blackbeard's greatest booty is buried there. So my family has hunted treasure for as long as we can remember. Of doubloons we have found many."

Here he motioned to Mr. Chapman to open the chest. The old man reached inside and drew out half a dozen gold pieces, about the size of a half dollar.

"Spanish doubloons," said Mr. Sterling. "Worth about twelve dollars apiece . . ."

I held the two-century-old coins in my hand wonderingly. But Mr. Sterling had barely begun. Now he said, "These are only a luck-piece, Ma'am. Here is the real heart of our heritage."

Again he motioned to Mr. Chapman. This time the old man pulled from the chest a stained piece of vellum. Suddenly I felt a surge of excitement and my fingers trembled as I held the old map. In the semidark Mr. Sterling turned a flashlight across the surface. I saw wrinkles and creases in the vellum, and a pitted and grainy surface. But shining out in clarity were outlines of the West Indian islands—the Spanish Main! There was a dotted line drawn from Havana, Cuba, to Vera Cruz, Mexico. North of the line was a high curved arc which included points on the Florida coast, points on the Mississippi Delta and on the southwest coast of Louisiana.

Now Mr. Sterling played his flashlight on the elaborately engraved name of the map and I saw that it read: "The Tract of the Flota from Vera Cruz to ye Havana, occasioned by ye Trade Winds." In the Gulf east of Havana, where the sea narrowed between Florida and the Bahamas, were these words: "The best passage of all the Islands." And at still another point there were the words: "The Gallions and Flota, usually joyning at the Havana, the whole Armada sails for Spain thro this Gulf."

I fingered the map, felt the crackle of ancient vellum in my fingers, and stared unbelievingly at the two triumphant old gentlemen whose faces glowed in the late twilight. Others had told me there was such a map. I had a friend who had a friend who claimed to have seen the original once, in some shop of antiquities in London, guarded by an old crone who said her father was the printer and had left this to her among his treasured possessions. Treasured possessions, indeed! With Mr. Sterling and Mr. Chapman I was about to learn the true meaning of the term.

Under the fancy scrolled title there were faint numbers indicating a date . . . 168? . . . The last numeral was too obscure to be seen clearly. At any rate this must surely be a copy of that prized chart which was published for the Brethren of the Main in the late 1600's. Whatever lucky buccaneer purchased a copy of this map in Bristol or old London Town, or came into possession of it in more bloody fashion, would have his path laid out for him. For along this well charted path of the Spanish Main there sailed each year the entire Flota (treasure fleet) of Iberian vessels carrying tribute from Vera Cruz, Porto Bello and Cartagena, to Spain. With such a map a pirate captain might take his pick of gold-laden galleons, cut out any one from the fleet which dared to lag a little behind in the great parade, and attack it with his own stout men and vessels.

In such a way, said Mr. Sterling, countless hundreds of ships had been sunk with their treasure cargoes intact, and other countless hundreds had been boarded and their cargoes divided and hidden in a thousand inner bays, lagoons and islands along the coasts of Florida and of Louisiana too.

Gingerly I handed the map back to Mr. Chapman. Then, at a signal from his partner, he pulled still another map from the battered chest and handed it to Mr. Sterling.

Silently, significantly, Mr. Sterling unfolded this smaller map and handed it to me. This was little more than a scrap of cloth carrying some symbols and a few lines of crude hand lettering. It was more faded and worn than the other for it seemed to have been made on an old piece of thin canvas. The lettering ran out to its tattered edges and it was impossible for me to see if words were thus torn off and omitted.

Bending over my shoulder to examine the map with me, Mr. Sterling whispered:

"Now, my lady, you see our real treasure! This marks the spot where a heavily loaded longboat of Lafitte sank in bayou waters while he was seeking a spot to bury booty from one of his greatest raids. Both these maps were left to my father by his father before him. For four generations we have searched for the sunken boat . . . and now we have, at last, equipment that will locate it for us!"

His happy sigh was echoed by Mr. Chapman, who slapped his hand affectionately on the curious Gold Witch.

Looking more closely I saw a wavering line run across the torn sheet from upper left to lower right corner. The map was crude . . . a dotted line, a compass bearing, a few jumbled figures, a large "X" and these words:

"Fm. Loon, 3rd passage s., Br. 4 arp. NW to Lost Bay,
10° S by E fm 80' oak tree mkd ax bld, ¼ arp. to
lg. bt."

I handed it back to Mr. Sterling hastily, for already I could feel the touch of gold, the tug at the heart that lures any incipient treasure hunter no matter how far removed he may think he is from a fated search for buried riches.

Now, in a swift outpouring of words, Mr. Sterling revealed his plan to me. After years of searching he had located Bayou de la Loon, a small silted-in waterway in the Bayou Barataria country near the village of Lafitte. This had been accomplished through the aid of his cousin, Sylvester Victoriana, himself a distant descendant of Lafitte's lieutenant known as Nez Coupé. *Couzan* Sylvester knew all the little bayous—old, new, and in-the-making—which cut the swamps and coastal marshes of that section. And so, after years of searching, he had been able to locate an abandoned water path once known to the oldest villagers as Bayou de la Loon.

"*Couzan* Sylvester himself, he saw it! Lafitte's own long-boat—big enough to hold a dozen men and a fortune in gold! It's been right there all the time, but it took last winter's freeze to kill the water hyacinths that was covering it in the bay's shallow edge. Just a year ago this month he saw it—an old rotten prow sticking out of the lilies, with the decks buried under mud. Then, when he got back with tools for digging out the wreck, he could never find it again. Finally, last month, he found the big oak tree again, with the ax blade buried in it. Now we're ready to go!"

As I looked more closely at the map, trying to distinguish the markings, Mr. Sterling continued.

"See, on the map, that pointed triangle . . . it means the long-boat . . . and this was the pirate's symbol for silver plate and gold doubloons! Just let *Couzan* Sylvester lead us there . . . my Gold Witch will do the rest!"

The plan was this: In two weeks' time, when the moon was full, we would meet at Cousin Sylvester's home, one quarter mile south of Fleming's Store in the village of Lafitte. From there Mr. Sterling's cousin would lead us to abandoned old Loon Bayou, and from this point the Gold Witch would take over. I was to bring my camera, with a proper synchronizer, and record the final triumph.

There were one or two mechanical bugs to work out of the Gold Witch, but these would be fact *accompli*, Mr. Sterling said, before the fortnight passed. The expedition to Bayou de la Loon could be delayed no longer, for it was now well up into October and the hurricane season was a threat with which all Gulf Coast mariners must reckon.

Two weeks from the night on which Mr. Sterling and Mr. Chapman revealed their secret to me, I stood in the late dusk near Fleming's Store on Bayou Barataria.

This was the last night in October—All Saints' Night— a very special night on Bayou Barataria. I wondered why my friends had chosen it for their treasure hunt. Perhaps Cousin Sylvester was a superstitious man and hoped to enlist the spirits of his ancestors in this important expedition. Or per-haps he chose a night on which all the other villagers would be gathered in cemeteries along the banks, not hunting or prowling the bayous on other missions.

Earlier in the afternoon I had seen him in the little family cemetery that lay on the bank of nearby Bayou des Oies (Bayou of the Geese), placing flowers on the graves of his parents and his wife. While I stood in the background and looked on, he had joined the large groups of visiting relatives there and had reminisced with them—retelling old family yarns, laughing again at family jokes, remembering nostalgically the old days and the old ways.

Tonight, when the relatives returned to the cemetery to place lighted candles on the graves, Sylvester would not be with them. He would be pulling a new, knife-thin pirogue down dark bayous toward a treasure field on Lost Bay. But none of this did he reveal during the afternoon of annual visiting among the family's graves. Toward the end of the day I saw him kneel again before the grave of his wife, cross himself, then light the first candle of the day and place it at the base of the tomb. He left then, nodding to me as he passed and giving a slight gesture that said he would see me later.

Now it was dusk—time for me to join Mr. Sterling and Mr. Chapman at Sylvester's cottage on the bayou. The night would be cold, I thought, from the sudden chill wind that rose in the north. Standing on the dusky bayou bank, I felt the winds pick up and cut through the tranquil twilight. I shivered a little, thinking how cold it would be out on the open bays.

Across the bayou, to the west, a great thunderhead had built up and now was lying ominously like a purple and black drapery behind the spire of the bayou church. A peculiar yellow-green streak seemed to line the dark drapery. As the setting sun struggled to break through heavy clouds, it cast an eerie yellowish light on everything. The wind was blowing, not steadily but in sudden erratic bursts that bent the bayou oaks in straining horizontal lines one moment, then straightened them the next and let their trailing strands of moss dip sulkily.

Out on Bayou Barataria the lights of returning shrimp luggers were beginning to cast shimmering reflections on the darkening water. The moon would rise in an hour. Now it was time to turn down the *banquette* toward *Couzan* Sylvester's home.

All along the bayou bank villagers were drawing into their

homes for supper, eating early so that they could return to the
cemeteries and place their lighted candles on family graves.
As first dark came down on the row of cottages which lined
the bayou bank, they busied themselves with the day's last
chores. There were shouts from inside the houses, to men and
boys who were securing boat lines to private docks, unloading
larger boats just in from the Gulf, storing fishing gear in proper
places under the house, finishing all the tasks that must be
done before they could go to the cemeteries.

Now, without warning, just as I was in sight of Sylvester
Victoriana's home, there came a growl of thunder out of the
west. I turned quickly to face across the bayou and saw a
second swift jagged slash of lightning as it streaked through
the forbidding black drapery of cloud. I felt the wind suddenly
blow stronger, colder, heard the sound of waves lapping more
loudly against the low *banquette*. Out on the bayou reflections
of passing boat lights gleamed across waves suddenly grown
rougher and higher.

"All Saints'! A rare and fit night for a treasure hunt," I
thought as I turned in toward Sylvester's lighted cottage.

Inside the three old men waited for me in the tiny kitchen,
drinking coffee and eating nervously from a big plate of boiled
shrimp which sat in the middle of the table. Cousin Sylvester
held the small map in one hand and read it to his comrades
carefully, bidding them to memorize its details.

"Ah, my lady," said Mr. Sterling, whose courtly manners
never left him, even in time of strain, "we wait only for you
and for the moon. Soon we must go. And how is your black
magic box?" They smiled wanly and I was conscious again of
their nervousness.

"All is ready now. Would you like to see the new pirogue
that *Couzan* Sylvester built to take care of the Gold Witch?"

They took me to a spindly dock in front of the cottage. Tied
there was a bayou man's dream of a pirogue, so slim, so
smooth, so lithe that it floated like a feather on the roughen-
ing water. In one end, where the gunwales met in a chiseled
prow, there was a small table-like shelf with two boat clamps

on either side.

Now I recalled that someone had told me months before that Sylvester Victoriana was the master pirogue builder of Bayou Barataria. Yet I had not realized that any craft could be so different from its kind as this shell was superior to all pirogues I had ever seen.

"He built this one like the racing pirogues," said Mr. Sterling. "And you have heard how Sylvester's grandson wins the Pirogue Race every Spring, *n'est-ce pas?* Next year is the fourth time for him, eh, *Couzan?*"

"*Oui, mais* sho," said the bayou man modestly. "But to race and to hunt treasure, they be two diff'rent horse of a single colours, no?"

While we talked, silent Mr. Chapman went about the business of the evening with dispatch, expressing himself in action. With a commanding motion of his flashlight he expressed disapproval of Mr. Sterling's chatter, and drew his partner toward Sylvester's back yard, motioning him to follow. In a moment they returned, the bayou man holding the light as the others carried the Gold Witch between them. At the dock they worked quickly, silently, grunting occasionally at the weight of the machine and the difficulty of bolting it into place on the pirogue's prow.

When they had finished, the strange looking machine rested as naturally in the pirogue as if it belonged there, and the three old men sighed happily and rested for a moment on the dock.

Then Mr. Sterling stepped into the pirogue and made some final adjustments on the machine. I saw that one of its radar screens and one radio tube were fitted carefully over a small open well built into the shelf on which it rested.

Chuckling happily, Mr. Sterling said, "Once we get near the gold we will hear our Gold Witch talk—and she speaks in two languages, her! You see this hatch she rest in, my lady? We call it our Witchin' Well!"

Now he settled himself comfortably behind the machine and

motioned Sylvester that he was ready. The pirogue builder took his place in the stern. Mr. Chapman stepped into a larger skiff nearby, motioned me to board her too. Going to my seat in the bow, I had to step carefully around a large three-foot-square box which lay on the floor of the skiff. This was the chest in which we would bring home the treasure! It gave one confidence just to look at its inviting emptiness and to think of the cargo it would carry soon.

The early moon was rising now, a huge red disk hanging like a child's cut-paper moon on the horizon of Bayou Barataria. Winds were picking up force and slapping talkative little waves against the flanks of the skiff as we pushed out from Sylvester's dock and headed down the bayou. But the men did not seem to fear the wind nor the low growls of thunder that came out of the indigo sky to the west, so I felt no worry either. We had a long way to go, said Mr. Sterling, and the waters might be calm before we got there.

Just below Cousin Sylvester's dock, and before reaching the point where Bayou des Oies entered Bayou Barataria, we crossed the stream and took a course close to the west bank. Huge oaks bent low from above and strands of trailing moss, whipped by the wind, reached out to clutch at us. Although a few scattered cottages lined the west bank, this shore was much more thinly populated and we were less likely to be observed by the villagers.

As we passed opposite the little cemetery on the peninsula of Bayou des Oies, we saw flickering lights from many candles reflecting in dark waters. From our passage across the broad bayou the little cemetery looked like a brilliant cluster of jewels. Each tiny spear of light from a brightly burning candle was reflected in the waters of the Bayou of the Geese and each cut its shiny path in the roughened water. I knew that before the night was over hundreds of other candles would be lighted there and in other private cemeteries further down the east bank. In many cemeteries of the bayou country around, on this All Saints' Night, villagers and townspeople would be gathering to light the little candles, to remember and commune with their lost ones.

Sylvester said quietly, *"Mam'selle,* you meet our *Couzan* Toinette yesterday afternoon? What you t'ink, *hein?"*

I knew that he sought my reaction to the stories told by an old crone who tended the private Perrin cemetery, not just on the days of All Souls and All Saints, but on every day of the year. It was her self-imposed task to leave her home across the road and to show any visitor who desired the wonders of the little cemetery. Solemnly and with awed whispers she told that Captain Jean Lafitte was buried here, and Napoleon, and John Paul Jones! She pointed out the graves, lingered over the strangely neglected one of Captain Jean, and told a fantastic tale of how the bodies of the great ones found their way here.

It seems that Jean Lafitte, determining to rescue the deposed Emperor, dispatched a sloop to the Isle of St. Helena and one night smuggled Napoleon out of prison. In his place the great pirate left one of his own men as a double. But Napoleon died on the passage to America and was buried here, sadly, by Captain Jean himself—unbeknown, naturally, to the rest of the world. Among the buccaneer crews was another whose sailing exploits were world-renowned. Fighting with the gallant Lafitte, and dying on one of the raiding parties, was none other than John Paul Jones. Sadly the corsairs laid him to rest beside the Little Corporal, leaving room between them to place the body of their leader when his time should come.

Today the graves lie side by side, with no inscriptions on any, but with an iron cross, made from a ship's file, marking the center one of Captain Jean who later followed his notable friends into the Beyond. Madame Toinette concludes her story by telling of a visitor who comes each year to the little cemetery, just before the day of All Saints'. The lady, said to be a distant descendant, spends hours at a time in meditation beside the unmarked grave of the Little Corporal, then pays Madame Toinette for caring for the spot for another year.

Madame Toinette told her story so convincingly that I found myself trying to figure ways it might have happened. For, after all, *mon ami,* don't you see . . . perhaps . . . ?

Yes, I knew what Sylvester sought, but I could not give an answer.

"*Mais* sho, *Mam'selle*," he whispered. "It might be, who knows for true?"

Overhearing our speculations, Mr. Sterling snorted his disbelief.

"That's Baratarian foolishments! What you say about half a dozen other graves I can show you, every one the final repose of Cap'n Jean?"

Thinking over the inconsistencies, he lapsed into Cajun

Once a year, on All Saints' Night, candles light the tombs in this private cemetery on Bayou des Oies where Baratarians claim Captain Jean Lafitte is buried.

speech and added, *"Non,* I don' believe it, me!"

We had left the little cemetery behind, had passed the lights of a second one, and now continued traveling southward. For an hour we kept our west-bank passage, unobserved by villagers whose clusters of homes had thinned out long since. Now the bayou waters reflected only an occasional beam of light from widely scattered, lonely cabins which clung precariously to dim banks of the broadening stream.

Looming ahead was the brilliant flare of a gas jet, lighting the whole sky like a giant's torch. It was the flare from an oil well, set on a peninsula of marsh created by a small canal opening off of Bayou Barataria.

Cousin Sylvester slowed the lead boat, turned into the canal and called to us.

"Voilà! It is the short cut to Bayou de la Loon."

We traveled for about half a mile down the straight canal before we saw Sylvester pause, slow his pirogue and turn the slender shell to starboard. Opening off to the right was a small water trail no more than ten feet across. I saw at once that it was an old, old bayou abandoned long before by navigators. Hyacinths, in beautiful but deadly clumps of green, clogged the banks and spread their bulbous growths across the water's surface. In places it was difficult to push our way through. Mouldering logs and fallen trees blocked our passage. As we stopped for Sylvester to grapple with his boat hook on one of these, we saw an even smaller water passage lead off to the south. Sylvester pointed to it and said to Mr. Sterling:

"See, *mon couzan,* it is the first passage south—lak it say on da map."

He heaved a great sigh as he pushed strongly on the pole and felt the log move in the mud, giving a few inches, enough to allow the pirogue to go through. The bow of our skiff entered the opening and Mr. Chapman forced it around the jammed log.

For the next hour we seemed lost in a world of shrouded swamps. Logs and hyacinths made an almost impenetrable maze of the narrow bayou. Oak trees on the bank, wind-swept and scraggly because of their proximity to the Gulf winds, dripped tentacles of moss into our faces. Like ghostly fingers they caressed our hair, as we bent low and pushed through the tunnel of woods and water. Moonlight could not penetrate the overhanging trees. Our way was lighted only by reflection, as we occasionally passed through a dense growth into a lighter one and caught the glow of thin, moonlit clouds. The swamp night was filled with a symphony of eerie sounds. Tree frogs, bullfrogs, crickets, owls, whistling cardinals, and far up the little bayou the bass roar of a solitary alligator—all sounded loud and resentful, as if trying by their tones to frighten us away from their watery kingdom. High, high above I heard the honk of geese, heading out to their island refuge in the Gulf. And from far back in the swamps came the spine-chilling scream of another winged creature, like a woman shrilling out a cry of terror. The wind had grown wilder now and whistled through the swamp forests, bending trees lower over the water and cracking off dried limbs and twigs. Bayou de la Loon! If this were the treasure trove of fabled Lafitte, he had found it well—for none but courageous souls would venture into such a haunted kingdom, no matter what the gain.

Twice during our tortuous passage down the bayou, Sylvester had hesitated briefly and pointed to water trails leading off to the south. Now he paused again, leaned heavily on his push pole and cocked his head, lifting his nose as if trying to smell the air before us. Suddenly I heard him chuckle:

"Ah, *mais oui!* The sea, I smell her good! We draw close to the lost bay, *mes amis.*"

Just as he spoke, we saw a third small water passage opening off to the south. Now Sylvester, turning into the water trail, motioned for Mr. Chapman to follow. They both strained harder on the push poles. It was true. This bayou widened a little, the trees draped less thickly over the water, and there was a smell of the sea in the winds which blew more recklessly now from the northwest.

We were through the deep swamps and were approaching

one of the thousands of bays which join the Gulf to marshlands and marsh to swamp. Now there were bigger waves on
the widening bayou, chuckling loudly against the skiff's sides.
Above us the sky opened like a great dark bowl. We saw that
the moon was gone and that the thunderhead in the west had
moved northward and was ripped every few moments with
jagged slashes of lightning.

Quite suddenly we seemed to come onto the grassy prairies
of marshland. Trees thinned out along the bayou banks. Then,
with startling clarity, we became aware of the bayou widening out into broad, flat waters of a little bay.

I heard a shout of joy come from Mr. Sterling, who had been
strangely quiet throughout the trip down Bayou de la Loon.
Sylvester laughed aloud too and called back to us.

"*Voilà!* That Lost Bay, she is found by us, for true!"

The wind, blowing relentlessly now from off the bay, flung
his words past us. In our skiff's stern Mr. Chapman laid
aside the push pole, placed the long oars in their locks, and
began to row with great effort against the wind.

I saw Mr. Sterling and Cousin Sylvester bending together
over the map, beaming it with a flashlight. Waves whipped
the bow of their narrow pirogue around in a frightening way,
but Sylvester seemed confident. Each time the narrow shell
lurched to one side he controlled it with his paddle deep in the
water.

They turned the flashlight off and began to pull more slowly
toward the bay, straining their eyes in search of the tall oak
which must stand out against the dark sky and mark our trail
from here.

Suddenly I heard Mr. Sterling shout:

"*Couzan!* I see her, yes! My God, that blessed oak!"

On a point of land near where the bayou entered the bay,
there stood a tall wind-beaten oak tree more dead than alive,
with withered trunk and great white arms bared to the sea
winds.

Our boats were close together now. I heard Sylvester mutter:
"Taller than three schooners' masts!"

From Mr. Chapman came a long sigh of relief and happiness, then a muffled curse as he strained to right the skiff and head her more straightly into the wind. From the bow of the pirogue Mr. Sterling shouted, "Quickly, *Couzan*, the compass . . . I mus' prepare the Gold Witch now!"

Sylvester, using his paddle with deep strong strokes, said, "Firs' we find ax blade, no? Maybe this not our tree, for true."

The oak was an ancient, weather-beaten giant. Straggling patches of moss clung to its gaunt frame like a torn shroud, whipped by ceaseless winds from the bay.

As we held our boats to its battered trunk, Sylvester played his flashlight over it. The beam caught a shine of metal buried in the first crotch of limbs and held there. All four of us must have seen it at the same time for we cried in unison:

"The ax blade! There!"

I felt a shiver of excitement. It was our last marker! One-quarter arpent, a few rods away, we would find the wrecked longboat, with its treasure of jewels and golden doubloons!

Breaking through the wind's roar came a cry of triumph from Mr. Sterling. He gave a shrill Rebel yell that might have been heard back at Lafitte Village:

"Yippee-Yeeooaah! . . . Cap'n Jean, we have come!"

As the shout was snatched by the wind and flung out over the marsh, Mr. Sterling stood up in the pirogue and waved his arms toward the sky. At just that moment there came a blinding flash of lightning, too close for comfort, and I saw the gaunt old man standing lean and straight in the narrow shell, his head thrown back, his arms outflung in triumph.

"*Mon dieu*, man, sit down . . . for Crissake, you sink us!"

Sylvester's urgent shout reached us just before the thunder roared over like a torrent of tortured sound.

Behind the thunder came blasts of wind that whipped the waves of the bay to a froth. It blew in gusts against us, hitting the sides of our boats in repeating blows, like punches from a giant's fists. Mr. Chapman muttered a curse that I could not hear—and suddenly I grew afraid.

I heard Sylvester shout to Mr. Sterling.

"Get dat dam' Witch goin' . . . dis nor'wester, she mean business, her!"

As the pirogue lurched again, Sylvester righted her, then tried to turn her snugly into the marshy shore of the bay. Mr. Chapman was having difficulty with the heavier skiff, but I knew that we were safer from the waves' pounding than was the slim shell that carried the two men and the Gold Witch.

Bending over his fantastic machine, Mr. Sterling worked quietly now, nervously turning knobs and pushing buttons. From the Gold Witch I heard a high-pitched, singing noise, on a steady uninterrupted beam. There was a dim light behind the tiny radar screen. It gave a ghoulish glow to Mr. Sterling's face as he bent closely to study it. Trying to protect the pirogue and its precious cargo from the waves, Mr. Chapman pulled alongside and asked me to grip the starboard gunwale while he stood and used the oars to keep both boats on an even keel.

Around us the wind whistled madly. The heavens had become a vast tortured abyss above. In livid slashes of lightning we saw one boiling black cloud pile on another in the devil's cauldron that was the sky. And through it all the thunder roared like cannon blasts.

What an irony! That our treasure-hunting night should be so tormented, after all the planning, scheming and dreaming during those long, tranquil twilights back in the Borrow Pit! We had done a bit of planning for the ghosts that Lafitte might have put to guard his treasure. But we had not thought of what to do if the night itself proved a jealous enemy.

What a sight we must make from the tumultuous heavens, for whatever ghosts of Lafitte's henchmen who looked down on us—two small boats clutched together in the stormy bay, four people hovering around a high-pitched, monotonously singing machine.

Slowly we moved down the shore, our boats clinging together for protection, our eyes and minds glued onto that peculiar machine in the pirogue's bow.

Then, above the winds and the thunder, I heard it! The

Gold Witch was speaking—in imperious, staccato notes. Short broken syllables of brassy sound, then a long whirring murmur, then more staccato notes. Over the machine Mr. Sterling bent closer, hunching his shoulders, gazing hypnotized at the tiny screen. He was very quiet now, his ear bent close to catch the Gold Witch's whisper, and it was Mr. Chapman who suddenly screeched a shrill shout of triumph.

"Yeeoooooooaaaaaaaaah!" he screamed, and strained over, trying to get a better view of the machine in the pirogue's bow.

At just that moment, while Mr. Chapman was off balance at our skiff's oars, there came a fierce blinding light out of the sky. The brilliant intensity of it sealed my eyes, streaked through my brain with a searing scorch.

Lightning! We were struck by lightning! The thought flashed numbly through my mind.

There was a deafening roar of thunder, rolling over and around us with heart-stopping blasts. When it passed, there was no sound at all from the Gold Witch—only frustrated cries from Mr. Sterling, curses from Sylvester, and a kind of moaning from Mr. Chapman. I realized that we were not hit by the lightning's stroke, only stunned by a nearby blast.

Then came another heart-shaking sound, the splintering crackle of wood, the tortured snapping of tree limbs, the bursting of timber as that great tormented tree trunk fractured and fell apart. The giant oak was sundered by the unleashed fury of the heavens! Suddenly there was a burst of flame, livid in the darkness. Heavy strands of moss, fired by the lightning, burned brilliantly against the tree's nakedness and lighted its death agonies.

In the brightness from the burning tree I caught a frightening view of the bay. Waves were bending before the wind's growing strength, tossing white spray from frothy crests, rolling toward us with vicious intent. I saw Mr. Sterling hunched over the silent Gold Witch, tinkering desperately with its wires and controls, an anguished look on his face. Sylvester was fighting grimly with the pirogue, trying to keep her upright against the pounding waves.

"Snug 'er behind us!" I heard Mr. Chapman shout, as he pulled our skiff forward and tried to protect the shell with our larger bulk.

At just that instant Mr. Sterling, numbed with desperation and fear for his prized machine, stood on his knees and bent over the pirogue's bow, trying to examine the Witch's underwater parts. The quick change in balance was too much for Sylvester. I saw the inevitable happen.

Swiftly, but silently and smoothly, the pirogue rolled over in the waves! In an instant it floated beside us, its shiny bottom glistening in the flame-lighted air. Clutched against the slender sides, the arms of its two passengers were gripping the slippery shell. Sylvester's face was contorted in anger and a vivid heat of curses flowed from his blue lips. It hurt me most to catch that glimpse of Mr. Sterling's face, for he was weeping—his face contorted with pain of frustration, tears streaming from his eyes.

Then Mr. Chapman and I fell to, preparing to haul the poor fellows into our skiff. With a quick staccato curse Mr. Chapman took hold of the empty box in the center of our boat and threw it overboard. So much for our treasure chest! Before we could pull them over the gunwales, Mr. Sterling and Sylvester got bitterly cold. Inside the skiff at last, they sat numbly, their teeth chattering, their limbs trembling. Mr. Chapman and I managed somehow to capture the pirogue's painter, tie it to the skiff's stern, and turn the two boats back toward the bayou's mouth.

Inside the bayou, close past the burning tree, we felt a temporary warmth. As our sad little crew traveled further into the swamps, away from the bay's bitter winds, the woods gave us some protection from the cold.

All was silent with my companions, though, for nothing at all could cure the coldness in their hearts. In the skiff Mr. Sterling and Sylvester huddled close together for warmth. Across their shoulders Mr. Chapman flung an old blanket, which he had brought along as extra storage for the treasure which might prove larger than our box. From behind his seat in the stern Mr. Chapman brought out a half-filled bottle of whisky, handed it wordlessly to the shivering treasure hunters.

Finally, after a few long draws from the bottle, Mr. Sterling broke the silence.

"It must have been the Gold Witch. She so good . . . she make the guarding ghost angry."

Sylvester was more literal.

"This guarding ghost . . . he is king of da nor'westers, him? *Non, mon couzan,* if it was a ghost at all, it was dat dam' nor'wester wind!"

"But my Gold Witch, she works!" cried Mr. Sterling, with some of the old enthusiasm returning to his voice. "You hear her talk when we ride close to the treasure, *hein?* You hear her whisper where the gold is buried, yes?"

Sylvester grunted assent and I hastened to assure the inventor that his machine had spoken for us all to hear.

"*So* . . . you see, my lady? We have only to dry out the parts . . . and wait for a night when the nor'westers don't blow! I think by the next moon, *hein,* Mr. Chapman?"

His silent partner, leaning heavily on the long oars to speed us homeward, proved that he knew when to speak and how to choose words of assurance.

"*Oui, mon ami.* We fix her . . . and return by next moon."

Two hours later our sad party was through the swamps, past the blazing flare of the oil well, and back on broad Bayou Barataria. The further we traveled from troubled Lost Bay, the quieter grew the northwest winds. Now the surface of the big bayou was smooth, though the air was colder than when we had left her to enter the swamps at first dark.

Was it true? Did the ghosts of Lafitte's henchmen, guarding their treasure well, send the nor'wester to Lost Bay to seek us out and ruin us?

As we tied up wearily at Cousin Sylvester's wharf, Mr. Sterling expressed best what we all must have felt:

"That Davy Jones be damned! He's the worst pirate yet, I guarantee you!"

Ole Man River's Delta Cajuns

xiv

A whole week went by—pleasant idling days among the charming Baratarians—before I found the courage to look my frustration square in the eye. Then . . . You might as well face it, *mon ami*, I said to myself . . . You're running out of leads. There's only a single thin and doubtful clue that you have not followed.

Allons! Have courage! You yet mus' finish your search, *mais* sho!

And so I found myself, at last, seeking the Cajuns who were Ole Man River's children—and following the first precept of my heart: never go by land when you can go by sea.

This dictate led me, after a minor detour or so, to New Orleans' Press Street docks and to a freight-boat packet heading straight down into the Mississippi's Lower Delta.

Captain Pete Taliancich, a man of great overflowing girth, filled the pilothouse of his freight boat *Victoria*. Somehow he managed to make the five-foot pilot wheel look like a toy. He leaned one big arm on the cabin window and yelled to his son, below on the foredeck, who yelled to lounging roustabouts standing by, to cast us off. I thought I felt the cabin shiver, above the increasing tremor from our motors, as Cap'n Pete's bellow reverberated down the length of the Press Street docks.

"Cast off and be gone, you lazy ones!" he shouted as he reversed the motors, putting a swiftly widening gap between us and the dock.

"Don' wanta see yo' ugly faces till next week," he muttered in a softer tone, and smiled. His great beef-steak hand on the tiller was as delicate as a girl's as he turned the *Victoria* about and headed downriver.

"See how she handle, my sweet lil colt," he said to his son who had come bounding up from the deck below to stand watchfully in the pilothouse.

Traffic was heavy in the port. The *Victoria* must be guided safely through crisscrossing ferryboats, through arrogant tugs which skittered about like water bugs, among ponderous up-river towboats pushing their long strings of barges, and smaller barges filled with yellow hills of sulphur, and finally through the bulky ocean-going steamships marching imperiously up the river highway.

"Lil Pete" Taliancich, who hoped someday to take over the *Victoria*, glued his eyes to the wheel, to his father's delicately caressing hands, and to the kaleidoscopic parade of traffic which dwindled as we sailed steadily along, passed through a lock and came at last upon the wide, free stretches of the great river.

I stepped from the pilothouse and joined my only fellow passenger, a solemn young priest who stood at the rail. Together we watched as the *Victoria* slipped through the heavier traffic and came to the open river.

Captain Pete had told me, slapping his big thigh and laughing hugely, "That one's the new pries' at Pointe à la Hache. Only been on the Delta for t'ree year now. He's a great scholar, Miss . . . knows all the about the old-old days . . . and he's plum in love wit dis Delta. You aks him. He talk you such talk! Mostly it's Dutch to dis ole Tocko . . . but I t'ink it worth givin' an ear too yet."

The young priest and I stood together at the rail for a long time without speaking. He seemed oblivious of me and I did not want to intrude upon his thoughts. I was enjoying memories of my own, memories of another riverboat, another captain, another crew. The same river? It seemed impossible that this was true, for all I could feel of the Mississippi now was a strangeness, an overpowering mystery and an odd heavy foreboding. Surely this was not the same water that the *Kursweg* had entered so gaily, that Captain Brown had laughed at and shaken his fist at companionably, and that the pixilated crew of the old bayou packet had sung songs to.

There was a new feeling about the wide waters we floated on . . . an undefinable quality that somehow rebuffed me. The *Victoria* was a small boat—a sturdy 110-foot packet-freight boat built like a tug—but she sailed on a vaster stream and she headed into a land more strange, more tantalizing and more forbidding than any I had seen so far.

Perhaps the young priest *could* interpret the new river and the new land for me, if he would take his eyes off the water long enough to talk. When I spoke to him timidly at last, he turned and I saw instantly that this indeed was a man in love. His dark eyes glowed fervently and in them I saw shadows of a thousand images that the river and this Delta land called up to him.

The things he told me of Father Mississippi and of deep Delta lands and peoples were strange and almost unbelievable, but I was to learn that he spoke truly of the land he loved. Speaking of the river's Delta and of the Delta's people, his imagery led us both into a kind of trance—eternal storyteller and eternal listener, cast in a mold as old as language itself. The river flowed around us, we floated on its vast bosom and approached its strange new world, all in reality, and yet somehow in a dream created by the hypnotic power of the priest's words.

For indeed the great hundred-mile-long Delta of Father Mississippi is like no other land on earth.

"Look at any map," the young priest said, using an oft-told simile, "and you will see that Louisiana is like a giant's boot, with a ragged toe dipping into the Gulf of Mexico. That frayed toe is deep Delta, torn and tormented, a wide, flat sea-marsh dipping toward the sea . . . a semiparadise, semihell . . . a trembling land of floating islands cut by surging currents, washed by waves from cyclonic winds . . . land ever-shifting, ever-changing, eternally in motion. The river gives to it the rich topsoil robbed from thirty-one mid-continent states and the sea absorbs these fertile deposits in great hungry gulps.

"It is war eternal, with Father Mississippi gaining along both upper and lower stretches. Patiently the Old Man builds ridges of higher land along his upper shores and laboriously he extends the soil at land's end, in broad brown reaches where he ends his journey among trembling prairies, floating islands and at last in blue sea itself.

"At other places along the whole jagged coast the sea wins pounding battles against weakened marshy shores, but here Father Mississippi is still dictator. He brings a million tons of earth from America's heart—topsoil from all the valleys of the Alleghenies and the Rockies—and spreads it recklessly to create new land, new islands which will attach to new shores and extend his Delta still further toward the enemy sea.

"So it happens that hunters, returning to the river's rich and teeming marshlands from year to year, cannot find their duck blinds, do not recognize the land as they left it, for different islands and different shores are there to greet them.

"So it is that geologists speak of the *weight* of the Delta, saying that its heaviness causes a regional tilt in surrounding lands, makes them dip sharply and become submerged, losing to the sea on one battle front what Father Mississippi gains on the Delta."

The poetic young priest paused, turned from his lyrical soliloquizing and looked at me as if he had forgotten my presence there. He smiled apologetically, ran thin nervous fingers through an unruly shock of black hair, and said:

"But you must pardon if I get a little lost. You see . . . the shining river and the sun, the marsh winds on trembling earth behind the river ridges . . . it makes all us Deltans a little crazy, I guess."

I smiled too, remembering that Captain Pete had said the young man had been a Deltan but three years. And yet he felt so deeply about the land and its great river and encroaching sea, I found an easy credence in his poetry and in his love for this curious country.

"And what of the other Deltans, who live in your weird and changing paradise?" I asked.

"Ah, but you should know them, Miss . . . It takes a formidable breed of men, you see, to match such a fabulous land. You wouldn't believe what a melting pot the Delta is . . . and how its peoples live in peace together. The English and French and the Tockos, Spanish and Irish, Italian and Chinese, Negro and Philippine . . . all living and sharing their work and their pleasures . . . the few big planters that are left and the *petits fermiers* in their narrow rows of truck garden, the orange growers and lily growers and the wine makers, the oystermen and shrimpers, frog hunters and trappers, alligator hunters and remedie men, the oil geologists and river pilots . . . and us few religious working among the whole great pack of them."

"Sounds like a formidable parish indeed, Father," I said.

"Ah, but you should see them. And you should hear their histories, Miss," he continued.

"Look now at the ruins of that old sugar plantation . . . and look just below at that avenue of live oaks almost hidden behind the chemical tank farm. Such a tale those oaks can tell!"

Along the unfolding shores, past spires and tanks of river-edge industrial plants which cut blackened scars against the sky, we had come through a country that once had been Louisiana's richest plantation land. Ruins of venerable mansions stood gauntly behind green levees, their huge empty windows sagging, staring moodily out to the river. Now the priest told stories of these houses and of others long since decayed and fallen away, burned in the fury of old wars or lost in the turmoil of financial ruin.

Foremost among all the great Louisiana plantations of its time was Versailles, the palace of the illustrious de la Ronde family.

Pierre Denis de la Ronde was a man of magnificent visions. Even on the Delta, where many sugar planters grew drunk with dreams of fabulous riches, he stood foremost. On his twenty-first birthday, picturing his mansion of the future, Pierre planted an alley of oaks stretching from the river for half a mile, back to this chosen site. In 1805 he built his great mansion, a house of such magnificent proportions and grandeur that Versailles seemed the only fitting name. To de la Ronde's neighbors—the de Marignys, Ducros, DeClouets, Philippons— the sugar baron's home was called simply "The Palace."

By then the avenue of oaks had grown grand and imposing, a symbol of this de la Ronde's dreams and schemes. Married to a daughter of another great Creole family of the Delta, he had sired a family as handsome and elegant as his château. On the great galleries, among the spacious gardens and under the oaks grown huge and towering in the lush Delta loam, frolicked nine daughters and a single son. They bore the classic names of Eulalie, Elizabeth Céleste Héloise, Joséphine Pépita, Marie Manette, Adélaïde, Adèle, Marie Félicie, Isabelle Émilie, Magdalena Azélie, and the son, Pierre Denis de la Ronde III—to their neighbors known as the Nine Muses and Apollo.

Pierre Denis de la Ronde had only begun to dream. Now he sat under his oaks, sipped his demitasse of *café noir,* and thought scornfully of Nouvelle Orléans, the scattered and ugly city just a few miles upriver. He would build his own city! Patterned after the French monarch's, it would be the beauty spot of the whole continent—a New Paris in a rich new land! He would set his city on the shores of nearby Lake Borgne, would build a channel to connect it with the Mississippi, would construct a road between his Delta mansion and the new city, a *Chemin de Paris* that would bear an ever-growing stream of traffic to an infant metropolis that would grow into a giant! Had he not built already a beautiful kingdom along the rich shores of this mighty river? Was it not clever how he and his Creole neighbors—the Villerés, Bienvenues, Jumonvilles, the Colombs, Rodriguez, Chalmettes and others—had devised ways to make their lands a paradise? Between each of the great plantations there were drainage canals which led overflow river waters "to the back" where smaller man-made canals streaked through the marshlands to flow into the coastal sea. Men who could perfect such designs, create and maintain such estates, could do anything!

While he dreamed in the shadows of his oaks, a war was brewing. The year was 1814. Flaring first in Europe, where the British had defeated Napoleon's armies, it would soon be fought on Delta shores sold so recently by Napoleon to the uncouth *américains.* Like all proud Creole planters, de la Ronde scorned the rough, uncultured *américains* and the booming commercialism they had brought to the French colony's Crescent City. But like all planters everywhere, the Creole loved his lands with a close and personal passion.

There appeared in New Orleans a gaunt frontiersman soldier who knew how to profit by the planters' love of homeland. Soon all the haughty Creoles and their gallant, dashing sons were rallying behind *"le général Gjacksong."*

The American general was to need them, as well as the ragged "Kaintucks" and Tennesseans whom the ungainly Indian fighter claimed as brothers—as well as the buccaneers whom pirate Jean Lafitte led in from Barataria bayous to the west and the brave Acadians from Bayou Teche and Lafourche. His was as conglomerate an army as any in American history.

Andrew Jackson was sick with fever. He had less than a fortnight to give his army shape and form. Eight days after he arrived in New Orleans, ill with malaria, the British armada arrived in sight of Louisiana shores. British land forces, commanded by Sir Edward Pakenham, brother-in-law of the Duke of Wellington, had sailed in from the east, past the Gulf Coast's Cat Island and Ship Island, the same route used by Iberville more than a century before. On board these vessels were some twenty thousand well-trained and well-equipped soldiers, veterans who had blasted Napoleon's legions and were now fresh from setting fire to the U.S. capital city. So confident were their regimental officers that they brought their wives along on the voyage—fastidious ladies in silks and satins who stood daintily at deck rails, watched the incredible new world unfold, and picked sites for their own plantations along rich shores of the Delta they felt to be doomed.

Against the British armada *Monsieur le Général* had pitted and lost five gunboats. Now there remained only a few schooners, among them the small but sturdy *Carolina*. Against General Pakenham's splendidly equipped regiments of picked veterans, the American had about five thousand soldier-civilians, carrying their own shotguns and rifles. It seemed an unequal contest indeed. Yet the American general had hopes. His was an army that fit the land it would fight upon. And he had faith in his greatest ally, the Delta itself—this half-water, half-land of marshy prairies, trembling earth, boggy alligator holes, mucky swamp slime, twisting river currents and sliding

shores—and always and forever the monstrous Delta mosquitoes which could drive a man into a screaming, tormented
animal. Britain's elegant army, dressed in resplendent white
and red, had yet to meet this kind of enemy.

A few miles to the east of the Mississippi, on the shores of
Lake Borgne near Bayou Bienvenue, the British made a landing and sent out scouts. Following them, laboriously dragging
themselves and their equipment through the swamp bogs, a
large part of the army arrived at higher plantation lands
belonging to Major Gabriel Villeré's estate. The Major was
supposedly in charge of local defense. The British surprised
and captured him in his own mansion. But his guards did not
realize the fervor and courage of a Creole aroused. Before
their eyes he leaped from a window, raced across his gardens
and escaped into nearby levee thickets. Eluding them, he
traveled swiftly to the adjoining plantation of Colonel de la
Ronde and the two men rowed across the river, secured horses
from a friend, and raced to New Orleans to give the warning.

General Jackson rallied his motley army around him—
Plauche's Creole battalion actually ran ten miles from Bayou
St. John into the city—and began an advance.

"By the Eternal, they shall not sleep on our soil!" shouted
the frontier general, and led his soldiers out of the city along
streets where strains of "Yankee Doodle" mingled with "La
Marseillaise."

It was dusk on the night of December 23, 1814, when they
reached the plantation country where the British were established. Across flat Delta lands the army advanced slowly, using
Indian tactics, slipping noiselessly past white-pillared châteaux until they approached the Villeré plantation. British
soldiers lolled around campfires, having supper under the
towering oaks, relaxing from their strenuous march through
the Lake Borgne swamps. Inside the mansion their officers ate
splendidly, enjoyed the rich wine cellar which was said to be
among the Delta's finest.

Jackson brought his men to a nearby avenue of great moss-
draped oaks and placed them strategically behind the Gar-

gantuan trunks. They were hidden among the de la Ronde oaks. Ragged Kentuckians and Tennesseans gaped at the dim outlines of graceful Versailles standing so nobly at the head of the long tree-lined lane and wondered at the elegance of Creole life they were here to defend.

Just over the levee the *Carolina* stood by, shrouded by a dense river fog, ready at Jackson's signal to fire the opening salvo.

Suddenly death roared in from the river, shattering the Britishers' calm, volley following volley in nerve-shattering rhythm. Rallying his startled and disordered troops, Sir Edward led them toward the river, expecting to meet the fire of many gunboats.

Silently the American land forces waited among the dark oaks. Then, at their general's signal, they rushed a screaming hell into the rear of the stupefied British camp. Fighting hand to hand in the dark, fighting with rifle butts and hunting knives, tomahawks and pistols and sometimes with feet and fists, the Americans routed the British recklessly and without mercy.

Quick to appreciate his advantage, Jackson withdrew. The first violent victory went to him. As the fog floated in more heavily, the British sent for reinforcements. The next attack would be theirs, they vowed!

Crossing several neighboring plantations, Jackson chose an abandoned drainage canal on the Rodriguez place and set his men to building a defensible barricade. With spades and shovels and bare hands they gauged the canal deeper and built a mud embankment behind it. Fence posts, cotton bales, old plantation gear of all kinds went into the barricade which must stay the force of Pakenham's revenge.

Against this homespun defense wall the British would throw the fire of heavy cannon they were now dragging with heartbreaking labor across bogs and swamps from Lake Borgne's shores. In the interim they blew up the gallant little *Carolina*, leaving but one sister ship to escape.

On the morning of December 28, five days after Jackson's

surprise attack in the de la Ronde oaks, Sir Edward Pakenham led his regiments against the crude barricade. Advancing with their heavy guns through the intervening plantations, British artillery tore at Jackson's wall with blasts of thunder. But the Americans had a few heavy cannon of their own, manned by the crew of the *Carolina* and by Lafitte's choicest marksmen. Behind their wisely chosen entrenchment, dominating the flat plains on which the British marched in neat, disciplined lines, the American woodsmen and Indian fighters made the most of their advantage. Their long-bore rifles, which they could load, fire, reload and refire with incredible speed, proved a greater advantage still. The British, baffled and unnerved, went down in havoc.

Shouts in several tongues rang out for *"le Général Gjacksong"* as he passed along his lines. Against frightening odds he had led his curious army to two victories! And yet the British, withdrawn now and planning another attack, must be met on still another day. Their numerically superior forces could be deployed in many formations. Would *Monsieur le Général* have the final victory?

Eleven tense days went by. The British struggled with their artillery, dragging more big guns across more boggy miles. When Jackson sent some of his forces to the west bank of the river, Sir Edward did the same. Weary, sweating Britishers cut a canal by hand, dragged cannon over the east-bank levee, loaded them on barges and prepared to float them across the wide river.

During the long days of terrible labor, Britishers came face to face with Jackson's ally, the Delta terrain. Stumbling through marsh bogs, falling waist-deep into alligator holes, dragging heavy guns through knee-deep muck and slime, their fatigue grew to a torment. And the everlasting mosquitoes, singing their sibilent and deadly tunes, would not let them rest.

Finally came January 18, 1815, the day of Sir Edward's attack. The plan was a good one. Men would be launched in barges, would cross the river to land on the west bank and begin the battle with Americans there.

At the sound of their fire, Sir Edward's east-bank regiments would move toward the Rodriguez Canal barricade, carrying with them the fascines and ladders to be used in crossing and scaling the wall. Attack would be before dawn, when the deadly aim from frontiersmen's rifles would be hampered by the dark.

The plan did not take into account that other tricky ally of Jackson's, the erratic Mississippi. On levee banks, British barges lurched and lunged, soldiers fell into the water, other barges buried their gunwales in mud. The launching took hours longer than expected. Once in midstream, the barge loads of men and cannon were swept by contrary currents, twisted in whirlpools, spun into the west bank three miles below the American forces they were supposed to attack.

Frustrated and livid with rage, Sir Edward finally ordered the advance of his main forces. But it was daylight now, a clear bright morning with no fog. Wave upon wave of brightly-clad Britishers, resplendent in gleaming red and white, advanced toward the American barricade. Frontiersmen awaiting them there had their general's orders: wait for the closest range, pick your targets well, give a single bullet to a single man.

It was a debacle, complete and terrible. The redcoats, re-filling their thinning ranks after each onslaught, advancing by inches, finally reached the canal only to face a deadlier onslaught. By some monumental error they had left their fascines and ladders behind. Three hundred badly-needed soldiers were sent back for this equipment. Before they could return their fellows were in mad retreat, diving into ditches, hiding in reeds and rushes. Attempting to rally his disordered troops, Sir Edward himself took a bullet in his right arm, felt his horse fall beneath him, leaped to the horse of his aide, then took a more terrible wound in his thigh and groin. Seeing their officers fall around them, the men turned retreat into chaos.

On the other side of the river the British fared better once their cumbrous forces met the numerically inferior American lines. They might even have pressed on to New Orleans. But news of the terrible collapse of the east-bank forces caused them to give up the battle.

The battle grounds among the east-bank châteaux were littered with British dead. Stretchers, long lines of them, took the wounded toward waiting vessels. Ladies on shipboard, waiting anxiously for their heroes' return, fainted at the sight of their husbands brought back dead or wounded.

Sir Edward Pakenham, mortally wounded, was carried to the rear, placed beneath the protective arms of a giant oak where he died. The oak tree was on the Colomb plantation, though legend tells that it was one of those planted by Pierre Denis de la Ronde. Thus the de la Ronde oak avenue saw a tumultuous battle, and met a destiny far different from what its owner dreamed. Today travelers are told erroneously that these are the Pakenham Oaks, because the British general is mistakenly thought to have died here.

Victory was sweet for the motley soldiers of *"le Général Gjacksong."* Incredibly, their loss in the three encounters was only thirteen killed, thirty wounded and nineteen missing. The British, outnumbering the Americans four to five times, reported seven hundred killed, fourteen hundred wounded and five hundred missing.

Today the plantations upon which the bloody contest raged have become a national cemetery. Visitors to New Orleans may drive down the east-bank road to the site, may walk among the shrouded oaks where Pierre Denis de la Ronde dreamed his great dreams so long ago and may recall the fierce battles where Americans, Creoles, Acadians, Choctaws, mulattoes and Negroes defended their common homeland against Britain's proud army.

After the Battle of New Orleans was fought on his estate, de la Ronde saw many changes in his homeland. Louisianians were more united than before and they took a greater pride in the Crescent City they had fought so desperately to defend. Thus his dream of a new Paris and a new capital were never realized. Versailles, which had served as a British hospital during the battles, remained a symbol of his magnificent dreaming until 1876 when it was destroyed by fire. Today, as

with the other noble châteaux of the Delta sugar planters, only
a few crumbling walls remain to remind you of its glorious days
long gone.

"That's the story the de la Ronde oaks can tell," the young
priest concluded. "Magnificent Versailles is gone and half a
hundred more . . . all of the shining châteaux of the Creole
planters, all wasted away in ruins."

The marsh has crept in from the back, the river has chewed
at the oaks where American batteries huddled through those
long fearful nights, and the Delta has won its own subtle war
for the land.

He showed me the very spot on which the *Carolina* had
hovered and fired the opening volley of the desperate battles.
Where the schooner had floated in fifty feet of water, the river
has deposited soils of a score of faraway states, building dry
land here, while it gnawed jagged holes in other parts of the
old battle field.

Standing beside the priest at the rail of the little *Victoria*,
I felt the power of the great river beneath us. Now its waters
swept us through abandoned sugar lands of the old plantation
country, past newer homes of humbler Deltans, on toward
the greater mysteries of the Lower Delta where it would split
into three mouths and pour its mighty flood into the sea.

As we sped downward, the shores grew more lush and fertile,
more exotically green with willows and cottonwoods weaving
a luxuriant drapery among the storm-torn oaks. Banana plants
and palmettos thrust upward through a morass of vines and
creepers. From our height at the rail we could see the encroaching swamp fighting to invade the highland ridges along
the banks, and further back, dim and dissolving into mists,
the swaying grasses of the water prairies. The city was but a
few hours behind us, yet it seemed another world away. For
this was like no other world I had ever seen.

Suddenly I was startled by a shrill blast of the boat's
whistle and by Cap'n Pete's bellowing voice: "Pointe à la
Hache ahead! All stand to!"

The priest said, "No! It is too soon!" and I agreed, for already the river and the Delta lands were weaving their spell on me.

It was our first stop of the trip, and a short one. Lil Pete and another crewman handled the unloading of thirty cases of beer and five cases of canned goods with alacrity.

The young priest spoke a hasty good-bye, smiling shyly. "Please do not think me always so garrulous . . . You *did* say you wanted to hear the old tales? I wish there were a week to tell them in . . . no, a month . . . perhaps a year, *n'est-ce pas?*"

As he stepped onto the dock and turned to wave, the *Victoria* reversed its motors and headed across river to West Pointe à la Hache. We sped along beside a west-bound ferryboat loaded with cars, wagons, carts, bicycles, and a milling crowd of Deltans. Captain Pete said this was one of few ferry crossings on the whole Delta and was used plenty-plenty by the natives. I saw Lil Pete down on the foredeck gesturing with wildly flaying arms, trying to attract the attention of a friend on the ferry. Then I caught the echo of a shout and a swift interchange of words in a guttural Slavic tongue.

The huge captain laughed loudly. "Them crazy Tockos! Ain't got no more sense to 'em than a Frenchmens!"

"What do you mean, Tockos?" I asked, for the term had caught my ear when the priest had used it awhile ago.

Captain Pete scratched one big drooping ear and thought for a long moment before he answered. "You don' know Tockos, Miss? Wal, now dat's a pretty long yarn for one man . . . and one river . . . but I oughta be able to tell you someways, seeing as I'm one of them myself . . ."

The beginnings of his story went back about a century, for it was then that the first schooners from distant Adriatic shores of Dalmatia sailed up the Mississippi and into New Orleans. Slavic sailors aboard looked at the fertile Delta earth, the widely scattered plantations of the Creoles and smaller farms of the humbler French, they looked at the bays and coastal waters where fishermen toiled and brought in their rich har-

vests—they remembered their war-shattered Balkan lands—
and they decided to make a new home.

They came to work and that was what they did, toiling from
pre-dawn till after dark, with a strength and a holding power
that shocked their Gallic neighbors.

"*Mon dieu*, them mens . . . ain' they need no res'? . . . Ain'
they need no good-time . . . no womens?"

The women they worked for were left at home—sweethearts,
fiancées, wives too, waiting for eight, ten, years and more
before their men could save passage money and return for
them or send them the money to make the long trip alone.

The huge, melancholy men lived to themselves, morosely,
a single lonely oysterman spending days and nights, weeks
and months and years by himself in his high one-room hut on
stilts in the grass-frayed marshes by the sea.

When they met occasionally at river ports, the greeting
was "*Kako ste?*" or "How are you?"

The odd syllables amused the French who began calling
them "*Kako ste's*." In time the nickname became "Tocko," a
Frenchman's approximation of the accent.

The French laughed at their surnames too, saying "if it
ain' got no 'itch,' it ain' Tocko."

Gradually the Dalmatian colony grew more prosperous.
When the women joined their men in barren oyster camps,
they worked as unstintingly as their mates, helped with oyster
tonging, cooked monstrous meals for a quickly growing family
which continued always to speak its native Slavic, follow its
ancient customs.

Young men, coming over from the old country, signed con-
tracts with their cousins, worked for the merest pittance for
four or five years or more before they could pay their sponsor
for transportation and become independent. Yet they too
prospered in time.

Communities grew up on both banks of the river—Empire,
Olga, Ostrica, Oysterville. Settling them were the Jurishiches,
the Popiches, the Zibiliches, the Luliches. Although Dalma-
tians always dominated, Balkans from Serbia, Montenegro,

Greece and Albania swelled the growing settlements.

After a time the Tockos began to feel at home on the Delta, softened a little in the warm, friendly atmosphere. The most successful of them took their hard-earned oyster profits and bought fleets of schooners for hauling, or bought orange groves, or they opened oyster shops and restaurants in the city, or entered a profession. They prospered. Some of the men looked appreciatively at gay, dark-eyed French girls and married them, to sire a new Slav-French admixture in this lush land of many hybrids. Although they retain many racial identities and speak English with strong Slavic accents, today only a few of the older men still wear the *brci*, the walrus mustaches which once marked the Tocko. They are true Deltans now, and proud of the term that ties them to their neighbors of many races, many tongues.

"Yah, the Tocko he a real Deltan now," said Cap'n Pete with pride. "Now take me, I come over from ole country when only fourteen. Work like a Missipp' mule for four year to pay back my cousin Albert who is sponsor for transportation. In cash I collect only nineteen dollar fi'ft cent a year and twenty-five dollar when I finish and go out on my own. Then I got my own oyster bed, nearly back o' Ostrica it was, and I mak' a little bit of start. It easy to work like Missipp' mule when it for myself and for my French-Slavonia woman I fin' here on da Delta. She help me work plenty hard, between our six baby boys and our girl. Pretty soon I buy my firs' hauling schooner. I haul my own oyster and plenty of my frien's into the French Market at N'Awlins. Then I lease more beds here in Ostrica. My boys grow up and we get another schooner. Pretty soon I build an oyster shed in Ostrica and buys other mens' oysters. Then I build a restaurant-bar too. Yah, you gonna see this evening. Then, my boys and me, we decide to lease the oyster luggers to our cousins and buy a river freight boat. Now we haul our oysters thisaway, and we haul plenty other freight up and down the river for our neighbors. Yah, da Delta she been good to us Tocko, Miss, you gonna see."

As the *Victoria* headed into the shore to make a landing at

Ostrica, I reminded Cap'n Pete of his promise that I should see the oyster grounds for myself.

Ostrica proved to be just a tiny settlement of a dozen or so flimsily built houses, looking more like fishing camps than homes. A few shone brightly in the late afternoon sun, but most were dreary, unpainted and depressing. They were centered around the oyster shed, with its small canal leading back into the marsh. Cap'n Pete's bar stood at the end of a long, narrow boardwalk ranging in front of the collection of huts. The whole community was built at least four feet off the ground—"clearin' the river mud."

Men, mostly Negroes lounging around the oyster shed, sprang into action when Cap'n Pete blew three short blasts on his boat whistle. Almost before he had tied up they were forming a line on the boardwalk, strapping fellows, each bearing an oyster sack on his shoulder. Once they started loading, they formed a double line of bent figures, passing each other in dreary monotony, one side shouldering the heavy hundred-pound oyster sacks, the other walking more straightly after leaving its burden, then pausing to pick up more sacks and joining the heavy-laden line leading back to the boat. The Negroes sang a low monotonous tune, more like a moan, as they trudged down the dock toward the *Victoria*. There was something acutely depressing about the scene to me. I was glad when Captain Pete led me off the boat, beckoning toward an old man whom I had seen standing on the bow of an oyster lugger in the canal.

"Heh . . . *Kako ste?*" he shouted in his bull-throated voice.

"*Dobro-dobro* . . . good-good," said the oysterman as we approached. "Twenty bushel-and-half sack I bring you dis trip, my frien' . . . why not I feel good?"

I noticed that the old man still wore his *brci* and pulled on it fondly as he talked. His little low-slung, broad-beamed lugger was neat and shining. He had just finished washing the decks after unloading his oysters. Captain Pete had told me of this special type of oysterman's lugger which the Tockos had modeled after the Louisiana shrimp lugger, but with modifications to fit their special needs.

Captain Carl Zibilich agreed to take me out to his camp on the sea marsh behind Ostrica.

As we pulled away from the dock at the end of the little canal, we were in reverse for fifty yards, until the oysterman could swing the stern around and head into another, tinier canal on the left.

This narrow man-made canal . . . "Mostly she dug by Cap'n Pete hisself" . . . was a straight blue-grey shaft through the tall weaving draperies of marsh grass that surrounded us on either side. Down it the little lugger traveled smoothly, taking us out of the world of the oyster settlement and into the great flat prairies of grass, water and skies that stretched far and wide around and above us. There was an immensity to this landscape that took away the need for speech. I felt suddenly that I could understand the Tocko's silent, melancholy ways. There was about this land the serenity and tranquility of a sleeping giant. When aroused, the giant could scream with terrible, cyclonic winds, could rip the marsh grass with great wild fists and churn canals and bays to frothy waves. But on an evening like this, with the sun slanting richly out of a mauve-blue sky, there was such peace on the land as I had seldom felt. Water, land and sky seemed one element together, and the oysterman and I a vibrant part of them all.

We rode silently together until we sighted a tiny hut far out upon the sea of marsh grass. As we came nearer I saw that it stood on spindly wooden legs like stilts, six feet above ground. Surrounding it and beneath it was a blanket of oyster shells, gleaming white and clean in the late sun's rays. No sprig of grass, no flowers, no unfunctional thing. Narrow, wobbly steps led up to the single room. Draped over them at the top was a throw net and leaning against the house were push poles, a boat anchor, a large coil of rope, several pairs of oyster tongs. Tied to one of the house piers were two skiffs, oars stacked neatly inside.

"Yah, it an oysterman's home," the old man said. "Ain't got

no womens since ten year now when my woman die from pneumonia."

Standing in classic simplicity against the immensity of blue sky and green-gold sea marsh, the oyster camp had an undefinable beauty of its own.

"She good strong house awright," said Captain Zibilich. "In '27 hurricane my woman and me was here all t'rough it. Winds like crazy hell . . . and waves ten-twelve feet, t'row spray lak bullets 'gainst these glass . . . turn my lugger upside-to, wash my skiffs out to sea . . . all aroun' us from here to Ostrica, nuttin' but sea-waves and tides. We stay like in a cage for five whole day . . . then a rescue boat get t'rough . . . da padre aboard say we got a miracle, us . . . plenty mens and womens and chil'ren drown on the marsh . . . yah, she good strong house here."

"You lika taste some fine oyster from my home beds, Miss?" he asked.

Jumping off the boat with the agility of a man half his age, the old man tied his lugger to a pier on the shell bank just under his home. Before I could follow him, he turned to help me off the boat with a kind of old-world courtesy.

Picking up a pair of long-handled scissorlike tongs, he went to the edge of the canal and began to search with them for oysters which lay in finishing beds around his camp.

"This special kin' of oyster tong, Miss," he said. "It was invent' by Tockos. You know da Frenchmens they good men, for sure, but they no good oystermen. The Tocko, he unnerstan' da oyster and unner'stan what is *work* . . . so he know how to make a proper oyster tong."

He was working now with hands full of the large oysters which he had tonged up so easily. Deftly, with a swift flick of his knife, he opened a dozen crusty shells, placed them on a little tin plate picked up from a nearby skiff. Then, with a smile that brought a glitter to his deep-blue eyes and a quivering of pleasure to his walrus-like *brci,* he presented the tray to me. Never have I tasted such succulent oysters as those we ate straight from the beds that evening. We ate as the native Deltans do, from the freshly tonged shells, without sauce to spoil the flavor.

And as we enjoyed the feast together, the old oysterman told me stories of his trade, a calling that the French Deltans had followed with characteristic *laissez faire* for almost a hundred years before the Tockos came and made it a leading Delta industry.

He told me how the "Frenchmens lef' their oysters to God" while Tockos "farmed" their oysters as carefully as the orange growers across the river cared for their groves. When nature's tricks of wind and wave tore at the natural reefs and ruined his oysters, the Frenchman shrugged his shoulders and hoped for a better season next year. The Tocko, born and bred to heavy, ceaseless labor, would have none of such uncertainties. By experimentation—"a little try at dis, a little try at dat"—Tockos developed a system of oyster farming that built a stable industry. In the process these water agriculturists found prosperity and sometimes riches.

He told how more than two years of back-breaking labor was required to turn wild oysters from natural reefs into the fat, succulent ones we were eating.

"First, a Tocko must get a lease on da bes' breedin' ground he can find, and that take plenty searching."

The Delta is peculiarly rich in these fine breeding spots. Here, in thousands of coastal bays and lagoons, there is a mixture of silted river water and saline water of the encroaching Gulf. To these natural breeding grounds the Tocko oysterman brings a lugger full of empty oyster shells, then transfers them to skiffs and scatters one heavy skiff-load after another onto the breeding beds. In the salty waters here, bivalves may "spat" or spawn, and "set" or attach themselves to a larger oyster shell or some other object.

After two years and several careful inspections by the oyster farmer, the crop is ready for gathering. The smaller crustaceans are re-bedded on the same grounds, but the largest, best oysters are carried to a new bedding ground near the sea. Here, washed and fed by salty Gulf waters, they grow fat. Soon they develop the delicate flavor which causes gourmets to say that the Louisiana oyster is the best in America.

Experience has shown that the best breeding grounds are on the west bank of the Mississippi, so oystermen like Captain Zibilich who live on the east bank must cross the river to fulfill the first step in their arduous oyster culture.

But the oysterman's work is not nearly done when he has re-bedded them near the sea. He may leave the oysters in their new, saltier beds for a week or for a couple of months—"a Tocko, he jus' *feel* when da time is right"—but when they have absorbed enough salinity, he must tong them up again, haul them back across the river and reset them in clean beds near his oyster camp. This time they are bedded close together, not scattered widely as in the first operation. When he tongs them up for loading onto his lugger, the oysterman will gather great tongsful at once. Two years of hard manual labor culminates in the heavily loaded lugger which the Tocko pushes off from his home bedding grounds and heads toward the shed at the river front. His last act—the loading of his precious crop—must be done just a few hours before the freight boat arrives at the oyster shed.

For time is of the essence from this stage on. In the old days, when oysters had to be hauled from Delta camps by cumbersome and slow sailing schooners, the two years of work might be lost at this final moment. Seeking out bays and lakes that lay to the east of the river, oystermen sailed with some assurance. But when these broad reaches gave out and they turned into the river, they faced uncertainty. Most times they paid motorized vessels to tow them upriver, hitching a tow from whatever genial captain would toss them a line, usually at a fee of about twenty-five dollars.

In those days even the Tockos who could afford more modern equipment preferred sailing schooners to motor vessels, for it was thought that the boat's vibrations shook the sensitive oysters too much, disturbing them. Now, however, this belief is discarded and oystermen travel regularly in luggers equipped with auxiliaries or full motor power.

Finally, as dusk began its somber march across the sea marsh, Captain Zibilich and I headed back to the oyster shed at Ostrica. On the way he pointed out a peculiar meshlike fencing that surrounded his oyster beds and those of some of his neighbors along the canal. This was the ultimate in water farming!

"We fence the devil drumfish out," said Captain Zibilich as if it were the most natural thing in the world to find fences staked in this watery wilderness. He told me then of many enemies which fed upon the oysters—boring sponges and clams, the sea conch or drill, and worst of all the "devil drumfish." They travel in deadly groups and when such a clan of fifty-pound invaders attacks an oyster bed they can destroy in a few hours' time the whole year's work of an industrious oysterman.

"So we buil' a fence and keep 'em out. It is the only way."

Our lugger bow broke the limpid stream. The marsh spread endlessly ahead. I was startled by the cries of birds which swirled in screaming circles before us. These winged creatures were as much a part of the vibrant, teeming Delta as were the scale fish and shellfish which crowded its bays and streams. Birds of every kind, of every size and color, and of raucous or silvery call were here . . . a Deltan paradise of swift-winged fowl, swirling and diving, dipping and winging over the sea marsh into the darkening sky.

Swiftly, as in a tropical twilight, the dark settled in. As the lights from the oyster shed and from the homes of Ostrica came flickering down the canal, I heard the *Victoria's* whistle sound a demanding call. We had over-stayed and Cap'n Pete was imptatient! I knew he was due to tie up in Buras this night, to make a *must* delivery to one of the orange growers. Saying a hasty good-bye to Captain Zibilich, I boarded the little freight boat apologetically. A roaring command from

Cap'n Pete and we were cast off from the dock. The surface was calm and the night winds had not risen. On the broad bosom of the river we floated as on a quiet sea, silently and swiftly.

Across the river we docked at Buras, orange capital of the Delta. From here to Pointe à la Hache above, the perfume of orange groves had sweetened the Delta air. Now we were engulfed in its fragrance.

At the landing stood Jean Pierre Buras, the orange grower who waited so eagerly for the *Victoria's* delivery of a new spray for his precious trees.

Cap'n Pete, seeing him standing there in the half-light of the dockside, shouted:

"Ah, Jean Pierre . . . come aboard, man! We gotta yo' poison. Tomorrow we unload you. Tomorrow you spray the lil trees and make a miracle . . . Tonight, you come aboard wit us."

In the flickering searchlights I could see the Frenchman shake his head as he shouted back, "*Non, mon ami,* firs' I mus' get her unload . . . and store' away from da moist . . . You come to my house now . . . We ope' a keg o' orange wine . . ."

Grumblingly, Cap'n Pete left his pilothouse and motioned me toward the dock.

"Crazy Frenchmens . . . tomorrow do as well for his tree dust!"

Disagreeing, the earnest grove tender helped Lil Pete and his deckman with the unloading of several cases of spray. When all the boxes were stacked in his worn-out pickup truck over the levee, he motioned us to crawl in too. Bouncing along the levee road, past the lighted windows of little houses which huddled there as if for protection from the river's wrath, we came finally to our friend's home.

As the noisy truck coughed to a standstill, a light-flooded doorway opened and a large blonde woman waved us inside. She had the huge rough hands, the soft dull eyes and the measured solemnity of the Slav. She was Tocko, the mother of Monsieur Jean Pierre's four lively bright-eyed children who clung to her skirts. With a wave of one big reddened hand she shooed them off to bed and welcomed us in. On the porch behind us, her sprightly husband stamped the mud from his feet and shouted:

"*Eh bien, ma petite.* The poison, she is here. Now we can res' and make da good-time, yes! Ope' that new keg o' wine, you. We show Cap'n Pete and the lady what is da bes' in Buras!"

I noticed that his head came only to the shoulder of his tall, solemn-faced wife, but it was obvious who was master in the house. The union was a common one on the Delta these days, although in the first and second generation of émigrés, it was Tocko men who married the dark-skinned, Gallic *jeunes filles* and Slavic women wed only the men of their own country.

When Madame Jean Pierre returned with the wine, it was served in tumblers.

Her husband raised his glass to us for a toast:

"Long life to *Mam'selle* aboard the *Victoria* . . . and many good passage to Cap'n Pete who this trip save my lovely lil trees!"

The orange wine had a bouquet different from any I had ever known. Also a warmth and a stealing slumbrous effect that loosened the tongues of Monsieur Jean Pierre and Cap'n Pete, causing them to spin yarns of their Delta with gusto.

I learned that almost the *whole* citizenry of their home town was named Buras. "Alla white mens here is my cousins, way back, and mostly now too," said *M'sieu* Jean Pierre.

'Way back—"a hunnert year ago"—when the seven Burat brothers sailed up this river from France and picked this site for their home, the Delta settlement had only a few fishermen and trappers' huts. They were a prolific breed, the Burat brothers, and peopled the Delta round with their Gallic sons and grandsons. After several generations the name was slurred, in the soft Deltan patois of their neighbors, to become "Buras" instead of Burat. It has remained so and now almost every family in the town bears this name and is related by blood or marriage.

Through the years many other racial elements have come in.
Today Buras is the cosmopolitan melting pot of the Delta.
Working side by side in the orange groves, in the oyster beds
and on the trapping lands, are French, Spanish, Dalmatian,
Slavonic, Chinese, Philippine, Negro, and the admixtures of all
these. In a tightly knit settlement on the northern fringes
is a group of mulattoes who are a blend of all these. Refusing
to share their neighborhood, their churches or their schools
with the darker Negroes, they remain aloof and self-contained.

Although oranges have been grown in this section for
almost two hundred years, it was not until fifteen or twenty
years ago that descendants of the Burat brothers led their
fellow Deltans in developing a modern citrus industry here.
Although they must confine their orchards for a short half-
mile along the river ridges, these growers have tended their
trees so lovingly that in a few short years they have established their "Creole Sweets" and "Louisiana Navels" as among
the finest in the nation. Through catastrophes of bitter frost,
hurricane, and devastating invasions of disease, they have continued to perfect their orchards. They have added mandarins,
tangerines, kumquats, Satsumas and grapefruit to their groves.
Several of the larger growers, forming the Buras Orange
Growers, Incorporated, have built modern plants where they
wash, dry and polish their crop along with that of their
neighbors, then wrap and pack them with a distinctive label.

Industrious and wine-loving Deltans have added still
another industry . . . the one we were enjoying around the
table of Monsieur Jean Pierre. For the making of orange wine,
once merely a family custom, is a business with several
growers who bottle the delectable juice for appreciative customers in New Orleans and serve it over the counter in tiny
bars attached to their homes or orange sheds.

In the midst of their talk, the men were interrupted by
solemn Madame Jean Pierre who had sat stolidly by with
little apparent interest.

"Tell da Miss about da blood orange," she said.

They recounted a Delta legend that has been told and re-told wherever there is talk of orange groves.

In the long-ago days when old Fort Jackson, across the river from Buras, had been an active fortress—before the time when the Confederates had fought unsuccessfully here to defend New Orleans from the Yanks—a young officer from the Fort had crossed the river and courted a Delta girl in Buras. When he overstayed his leave, he was severely reprimanded for "frat'nizing with river sluts." Resenting such a description of his dark-eyed sweetheart, he argued brashly with his commander. For this audacity he was court-martialed and executed. On the ground where his blood spilled there were a few scattered orange seeds. Deltans say that from this spot there grew a tree whose fruit was streaked with red—and there grew the legend of the "blood orange of the Delta."

Cap'n Pete pushed his chair back from the table and helped me rise from mine.

"Thanks for da treat, ole friends. It's late-late now an' we mus' go."

It seemed a swift parting from our gracious hosts but it was the practical Delta way.

Monsieur Jean Pierre drove us back to the dock and Lil Pete welcomed us aboard the *Victoria* again, motioning us into the pilothouse with a quick gesture. He wanted to show his father a new set of river charts which he was studying. Indicating various channels and depths on the charts, he talked confidently and proudly of the navigational points he was learning. Like all Delta youths, Lil Pete was afire with ambition to become a river pilot, to be accepted into the proud Pilots Association of the Delta. His eyes burned with eagerness as he told me about the rigid tests and standards of those who piloted ships through intricate channels of the Mississippi.

Cap'n Pete smiled indulgently.

"What you t'ink Miss? My boy gonna leave da *Victoria* some day and take da big ships into N'Awlins? Me, I don' believe he gonna want to, when comes da time."

Lil Pete grinned, and his father reached under the pilot
wheel to pick up a gallon bottle of orange wine. Pouring a
small glass for each of us, the big captain said, "Anyways,
we gonna drink a nightcap . . . to Lil Pete and his Pilots
Association . . . and to *Mam'selle* and her Cajuns."

Out on the river moved the silent silhouette of a great
steamer, reflecting its lights in the rough waters. She moved
slowly, with a proud, calm majesty. Lil Pete tilted his glass in
her direction then turned with his father to lift his glass to me.

"An' how it goes wit your search, Miss?" asked Captain
Pete. "You fin' yo' Cajuns here on our Delta, no?"

"No," I admitted. "I find many peoples, many Frenchmen,
even, but not the true Cajun I'm seeking. I don't know . . .
maybe there is none anywhere . . ."

Cap'n Pete considered the thought, studied me a moment
quiet seriously, and said:

"Miss, I give you da good idea! I don't believe you fin' a
for-true Cajun here. Us Deltans is some mixed-up peoples,
sure. I give you, though, da bes' idea I got—you go to one
man I met a couple years ago, way up in da bayou country.
He gonna fin' you a true Cajun, him. You go to Monsieur
André Olivier! You fin' him on . . ."

"Bayou Teche!" I said, and we all laughed together, for
Cap'n Pete and Lil Pete must have known that I had been
there already.

Back to M'sieu André

XV

Where my search began it came to an end.

I found *M'sieu* André back in St. Martinville, still hovering over the mouldering relics of his Evangeline Museum, still looking like a character out of Molière—or was it Racine?

He greeted me with the same formal bow. There was a twinkle in his eyes when he lifted his pince-nez, studied my face inquisitively and invited me into the little garden behind his cluttered store.

He opened the bottle of orange wine I had brought from the Delta and poured the golden liquid carefully.

"And so, *Mam'selle,* your search is *finie?* You come back to *M'sieu* André, yes? And you find your true Acadian?"

I pulled out the tattered map, more frazzled now than when he gave it to me, and pointed out places I had seen. And I told him many things that I had learned along the bayous.

I had found Acadians everywhere—on bayou, swamp, marsh and Delta—yet nowhere were there those who would call themselves Cajuns.

Wherever there were Acadians, there were mixtures too—with Spanish, English, *américain,* with Italian, Irish and Tocko, with Filipino, Indian, and yes, with Negro too.

Wherever there were French, along dim reaches of swamp or vast flat prairies of marsh, there were the Gallic traditions —of strength, resourcefulness, adaptability, and gayety.

Acadians of this strange, wild country lived out the patterns of far distant Normandy, Brittany, Picardy and Gascony— transplanted the virtues and weaknesses, blended their character, personality and traditions midst the new land's necessities.

So the sailor became a jumbo shrimp man, the *petit fermier* planted his rows of truck in the front and trapped foraging muskrat and mink in his "lan' alon' da back"; so the lowland peasant let his cattle wander lazily along lush levee banks, and the French canal man's great grandson pulled moss from the swamp's bearded cypress giants.

While they re-created their small farms of France and *Acadie* in this watery wilderness, *les petits habitants* clung tenaciously to many of their ancient patterns of living— remaining after ten generations still in the Gallic mold, romantic, quixotic, excitable, yet with a wise serenity, an instinctive understanding of life's best values. With laugher in their eyes, a joke on their facile tongues, a *joie de vivre* in their hearts, they held to their own world and called it good.

Yet like many peoples of this new, fabled land, the culture they created was hybrid—not rigidly French, nor Canadian, nor Creole, nor English, nor American, but a blending of all of these. Transformed by a subtle "sea change" in this watery land of bayou and marsh, the people's life patterns became a rich tapestry woven with threads of many old lands.

By now I knew the futility of trying to unravel these threads. Nor would I again try to follow a single thread through the variegated fabric. For to find a single man who called himself Cajun—this was an impossible thing, *mon ami.*

Was this perhaps the secret of Louisiana's Acadia? It seemed a small thing to have learned, out of all my rare adventures.

I offered it rather apologetically to *M'sieu* André, then reminded him of his promise to reveal the secret of his people to me.

The Frenchman sipped his wine quietly for a moment, then said with a curious smile, "The truth, *Mam'selle,* is only this . . . that my land and my people are a myth. You may search for them forever and always you will find this true . . . They are only an illustion, a myth of their own making . . . *n'est-ce pas?*"

So I had found the true Cajun after all!

Many say it is a myth—this land of Evangeline's people—and I believe it with them.

Yet it is more than a myth. It is rich, rich earth and old, old trees—and ancient moss drooping always down, and young green cane springing always up. It is bayou meeting bayou in far, dim swamps; and sweet water meeting salt along a flat marsh coast. And it is many kinds of people—serene ones and wild. Farmers tilling the earth by day and traveling the swamps by night. Trappers hip-deep in the cold wet marsh; alligator hunters on the bayous at dawn; cane planters along the front and moss gatherers in the back; riverman and swamper, crab fishermen, cray fishermen, shrimp fishermen and oystermen.

And the strange, strange mixtures down on the coast, where Acadian peasant stock meets the reckless children of Lafitte!

This is the mythical land and these the mythical people—And who could name a better search than the one which had revealed them to me?

It is now more than ten years since most of these adventures began. Dramatic changes have come to the Cajun country.

Many of the old things have gone and many of those lovely characters I met have passed away. Tied to a levee at Baton Rouge you may see the ghost of an old stern-wheeler, used today as a wharf boat. Its greyed decks droop dejectedly, its paddle wheel sags in the river mud, and in front of the pilothouse sways a broken board bearing dim letters of a once-proud name, *V. J. Kursweg.*

For a few years after his beloved old packet was retired, Captain Brown Blakeman piloted the Canal Street ferry back and forth across the Mississippi in New Orleans. We had several fine reunions there and the pilothouse rang loudly with his tall stories and remembrances of Mr. Joré, "Our Saviour" Kelly, Albert, Preacher and the others. But for a man who has captained a gallant old stern-wheeler on winding bends and reaches of Bayou Teche, the ferryboat at Canal Street spelled a killing monotony. I was not surprised to hear last year that Cap'n Brown was dead.

Many of the oldsters have gone—*Grandpère* and *Grandmère* Boudreaux, Captain Pete Taliancich, Mr. Joré, *Grandpère* Verret, and Mr. Sterling.

Another breed of outlanders—"men in tin hats"—have poured in from Texas and brought roaring oil excitement to the swamps, rivers and finally to the sea itself. New jobs, new money, big and bigger riches—these have changed bayou towns and villages of the deepest swamps more than anything since the invasion of Evangeline's people two hundred years ago.

Jumbo men of Morgan City have found their new horizon in Mexican waters four hundred miles away. In the great hulking shadows of The Greek's old boat shed a new company builds bigger lugger hulls than that master-builder ever dreamed of, and builds them of steel. Other boat factories work around the clock turning out steel barges, cruisers and crew boats for booming offshore oil explorations. Supplanting jumbo men in fields of derring-do are the brave, brash "offshoremen," symbols of fabulous new sea-going petroleum developments.

Out in the trapping lands of the coastal marshes a big, tough fur-bearing animal, the nutria, has appeared and is changing the whole economy and way of life for cousins of the Boudreaux. A new land company, known as Marshlands Incorporated, has brought a new system of operation, offering fine benefits to trappers and engineering many structural improvements in the marsh itself. There are problems yet in the ever-changing marshlands, but in many large sections of land the injustices that necessitated an annual funeral for *Tante* Cloe are gone.

A road has been built into Isle au Jean Charles and runs straight alongside 'Ti Canal, changing the weirdly beautiful landscape there and removing the pleasant necessity of traveling to the island by lugger and pirogue.

At Grand Isle towering oil rigs stand on legs of steel, planted in waters of Bay Rigaud, their tall derricks soaring into the sky.

Yet in the midst of change many things remain indestructibly the same.

Up on Bayou Teche *M'sieu* André still dispenses wisdom, charm and gallantry along with groceries and Evangeliniana—and his country store-museum remains one of the most curious and fascinating shops in America.

Though the derricks rise off Grand Isle's back shores, they are used today to mark shoal waters for a booming fleet of "lil swimp and jumbo mens" who still choose to follow the old fishing paths of their fathers.

You can still look for Maxim at the shrimp wharves of Bay Rigaud. Now he manages his own modern, well-equipped dock. And when the fleet is out, he stands proudly behind the long shiny bar of his café close by the dockside—a handsome restaurateur beaming as brilliantly here as ever he laughed and shouted from the pilothouse of his shrimp lugger or along the docks on backwaters of the quiet old bay.

In the Borrow Pit at Morgan City, more campboats than ever float peacefully on the still water, making this truly the largest shanty-boat metropolis in America. The campboats are brighter with paint these days, Cadillacs stand on the levee bank beside many of them, and there is a cluster of TV aerials shining from rooftops as far as you can see down the watery pit. But the tinsmiths and basket weavers, the net makers and blacksmiths still work beside their floating homes, their wives still catch tasty river shrimp on myrtle bushes staked out in the river, and there remain the inevitable signs to tempt motorists on the levee road: "River swimps and crabs sole here."

Captain Dew Robert Vuillemont still takes his *Elaine* into Great Basin swamps each week. On a new levee road atop the high-flung Morganza Spillway, you may drive your car from Morgan City to Belle River, then cross a ferry to Pierre Part—straight through America's greatest water wilderness, along the same course used by the *Kursweg* and by the fishboat *Elaine*, past tarring pits of the cat fishermen, into picture-book villages of the moss pickers.

On Bayou Lafourche *les petits habitants* are enjoying new wealth from a booming oil field of their own. Rambling brick ranch-style houses, stiff and ill at ease on the bayou road, are replacing Cajun cottages. But there are many of the old type left—their huge cisterns, shuttered gallery windows and outside stairways giving them an ebullient and happy look. Jules Verret has a shining big store at the foot of the bayou's newest bridge and his son is now the *marchand-charrette*, proudly driving a bus as crowded and as decrepit as the one I rode in with his father.

Across the bayou you will no longer find the shattered ruins of Woodlawn, with classic doors and windows bulging with stores of hay. It has been torn down to the ground and all that remains of glory and magnificence are the Ionic capitals to its soaring columns, used now to mark the driveway entrance at Madewood just below. Yet, on the east bayou bank at Thibodaux, the changeless beauty of Rienzi remains, a symbol of eighteenth-century grandeur among the brilliant Creoles.

Although Cap'n Pete Taliancich and his *Victoria* no longer ply Father Mississippi's broad Delta waters, a friend of his, Captain Marine Gerica, pilots a beautiful little packet freight boat, the *New Majestic*, on the same thrilling river passage.

And with these things there remain other symbols of an older day. For there is a timeless quality to Louisiana's bayou country. In spite of the outlanders' booming industrialism, life in the Cajun country moves much in the same old rhythm. This is a land of little men, happy with ancient patterns, and of little occupations served fervently and with flair.

On All Saints' Night, each October 31, you may still find candles burning brightly around graves in the little cemeteries of Bayou Barataria, still find the oldsters and the young gathered to honor their dead, to gossip, to tell old tales and to whisper about the new tomb that *Couzan secondaire* Ned has built this year over the grave of *Couzan* Jean Lafitte— *mon dieu!* What you t'ink?

On moonlight nights along ghostly banks of a dozen or more dim bayous, you may still join treasure hunters bending faithfully over their tattered maps and digging eternally for treasures of the bloody buccaneers.

There are adventures yet and to spare along a hundred smaller bayou passages. You need c ly seek them out. For wherever Gallic blood runs strong in this strange and beautiful world of the bayous, there are men and women born to live in adventure and eager to share with you the poetry and wonder of their lives. They have found their own secrets of living and they love life complete—pain and joy, defeat and glory.

And always there is the green-gold marsh, flung like a frayed carpet along the Gulf's sweeping curve. And always the trappers, living out their annual Great Adventure as faithfully as I would relive my own adventures in their misty, haunting land.

It is late October now, and the little winds are beginning to whisper through the tall roseau-canes along a thousand hidden *traînasses*, a hundred lonely bayous.

Comme ça, mon ami? It will soon be the time, yes? Let us go now. The bayous and marsh, they wait for us. Tomorrow is the Big Day, *hein?*

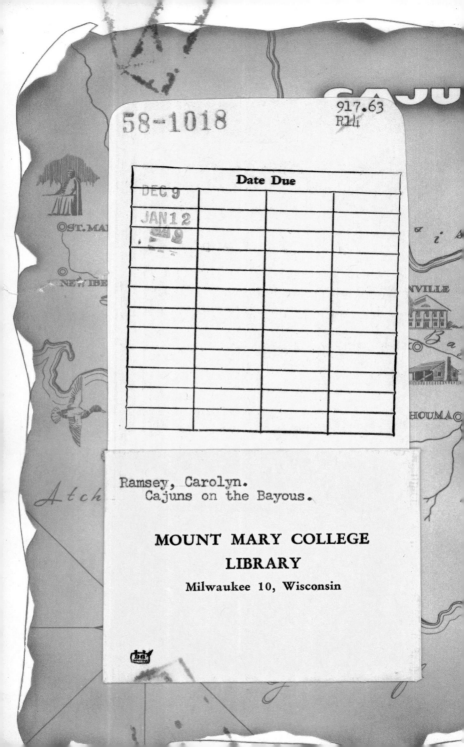